A KNIGHT ON THE BOX

40 Years of Anglia Television

ANGLIA
Television Limited

ACKNOWLEDGEMENTS

Writers:
Tom Walshe, Colin Bevan, Ruth Sealy, Naomi Phillipson.

Editor:
Crawford Gillan.

Production Editor:
Robin Bray.

Anglia Staff Photographers:
Dave Dawson, Philip King, Bob Hobbs, Cati Majtenyi, Mike Harrington, Ian Barringer-Allen, Don Bennett, David Wheeler.

Other pictures by freelance photographers and *Survival* camera teams.

Picture Research:
Colin Bevan, Tom Walshe, Maureen Monk, Bob Hobbs, Teresa Hopper.

Design and Reproduction:
Graphico Limited, Norwich.

Indexing:
George Hammond.

Printed in the UK by:
Fuller-Davies, Ipswich.

Bound in the UK by:
WBC Book Manufacturers Limited, Bridgend.

The authors gratefully acknowledge the help and support of the following: Graham Creelman, Martin Morrall, Bob Ledwidge, Harvey Buck, Eddie Anderson, David Brooks, Trisha Goddard, Dick Joice, Nicholas Parsons, Guy Adams, Surrey Beddows, David Jennings, Rebecca Atherstone, Greg Barnes, Steve Aldous, Kevin Piper, Richard Foxton, Paul Freeman, Sue Heard, Emma Jenkinson, Judy Ball, Susan Littlemore, David Leverett, Tracey O'Connor, Petra Regent, Bill Smith, Wally Sparrow, June Wright, Alison Aitken, Trevor Heaton, Derek James, Mike Hay, Peter Hansford and all the many celebrities who have contributed information, anecdotes and greetings.

Published in the United Kingdom in 1999 by

Anglia Television Limited
Anglia House, Norwich, Norfolk NR1 3JG.

A catalogue record for this book is available from the British Library.

ISBN 0 906836 40 9

UM A United News & Media company

Contents

Foreword

David McCall.

ANGLIA TELEVISION today is a successful regional station and a vibrant producer of programmes for ITV and other networks. Many viewers may not realise that we make programmes for Channel 4, Channel 5 and even Sky. Our staff are involved in everything from Formula 1 motor racing to fly-on-the-wall documentaries, from top-rating talk shows to *Survival Specials*. The company and its staff have been innovative and ambitious from the start.

The group which was awarded the contract to bring commercial TV to the East of England was led by **Lord Townshend** and **Aubrey Buxton** (now **Lord Buxton**) – both quintessential rural English gentlemen – together with **Laurence Scott**, a member of the famous Scott newspaper family and chairman of the *Manchester Guardian* and **John Woolf**, a renowned international film producer.

These four founding directors were very much 'hands on', heading up the key areas of programme planning and production, sales and marketing, and finance and administration, through a committee system.

The regional service was a great success with the star find of **Dick Joice**, a Norfolk farmer who presented the first farming programme. Despite being dyslexic, he was a television natural. He was soon presenting the nightly magazine programme and then running the whole regional output. Sadly, Dick died just as this book was going to press.

Anglia's regional service had a number of firsts; among them, the first company to have its own weather forecaster, and the first to produce video-edited football highlights of Saturday afternoon soccer.

The founder directors also had their sights firmly set on producing programmes for the national ITV network. John Woolf headed up the Anglia drama department and, because of his reputation, was able to secure a network slot for Anglia's first drama on the very first evening of Anglia's transmission. It began a great tradition of some six or so star-studded Anglia dramas being produced in Norwich every year for the network.

Another great success, the natural history series *Survival*, continues to sell to more than 100 countries today. It spawned from the regional programme *Countryman*, fronted by Aubrey Buxton, who was the creative genius behind the *Survival* series. Its excellence and world-wide acclaim also attracted star names such as **David Niven**. I remember Niven, a brilliant and witty raconteur, walking through the old Agricultural Hall, which houses Anglia's studios but retains some of its original design features, saying "working here is like working at 19th Century Fox". He was referring to the wrought ironwork and not the production methods!

There is no doubt that Anglia has been at the forefront of technological change in the industry and it has a proud record of fostering and nurturing creative talent, much of which is graphically illustrated in this anniversary book. There are many who have contributed to Anglia's success who have not been mentioned, but I hope that they and our viewers enjoy reading the book as it rekindles memories and reveals what Anglia is doing today. Anglia is now part of the large United News & Media Group which, in today's high-tech, competitive economic environment, enables it to continue to provide an outstanding and innovative regional service, contribute a record number of hours to the ITV network and find and foster new talent like **Trisha Goddard**.

Here's to the next 40 years!

DAVID McCALL
Chairman of Anglia Television

Anglia Television's headquarters in Norwich.

Anglia takes to the air...

It is hard for many of us today to imagine how limited the choice was for viewers and listeners in the late 1950s. One TV channel, three radio stations... and that was it. Yet more and more people were buying television sets and there was excitement in the air about the arrival of commercial broadcasting.

Speculation was rife in February, 1958, about who was in the running to provide the new regional ITV service for the East of England.

A number of rival interests were expected to compete for the franchise. One group, representing Eastern Counties newspaper interests, included the Norfolk News Company (publishers of the *Eastern Daily Press, Eastern Evening News* and *Norwich Mercury* series of newspapers), along with the East Anglian Daily Times Company, of Ipswich, the East Midlands Allied Press and other local interests under the chairmanship of the Earl of Cranbrook.

The *Manchester Guardian* was reported to be actively associated with another group – and leading Norfolk farmer the **Marquess Townshend**, of Raynham Hall, was understood to be its likely chairman. A third contestant, according to reports, was thought to be a group headed by Odhams Press, publishers of the *Daily Herald* and many periodicals.

Several months later it was revealed that another consortium included *Reynolds News,* of London, and 15 East Anglian Co-operative Societies.

At the end of June it was announced that the contract for provision of commercial television programmes in East Anglia (the eighth ITA station nationally) had been offered to a group headed by Lord Townshend. Among local interests represented were the Norwich Union Insurance Societies, King's College and Selwyn College, Cambridge, May Gurney and Company (civil engineering contractors), of Norwich, and The Dairy Farmer Ltd. (publishers of agricultural periodicals and books), of Ipswich.

It was also reported that the Norfolk News Company, the East Anglian Daily Times Company and the East Midlands Allied Press had accepted the group's invitation to become shareholders with representatives on the board.

The next day it was announced that, subject to full council approval, the new broadcaster – having submitted the highest of four tenders – would be leasing the Agricultural Hall, in Norwich, for use as its studios for

Lord Townshend.

Directors were listed as:

The Marquess Townshend, of Raynham *Chairman*

Sir Robert Bignold
President of Norwich Union Life Insurance Society and chairman of Norwich Union Fire Insurance Society

Mr Aubrey Buxton
The author and naturalist, of Stansted, Essex

Dr Glyn Daniel
Fellow of St John's College, Cambridge

Sir Peter Greenwell
Farmer, of Woodbridge, Suffolk

Miss Audrey Richards
Vice-principal of Newnham College, Cambridge

Mr Donald Albery
Later Sir Donald Albery, managing director of Wyndham Theatres

Mr Laurence Scott
Chairman and managing director of the Manchester Guardian and Evening News Ltd.

Mr John Woolf
Later Sir John Woolf, chairman and managing director of Romulus and Remus Films Ltd.

Plus a representative of local newspaper companies.

75 years at a rent of £5,000 a year exclusive of rates. This figure, however, would be reduced to £3,500 a year for the first seven years "in view of the heavy initial expenditure".

The old hall, which was opened in 1882 by **Edward VII** when he was Prince of Wales, had a chequered history. It had hosted a blindfolded tightrope walk by a celebrated artist called **Blondin** a few days before his 70th birthday in 1894, and also featured Whimsical Walker and **George Lockhart's** Elephants.

Grand Opera had been staged in the main hall in 1885, Gladstone had spoken there in 1886 and regular fat cattle shows were interspersed with everything from 'quack' medicine men to rodeos and indoor fairs with steam roundabouts. In the early days of films a small theatre at the front of the building was used as an improvised cinema – before any others were built in Norwich – and **Oscar Wilde** lectured there 10 years before any of his plays were ever seen.

The hall was also reputedly haunted by the ghost of an auctioneer. Sadly, it has never been seen, although mysterious footsteps were reported in empty corridors late at night.

As the builders completed work in Anglia House the company took on its first employee, chief engineer **Tom Marshall**, to supervise the equipping of the studios and technical areas. Executives, technicians, entertainers, journalists and secretaries followed in his footsteps – 300 in all with more under contract for particular programmes.

> **"East Anglia has taught the world something about agriculture. Perhaps it may teach the world something about television."**
> **Chairman Lord Townshend**

Converting the Agricultural Hall to Anglia Studios.

Aubrey Buxton.

Writing in the *Eastern Daily Press*, Anglia director **Aubrey Buxton** said Independent Television could represent a minor revolution in the life of the community — with the job opportunities it brought. For the first time it would be possible for a few young people to make their careers within daily distance of their homes and to earn rewards comparable to anything they might achieve in London, Birmingham, Glasgow or anywhere else.

He emphasised, however:

"There will be no free-for-all for Tom, Dick and Harry. If ever there was a specialised industry, this is it."

Independent Television could also introduce a new phase to regional life in another sense, he added. "Whereas hitherto London and other great centres have acted as magnets in the world of entertainment and culture, the process may now be reversed in a small degree by the establishment of new magnets in provincial centres.

"The creation of an Independent Television centre in Norwich. . . will attract personalities, stars and notabilities from all walks of life into the heart of the area. The glamorous pop-singer or the distinguished archaeologist may soon be heard declaring with undisguised relish: 'I'm off to Norwich!'"

Chairman Lord Townshend, meanwhile, was quoted as saying:

"East Anglia has taught the world something about agriculture. Perhaps it may teach the world something about television."

No escape from television now...

IN September, 1958, it was reported that Jordan's Daily Register of New Companies had announced that Anglia Television Ltd. was registered on September 11 with a nominal capital of £110,000 in £1 shares.

The following month, the company's new chief executive was named as **Donald Stephenson**, who had been with the BBC for just over 20 years and a controller of the corporation since 1949. By December, Mr Stephenson was talking to Norwich Rotary Club at the Samson and Hercules meeting rooms and insisting that to be without television was to cut oneself off from a major factor in modern life.

"You can no more get away from it in the days to come than you can get away from running water and electric light," he declared.

By January, 1959, work was forging ahead on conversion of the Agricultural Hall into studios and signal reception areas were outlined with the hope that 200,000 of the 350,000 homes with television in the area would view the new channel.

Not everyone was happy about the new arrival, however. Labour MPs, led by BBC personality **Christopher Mayhew**, were reported to have been 'working furiously' attacking the ITA. In particular, Mr Mayhew complained about the interruption of serious programmes for advertisements and the abuse of the term 'natural break', used in the Television Act to specify periods during which advertising could be introduced.

A controller of programmes, **Stephen McCormack**, had been appointed in February and was by now doing the industry rounds, including the laying of the foundation stone of Associated Rediffusion's new studios at Wembley.

Unfortunately, he needed a dark suit for the occasion, but had left his in the car when his wife had dropped him off. Undaunted, he borrowed a suit from the London television company's wardrobe department. The trousers were a little large and no braces could be found so Mr McCormack steadfastly kept one hand in his trouser pocket throughout the opening ceremonies.

"If I'd given anybody a big hello and clasped their hands between mine, my trousers would have fallen down," he reported afterwards.

A low-power test signal for the new station in East Anglia, with full power test transmissions scheduled for September, was announced for July by area sales manager **S.M. Robertson** at a Norwich meeting.

Stephen McCormack.

Norman Hackforth.

He also assured his listeners that, in all but about five per cent of cases, the cost of converting an existing set, mainly through aerial changes, would be between £3 and £8. Only sets more than four years old would cost more to adapt as these would need a new coil.

Meanwhile, more than 780 job applications from prospective announcers and newscasters were flooding into the station and first auditions were held in the Royal Hotel, Norwich, on June 9. Candidates had to read news items, make announcements about forthcoming programmes and conduct an off-the-cuff interview with a member of Anglia's staff, **Philip Bray**, who posed as an American film actor, an Irish playwright, an Australian sheep farmer and a guardsman who had refused to go on guard!

One of the assessors was **Norman Hackforth**, whose voice could be heard on radio's *Twenty Questions*, announcing: "And the next object is…" The outside broad-cast equipment for the auditions was borrowed from Pye Television Transmission Services, of Cambridge, who had been awarded the £500,000 contract to equip the station.

Anglia's first newsreaders – 'Sandy' Newman Sanders, Drew Russell and Colin Bower.

Together for 40 years...

THERE is only one man who can claim to have seen it all at Anglia – Wally Sparrow, the sole employee with 40 years' unbroken service.

Having joined as a trainee technician in the autumn of 1959, he was the man who inserted the tape into the machine to launch the station on air on October 27 that year.

Wally Sparrow is a sound man in every sense. He spent most of his career in the sound department, rising to the post of head of production services. His first few weeks as a trainee were spent soldering wires to get everything connected for the big switch-on.

"Those early days were totally exhilarating and great fun. We were all new to Anglia and many of us new to television," he recalls.

There have been enormous changes since, of course, in technical terms, personnel and production techniques.

"As far as the equipment is concerned, reliability is one of the biggest differences," he says. "Nowadays when you switch on a piece of kit, it actually works. I can remember when we had to do a daily inspection of the huge racks of equipment to make sure all the valves were glowing. Those that weren't had to be changed.

"When drama was shot using special sets in the studio, all the sounds were put on at the time via tape recorders in the control room to generate effects and background noises. Now it is all done after the programme has been shot."

He especially remembers a replica Centurion tank being built in the studio for a desert war scene. "It even came complete with real sand, which was a blessed nuisance because it got into every piece of equipment."

Wally Sparrow.

Philip Bray.

D-Day arrives...

DESPITE initial fears over the spread of television, newspaper industry leaders were confident their product would continue to have a place in people's homes.

"It may take reading time away from the national newspapers but certainly not from the local newspapers," the Newspaper Society's advertising liaison officer told the Publicity Club of Norwich.

When the station went on air as scheduled, on October 27, 1959, the launch was recorded simply by *The Times* (price 6d) on an inside page: "Anglia Television Starts Today".

The accompanying report, with a dateline of October 26, noted: "The youngest of the commercial television companies — Anglia Television — which will bring an alternative programme (sic) within reach of just over two million people in the Eastern Counties, goes on air tomorrow."

It added that the new station had three studios and, in the control room, a 'robot machine' devised by the chief engineer, **Mr T. Marshall**. This automatically performed such functions as switching and starting up tape and telecine machines, "all of which would normally be done by pressing individual buttons".

This Tape Operated Switching and Indicating Equipment, the report added, was familiarly known as 'Topsie'.

In the same edition of the paper a display advertisement placed by British Insulated Callender's Cables (BICC), of Bloomsbury Street, London, heralded the start of high-power transmission from the Mendlesham transmitter mast. This, it said, meant that more than one million viewers would now be able to receive a first-class service from the ITA station.

At 1,000 ft high, it added, the mast was the tallest structure in Britain and among the 10 tallest in the world — surpassed only by the KKWTV mast in Oklahoma City, the 1,472 ft Empire State Building and other TV masts in various countries — and yet each side of its triangular framework was only 8 ft 6 in across.

In contrast to the lavish way listings are published in newspapers today, the evening's radio and television programmes were buried away in two columns at the bottom of a page in *The Times*.

**Chief engineer
Tom Marshall.**

Lord Townshend watches intently from the control room as Anglia goes on air.

Opening night...

PROGRAMMES for Anglia viewers started at 4.15 pm with *Introducing Anglia*, in which viewers saw film of a tour of the region, much of it shot from a helicopter, including aerial views of the Mendlesham transmitting mast.

They met newsreaders **Drew Russell**, **Newman Sanders** and **Colin Bower** for the first time and saw previews of *Farming Diary*, *Town and Gown* and *The Midday Show*. An extract from *The Violent Years* – the first of many Anglia plays which were to gain the comparatively small regional company a special reputation in the field – was also screened.

The programme ended with coverage of the simple but historic official opening of the new Norwich studios by the chairman of the ITA, **Sir Ivone Kirkpatrick**.

Anglia Television was 'on air' and the first of many deadlines had been successfully met, apparently without hitch. This in itself was quite an achievement as Anglia had made the bold decision, not many weeks before going on air, to open two days earlier than planned.

Introducing Anglia was followed at 4.45 pm by *Small Time*, at 5 pm by *Lucky Dip* (television's junior newspaper); then 5.25 pm *Romance of the Railways* (the story of British Railways), 5.55 pm *News from ITN* and 6.05 pm by *Anglia News*.

Programmes continued with *This Wonderful World* (the wonders of the world as seen by the camera), *Birth of a Regiment* (a 15-minute programme marking the merger of the Royal Norfolk Regiment and the Suffolk Regiment to form the first East Anglian Regiment a month earlier) and *Song Parade*.

Then came *Emergency Ward 10*, *Concentration* (a test of memory and observation with **David Gell**), *Knight Errant '59*, *News* and Anglia's first network production – a drama of romance and tragedy between the wars entitled *The Violent Years*, starring German actress **Hildegard Neff**, **Laurence Harvey** and **Margaret Leighton**.

It was Miss Neff's first TV play and she admitted being nervous when cameras and sound booms moved towards her. According to **Philip Purser** in the *News Chronicle*, it was Harvey's first TV play since *A Month in the Country* four years earlier.

The actor was busily telling people it was probably the last for a good while, too. "I am not very keen on television. There is too much of it," he said.

At 11.08 pm there were further ITN news headlines and at 11.10 pm coverage of the opening of Anglia was repeated. *The Epilogue* sent viewers of the new broadcaster off to bed at 11.40 pm.

Closing knight...

FOR almost 30 years, until 1988, the image which instantly identified Anglia TV for viewers was the silver knight. The figure was discovered in the window of a London jeweller's shop when the company was looking for a symbol of its identity.

More than 100 years old, the knight was originally commissioned by the King of the Netherlands, who was patron of a society called the Falcon Club which met once a year to compete in horse races, falconry and other sports. In 1850 the king was so sure he would win the contest he commissioned a trophy from London silversmiths. It was modelled on the statue of **Richard Coeur de Lion**, which stands outside the Houses of Parliament, but made to represent the Black Prince.

To the king's dismay, however, the trophy was won by an Englishman and brought back to Britain, where it remained in the possession of the victor's family until the year Anglia went on air.

A firm of Bond Street jewellers and goldsmiths was commissioned to make certain modifications, including the pennon on the lance. The magnificent sterling silver trophy became the symbol of Anglia Television.

In 1987, however, it was announced that the knight was being 'retired' the next year.

"The main reason is that it is impossible to adapt to the sophisticated demands of modern screen technology," said **David McCall**, then the company's chief executive, now chairman.

Lord Buxton, who was company chairman at the time, said the decision to replace the knight had been particularly hard as it was one of the most widely-recognised symbols in British broadcasting.

In the previous two years, however, he said, the company had made great strides towards gearing up for the competitive new era of broadcasting on the international scene: "We need to show that Anglia can move with the times."

Design specialists **Robinson Lambie-Nairn** were called in to work on a symbol as part of a new corporate image for the company. They were behind the original 'exploding' Channel Four symbol and, more recently, the 'imploding' Channel Five logo, as well as the BBC's 'transmitter' and 'balloon' images and its new beige, cream and ivory Six O'Clock News set.

When the new Anglia symbol for the 1990s and beyond was unveiled – at presentations in Norwich and London on March 21, 1988 – it was revealed to be a distinctive triangle in Wedgwood Blue, Cambridge Blue and Gold to represent the

company's initial letter. On screen, elements of the triangle came together to form an animated Anglia standard.

New title music, an orchestral fanfare, replaced the **Sir Malcolm Sargent**-arranged snatch of **Handel's** *Water Music* as the introduction to all programmes and commercial breaks.

David McCall said research showed that although the public admired the exceptional quality of Anglia's programmes, they felt its presentation style was old-fashioned. The brief for the new corporate image had been 'evolution not revolution,' he emphasised.

"The new symbol and corporate image will ensure that our programme service is attractively packaged, presented and promoted in the competitive new broadcasting environment – in which all television companies will be fighting to attract and retain viewers," said Mr McCall.

1959 – That was the year that was...

FORTY years may not be a lifetime but comparisons between then and now – from the music you could hear on the radio to the value of money – reveal just how much life has changed since Anglia first went on air.

If you need a musical key to 1959 it was, according to American singer **Don McLean**, the year "the music died". The reference is to the plane crash near Mason City, Iowa, on February 3 of that year, when bespectacled rock star **Buddy Holly**, along with **The Big Bopper** and **Richie Valens**, perished. They had all been appearing on the same tour bill.

Music died with Buddy Holly.

Holly's *It Doesn't Matter Anymore* became a number one hit on a wave of grief and Valens had the unenviable distinction of becoming the first person to make his chart debut posthumously with *Donna*.

One of the main stars on the British pop scene was pianist **Russ Conway** who cantered to the top of the charts with *Side Saddle*. He could afford to smile – and flutter the hearts of thousands of female fans – as he enjoyed further hits with *Roulette* and *Snow Coach*.

Meanwhile, **Cliff Richard's** career was taking off. He made the number one slot with *Livin' Doll* at the end of July and repeated the success in October with *Travellin' Light* – the last record on which the **Shadows** were listed under their previous name – **The Drifters**.

Other number ones in 1959 included:

The Day the Rains Came Down *Jane Morgan*

One Night *Elvis Presley*

As I Love You *Shirley Bassey*

Smoke Gets in Your Eyes *Platters*

A Fool Such as I *Elvis Presley*

Dream Lover *Bobby Darin*

Only Sixteen *Craig Douglas*

Here Come Summer *Jerry Keller*

Mack the Knife *Bobby Darin*

What Do You Want? *Adam Faith*

What Do You Want to Make Those Eyes at Me For? *Emile Ford and the Checkmates*

Another hit item which went round and round in 1959 – but not on the record turntable – was the hula-hoop. At least the hula-hoop was fairly cheap which was probably just as well as the average weekly wage was only £13.54. Mind you, a pint of beer cost just 1s 2d (about 6p today), petrol was 4s 8d (about 24p) a gallon, a Simpsons suit cost 20 guineas and the average house price was £2,410.

You could buy a Ford Anglia de Luxe for about £500 or, if you felt like splashing out, drive away in a new Rolls-Royce Phantom V for a mere £8,905.

Unlike today, there was no all-night programming on television but the licence fee cost just £4 a year. In 1959 the number of TV licences in the UK was 10 million, almost double the figure of four years earlier.

As one commentator put it: "Television sold faster than ever. It was the perfect commodity for the suburban Fifties – a piece of furniture that did something. And what it did was bring entertainment into the home."

The small screen had begun to hit cinema audiences but the movie industry was not giving in without a fight and there was still money for big-name productions and lavish launches. In December, 1959, a film described as "the biggest story of our time" premiered simultaneously in capital cities all over the world. The film? **Stanley Kramer's** production of *On the Beach*, starring **Gregory Peck**, **Ava Gardner**, **Fred Astaire** and **Anthony Perkins**. Another American success released the same year was *Some Like It Hot*, starring the legendary **Marilyn Monroe**.

On this side of the Atlantic films like *Gigi* and *Room at the Top* were making their mark. Academy award winner for the year was *Ben Hur*, starring **Charlton Heston**. An even more significant picture, however, was beginning to emerge from outer space as the US Explorer VI spacecraft beamed back the first television pictures of Earth. The Soviets were getting in on the act as well, launching Luniks which photographed the far side of the moon.

One of the biggest cinema hits of recent years has been *The Full Monty*. Back in 1959 Monty meant one thing – the soldier, **Viscount Montgomery**, of Alamein. And if you wanted an intimate portrait of 'The Real Monty' you could read "The Fascinating Story That Has Never Before Been Told" in *John Bull (Everybody's Weekly)* for just five old pennies.

By 1959 things had come a long way from the military hardware the Second World War commander was used to. The atomic age had dawned with Britain launching Dreadnought, her first nuclear submarine, and Russia the nuclear-powered ice-breaker Lenin. Political links with Russia were strengthened, however, in the February when Prime Minister **Harold Macmillan** – acknowledged as probably the first British politician to master the art of appearing on television – visited Moscow.

OTHER KEY EVENTS IN 1959

January Fidel Castro takes power in Cuba. Charles De Gaulle proclaimed president of the Fifth Republic in France. Alaska becomes 49th state of America.

February London Transport unveils details of £50 million Victoria underground line from Victoria to Walthamstow.

March Oxo wins the Grand National.

April Mao tse-Tung succeeded by Liu Shao-Chi.

May Nottingham Forest beat Luton Town 2-1 in the FA Cup Final.

June Singapore becomes independent.

July Postmaster General Ernest Marples inaugurates the first post codes and post code sorting machine in Norwich.

August China invades north-east frontier of India. Hawaii becomes 50th state of America.

September The number of people going to university in Britain has doubled since 1939.

October A survey shows that a third of 15-year-old boys are regular smokers.

November The Lords oppose the introduction of commercial radio.

December Archbishop Makarios becomes president of independent Cyprus.

AND FOR THE FIRST TIME...

- New MPs included Margaret Thatcher.
- Air speed of 1,520 mph established by USAF pilot.
- Barclays Bank orders computer for branch accounts.
- Boxer Ingemar Johansson becomes Sweden's first world heavyweight champion.
- Car designer Alec Issigonis's Mini car first shown in UK.
- Commercial Xerox photo-copier introduced.
- Fashion designer Dior announces skirts are to rise above the knee.
- First section of M1 opens.
- Flashing indicator lights become legal on motor vehicles.
- Hovercraft's maiden cross-Channel voyage.

FOR THE LAST TIME... OTHER 1959 DEATHS

Actor Errol Flynn, jazz singer Billie Holiday, painter Sir Stanley Spencer, singer Mario Lanza, racing driver Mike Hawthorn, film director Cecil B de Mille, comedian Lou Costello, author Raymond Chandler, architect Frank Lloyd Wright.

Cliff Richard – top of the pops.

Marilyn Monroe – hot stuff.

The stars come out to play for Anglia...

RIGHT from the start, Anglia set out to make its name in television drama. Under the guidance of film producer **Sir John Woolf**, who won international acclaim for big-screen productions such as *Room at the Top, The African Queen* and *Oliver*, Anglia's drama output was geared to provide maximum popular appeal. Strong stories and star names were the watchwords.

The impact was immediate. The first play, *The Violent Years*, on Anglia's opening night starred one of the hottest screen properties of the time, **Laurence Harvey**, who had played the central character in *Room at the Top* the previous year. Co-starring **Hildegarde Neff**, *The Violent Years* was a powerful tale of a man on trial for his life in an American court, and it reached number nine in the national top ten programmes for the week.

Sweet Poison, which followed in December, 1959, was another courtroom drama, with **Dawn Addams** and **John Ireland** in the lead roles. It shot to number four in the ratings, while *Carrington V.C.*, starring **Richard Todd, Ann Todd** and **Dorothy Tutin**, and centring on a court martial, achieved a fifth place in January, 1960.

It was a startling beginning – but Anglia knew it had to make an immediate impact if it wanted to compete alongside the 'Big Four' ITV companies for network slots. Before Anglia went on the air, there had been a reluctance in some quarters to entrust network drama slots to an unknown newcomer. But the involvement of **John Woolf**, as a founder member of the Anglia board, and the appointment as head of the drama department of **George More O'Ferrall**, who had directed the world's very first television play, in 1936, went a long way towards bolstering confidence.

Sir John Woolf.

London ITV company Associated Rediffusion agreed to provide time for up to eight Anglia plays a year – provided they were made at its Wembley studios using its technicians. So it was that the first-night play was credited as "An Anglia Television production networked by Associated Rediffusion." Anglia was keen to use its own technical staff in Norwich, however, and proved it could do so successfully with *Sweet Poison*. Although some plays continued to be recorded at Wembley until 1962, Anglia's reputation became so well established that it was soon able to move production permanently to Norwich and present the plays in its own right.

Richard Todd and Ann Todd in *Carrington V.C.*

Laurence Harvey in *The Violent Years*, **Anglia's first play.**

First television appearance...

GLADYS COOPER, **Margaret Leighton** and **David Tomlinson** were among top stars appearing in Anglia dramas in 1960. The next year's output included *The Burden Of Proof*, starring **Richard Pearson** as an innocent salesman who agreed to make up the numbers in an identity parade in an assault case, only to find himself accused of being the guilty man. Pearson achieved an Anglia link spanning 35 years when starring with **George Cole** in the 1996 comedy drama *My Good Friend*, produced by Hartswood Films and presented by Anglia on ITV.

Another star who has enjoyed a long association with Anglia is **Francesca Annis**. She made her debut for the company in October, 1961, as a 16-year-old in *Children In The Sun*, which was based on the true story of one man's efforts to protect the starving urchins of Naples. And the following year she appeared in a 'Play of the Week' thriller called *The Gentle Assassin* which attracted more than 14 million viewers — a record at the time for any Anglia production and one of the largest for an ITV 'Play of the Week'. Annis went on to appear in *The Explorer* in 1968, and *Orson Welles' Great Mysteries* in 1974 before co-starring with **Roy Marsden** in *Inside Story* in 1986.

A Letter From The General another 1962 'Play of the Week' marked a first appearance in a television drama by **Anna Neagle**, a star of more than 30 movies. And a much-loved doyenne of British stage and screen, **Margaret Rutherford**, took the lead role in *The Kidnapping Of Mary Smith*.

Oscar Homolka, the Austrian actor who cornered the market in playing Russian intelligence chiefs in **Michael Caine** films such as *The Billion Dollar Brain* and *Funeral in Berlin*, made his first British TV appearance with Anglia in 1963. The production was *Danger Zone*, a tense drama about the crew and very special passengers of an airliner flying into an American nuclear test area just as a detonation was about to take place.

A large mock-up of a Boeing 707 was built in the Norwich studio — by no means the only time Anglia designers and scenery constructors created lifelike illusions for drama sets. In 1967, a Dublin square was recreated in the studio for a production called *Little Moon Of Alba*, and the construction department built a replica tank for a play called *The Enemy*. In the 1980s, filming for the P.D. James thriller *The Black Tower* brought a terrace of facsimile Dorset stone cottages to a North Norfolk location, along with a black tower replicating the original on the south coast.

Richard Pearson is picked out in an identity parade in *The Burden of Proof* **in 1961.**

Anglia Television 40th Anniversary — Drama

Margaret Rutherford in *The Kidnapping of Mary Smith.*

Anna Neagle's first appearance in a TV drama,
A Letter From The General, **1962.**

Mock-up of a Boeing 707 cockpit built in the studio for
Danger Zone.

Collect Your Hand Baggage, written for Anglia by **John Mortimer** and screened in 1963, was another film with an aviation setting. This time all the planes were for real – the action taking place at London Airport with **Kenneth More** as an extrovert seeking to retain his youth.

In 1964, **John Jacobs** – brother of broadcaster David – succeeded **George More O'Ferrall** as head of drama and produced or directed almost all Anglia's output for the next 13 years. A much respected figure, he was known as 'the actor's director' in the television business. That same year saw **Anna Neagle** return for a second Anglia role in *Shadow In The Sun*, playing the headmistress of a fashionable school in a story set against a background of apartheid and prejudice in South Africa.

Anglia had to wait until 1968 to achieve its first number one position in the TV top ten, with *Countercrime*, starring **John Gregson**. It heralded the start of a golden era for the company's drama, coinciding with the advent of colour transmission. That year, 1969, *Speaking Of Murder*, which again featured Gregson and also starred **Jill Bennett**, became the first ITV drama to reach an audience of 25 million, reflecting the rise in television viewing that had taken place during the decade.

Jill Bennett was also at the head of the credits, along with **Peter Barkworth**, in *Intent To Murder* which gained Anglia another number one position in 1974. Two years later, the highly acclaimed *Dame Of Sark*, starring **Celia Johnson** (in her fourth Anglia play) as the wartime Channel Island heroine, also achieved the top spot.

There were some disappointments along the way, of course. In 1965 **Rupert Davies**, of *Maigret* fame, played the Pope in *The Successor*, a story about a papal election. At the time it was Anglia's most expensive drama and involved Vatican scenes being accurately reproduced in Norwich. But viewing figures in the UK were moderate, although the production was praised by critics and was sold to America where it was nominated for an Emmy.

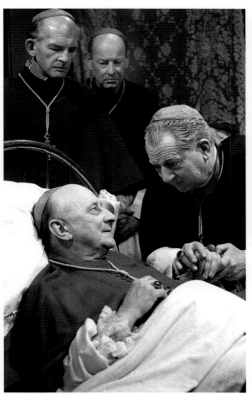

Rupert Davies (right), as the Pope, in *The Successor*.

Francesca Annis and **Michael Bryant** in *The Explorer*, **1968**.

Kenneth More in John Mortimer's *Collect Your Hand Baggage*, **1963**.

Jill Bennett and **Peter Barkworth** in *Intent To Murder*, **1974**.

Celia Johnson starring in *Dame of Sark*, **1976**.

Studio reconstruction of a Dublin square *Little Moon of Alba*, **1967**.

Anglia drama in the 1970s diversified further to include more half-hour productions, among them its first comedy series, *Backs To The Land*, and two lavish series of sting-in-the-tail stories, first *Orson Welles' Great Mysteries* and then, from 1979, the much celebrated *Tales Of The Unexpected*.

One-off plays continued as well, however, along with notable casting. **Telly Savalas**, at the time TV's best-known detective as the lollipop-sucking *Kojak*, came to Norwich to star with **Gayle Hunnicutt** and **Liz Fraser** in **Terence Rattigan's** *Man And Boy*.

In 1974, **Joan Collins** took the first of many roles for Anglia, appearing with **Susannah York, Michael Aldridge** and French singer **Sacha Distel** in **Noel Coward's** *Fallen Angels*. And **Kenneth More**, another great Anglia favourite, returned – first starring with **Nigel Davenport** in *Goose With Pepper*, a 1975 story of tensions between a retired brigadier and his former sergeant-major, and then teaming up with **Claire Bloom** in an emotive drama *In Praise Of Love*.

Frank Finlay appeared in two productions in 1978. He played a retired army officer who struck up an innocent but dangerous friendship with a teenage boy in *The Last Campaign*, and then starred with **Lucy Gutteridge** in **William Douglas Home's** *Betzi*, a Napoleonic love story.

Frank Finlay, as Napoleon, and Lucy Gutteridge, as his lover, in *Betzi*.

Alistair Sim in one of his last TV roles as a priest in
The Prodigal Daughter, 1975.

Douglas Home's play *Lloyd George Knew My Father* had also been produced by Anglia three years earlier, with **Celia Johnson** and **Roland Culver** in the lead roles. And there was a typically characterful performance in 1975 from **Alistair Sim**, in one of his last television roles, playing a priest in *The Prodigal Daughter*. **Jeremy Brett** and a young **Karl Howman** were also in the cast.

In the early 1980s, **Sir John Woolf** and head of drama **John Rosenberg** brought three prestigious films with top British stars to the screen. In 1981, **Wendy Hiller, Cyril Cusack** and **Hannah Gordon** starred in the two-hour film *Miss Morison's Ghosts*. The following year, **Wendy Hiller** and **Cyril Cusack** were back, this time alongside the legendary **Rex Harrison** making one of his rare television appearances in the frothy Douglas Home comedy *The Kingfisher*, a Christmas special for ITV.

Another Anglia coup cast **Alec Guinness** in the **John Mortimer** play *Edwin* as a crusty retired High Court judge who conducted his private life as though still dispensing justice in court. The 90-minute production also starred **Paul Rogers** and was shown on Channel Four in 1984.

The 80s marked the beginning of another important chapter in Anglia drama with the introduction of the long-running series of murder mysteries based on the novels of **P. D. James**. Acclaimed actor and theatre director **Roy Marsden** has made the role of James's poetry-writing detective Adam Dalgliesh his own since Anglia introduced the enigmatic character to ITV viewers in the adaptation *Death Of An Expert Witness* in 1983.

The dramatisation of the crime author's latest thriller, *A Certain Justice*, 15 years later, marked Marsden's tenth appearance as the cerebral cop. Not bad for someone who, as early as 1985, was hinting that he did not see himself continuing in the role.

nneth More and Claire Bloom in *Praise Of Love*.   **Wendy Hiller and Hannah Gordon** in *Miss Morison's Ghosts*, **1981.**   **Joan Collins, Sacha Distel and Susannah York** in *Fallen Angels*, **1974.**

ove, left: **Rex Harrison** making a rare TV
pearance in *The Kingfisher*, **1982.**

**Telly Savalas
and Liz Fraser in**
Man And Boy.

The first adaptation was seven one-hour episodes, and
P. D. James was an early visitor to the location in the
East Anglian Fens, her own setting for *Death Of An
Expert Witness*. "I'm very excited about it," she said, "and
so pleased they have kept so closely to the original
story."

She revealed that Marsden's Dalgliesh was not quite her
conception of the character. "But there must be millions
of Dalglieshes; everyone who reads the book must have
an individual interpretation and view of the character I
have described."

Anglia's drama chief **John Rosenberg** described the
P. D. James link as "an exciting opportunity to
move into what for us is a new field of
drama with a production rooted in our
home territory."

It was indeed a case of Anglia
leading the way. By the time the
second adaptation, *Shroud For A
Nightingale*, was screened in 1984,
Evening Standard TV columnist
Geoffrey Phillips mused: "The strange
thing is that Anglia should virtually have

the field to themselves... while the TV networks are
desperate to attract bigger audiences, the viewers are
often curled up with their P.D. James, Dick Francis or one
of the other thriller writers whose books sell by the
hearseload. Why, then, so few good, old-fashioned
murder mysteries on TV?"

The question was soon answered, to borrow Phillips's
word, by a hearseload of classic thriller stories on both
BBC and ITV . . . **Jeremy Brett**, as Sherlock Holmes, **Joan
Hickson**, as Miss Marple, **David Suchet**, as Hercule
Poirot and **George Baker**, as Ruth Rendell's *Inspector
Wexford*, all followed in Dalgliesh's footsteps.

Anglia outstayed them all with other acclaimed
adaptations of the James novels *Cover Her Face* (1985),
The Black Tower (1985), *A Taste For Death* (1988), *Devices
And Desires* (1991), *Unnatural Causes* (1993),
A Mind To Murder (1995), and *Original Sin* (1997).

Strong supporting casts have been the order throughout
— **Geoffrey Palmer, Joss Ackland, Pauline Collins,
Rachel Kempson, Kim Thomson, Frank Finlay, Bill
Nighy, Mel Martin, Susannah York, Gemma Jones,
Jerome Flynn, Penny Downie, Ian Bannen** and **Tim
Dutton** among them.

Roy Marsden in *A Certain Justice*.

A classy formula

BY the mid-1980s, the Anglia formula of classy, traditional productions had served the company well for 25 years. Increasingly, however, TV chiefs were developing an appetite for action thrillers and plots that embraced contemporary realism. *The Guardian's* TV critic **Nancy Banks-Smith**, writing about Anglia's *Edwin* in 1984, was fulsome in her praise, but noted: "Anglia have cornered the market in plays with a butler, a French window and Dame Cecelia Molestrangler in the lead. It is not a market in which there is much competition. They are firm believers in established playwrights, proven plays and a good, big, banging star name over the title. And they do them very well. It is all so strikingly against the tide of the time, it must be like driving the wrong way down a one-way street."

Anglia was already heading in new directions, however, with **John Rosenberg** exploring a range of topical ideas for a new wave of productions in the second half of the decade. One that had been in mind for some time was a thriller series set against the background of banking and the Stock Exchange. The workings of the City of London had become high profile with financial scandals, mega takeovers and suspect share-dealing seldom out of the headlines.

A Cambridge setting for *Anything More Would Be Greedy,* **1989.**

Alec Guinness and Paul Rogers in *Edwin.*

Douglas Lambert and Roy Marsden in *Inside Story*.

Former Prime Minister Harold Wilson makes his TV acting debut in 1986 with Francesca Annis in *Inside Story*.

The area yielded two successful six-part series. First, in 1987, came the murder thriller *A Killing On The Exchange*, starring **Tim Woodward, John Duttine, Gavin O'Herlihy, Joss Ackland** and **Kim Thomson**. Writer **Paul Ableman** skilfully planted his tense whodunnit in the midst of the Square Mile, ensuring authenticity in the financial nuances of the plot by engaging merchant banker **Anthony Brown** as a technical adviser.

It was followed by *Anything More Would Be Greedy*, screened in 1989, a raunchy six-parter following the fortunes of six Cambridge high-fliers as they carved out careers in the hi-tech business and political world of the Thatcher era. Described as 'a yuppie morality tale', it was written by *History Man* author **Malcolm Bradbury** and was his first original screenplay for television. **Martin Wenner, Robert Bathurst, Matthew Marsh, Alison Sterling, Sharon Holm** and **Tessa Peake-Jones** took the lead roles.

Meanwhile, **Roy Marsden** had taken time out from his detective role to play Press baron John Bennett in *Inside Story*, screened in 1986. The change of character also marked a change of hair-piece for the naturally bald actor. From the police regulation cut of Dalgliesh's hairline, Marsden switched to a more racy style of permed curls for his Bennett toupee.

Inside Story dealt with the topical issue of powerful newspaper proprietors, with Bennett becoming owner of a top Sunday title and falling for its ace foreign correspondent, Paula Croxley, played by **Francesca Annis**. As befitted a Press drama, stories surrounding the series generated plenty of copy for the real-life news pages. First came the involvement of former Prime Minister **Harold Wilson** (by then Lord Wilson) who agreed to appear presenting an award to Paula Croxley. His participation initially caused a difficulty with Equity, the actors' union, but Lord Wilson, who was not paid for the part, eventually made his TV acting debut at the Ocean Rooms, Gorleston, near Great

Yarmouth, which masqueraded as a top London hotel. He was word-perfect in his 15-line scripted speech, but asserted afterwards: "I'm not planning a career as an actor. I enjoyed it for a day, but I think I prefer politics."

The other big 'inside story' to emerge concerned American-born actor **Douglas Lambert**, who played a sharp lawyer in the series. He was diagnosed with AIDS while filming was taking place, but the fact did not become widely known until later, at which point everyone who had worked on the production was offered a precautionary HIV test. When the newspapers discovered the story, Lambert spoke bravely of facing up to his illness which had struck at the high point of his

career. He died, aged 50, a few months after *Inside Story* was screened.

The sinister world of computer crime was the subject of *Menace Unseen*, screened in 1988. This three-part mini-series starred **Judi Bowker** and **Ian Ogilvy** – in his biggest TV role since he played Simon Templar in the 1970s series *The Saint*. Some of the filming for *Menace Unseen* took place at Blickling Hall, the National Trust property in Norfolk, around the time of the hurricane in October, 1987. Many important trees were destroyed on the estate, and Anglia donated its £1,000 filming facility fee to the National Trust's Tree Appeal, with Ogilvy presenting the cheque.

Taking the plunge... *Menace Unseen*, **1988**.

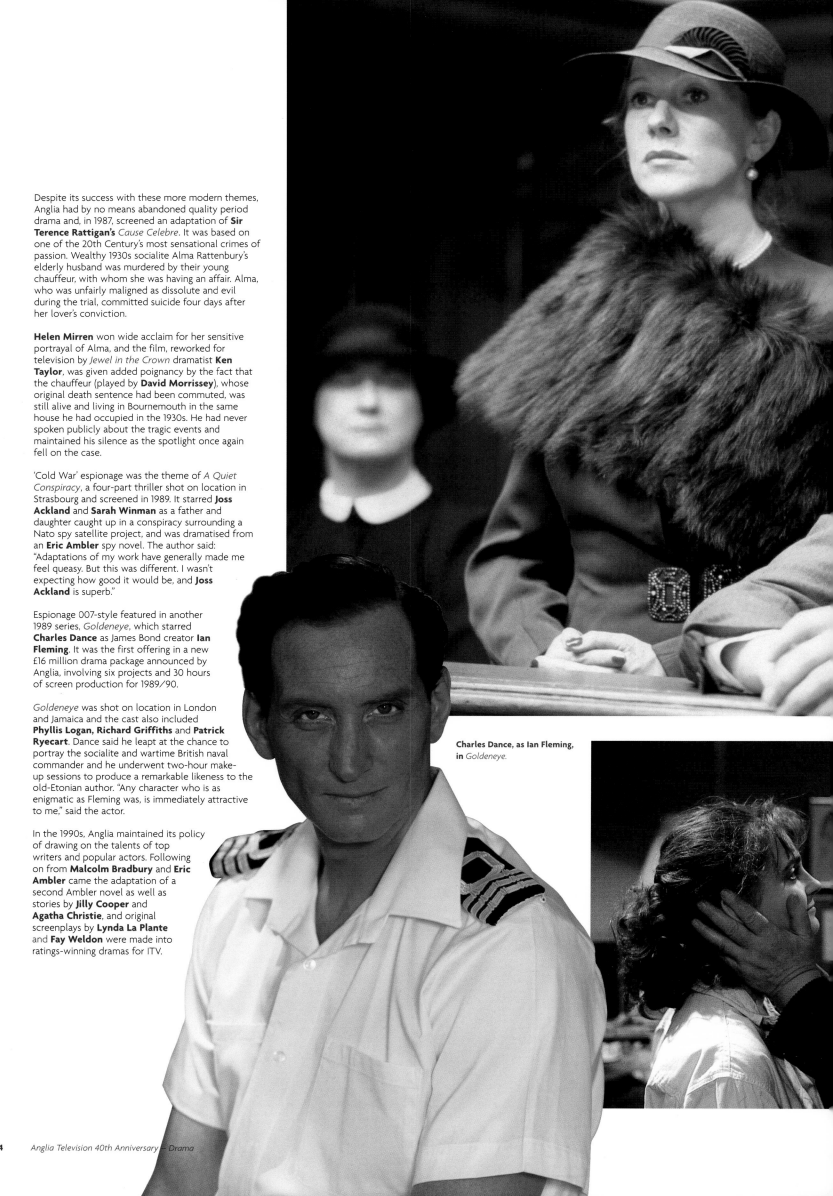

Despite its success with these more modern themes, Anglia had by no means abandoned quality period drama and, in 1987, screened an adaptation of **Sir Terence Rattigan's** *Cause Celebre*. It was based on one of the 20th Century's most sensational crimes of passion. Wealthy 1930s socialite Alma Rattenbury's elderly husband was murdered by their young chauffeur, with whom she was having an affair. Alma, who was unfairly maligned as dissolute and evil during the trial, committed suicide four days after her lover's conviction.

Helen Mirren won wide acclaim for her sensitive portrayal of Alma, and the film, reworked for television by *Jewel in the Crown* dramatist **Ken Taylor**, was given added poignancy by the fact that the chauffeur (played by **David Morrissey**), whose original death sentence had been commuted, was still alive and living in Bournemouth in the same house he had occupied in the 1930s. He had never spoken publicly about the tragic events and maintained his silence as the spotlight once again fell on the case.

'Cold War' espionage was the theme of *A Quiet Conspiracy*, a four-part thriller shot on location in Strasbourg and screened in 1989. It starred **Joss Ackland** and **Sarah Winman** as a father and daughter caught up in a conspiracy surrounding a Nato spy satellite project, and was dramatised from an **Eric Ambler** spy novel. The author said: "Adaptations of my work have generally made me feel queasy. But this was different. I wasn't expecting how good it would be, and **Joss Ackland** is superb."

Espionage 007-style featured in another 1989 series, *Goldeneye*, which starred **Charles Dance** as James Bond creator **Ian Fleming**. It was the first offering in a new £16 million drama package announced by Anglia, involving six projects and 30 hours of screen production for 1989/90.

Goldeneye was shot on location in London and Jamaica and the cast also included **Phyllis Logan, Richard Griffiths** and **Patrick Ryecart**. Dance said he leapt at the chance to portray the socialite and wartime British naval commander and he underwent two-hour make-up sessions to produce a remarkable likeness to the old-Etonian author. "Any character who is as enigmatic as Fleming was, is immediately attractive to me," said the actor.

In the 1990s, Anglia maintained its policy of drawing on the talents of top writers and popular actors. Following on from **Malcolm Bradbury** and **Eric Ambler** came the adaptation of a second Ambler novel as well as stories by **Jilly Cooper** and **Agatha Christie**, and original screenplays by **Lynda La Plante** and **Fay Weldon** were made into ratings-winning dramas for ITV.

Charles Dance, as Ian Fleming, in *Goldeneye.*

Helen Mirren and David Morrissey in court for *Cause Celebre*.

Timothy Dalton, as a Spanish playboy, in *Framed*.

Timothy Dalton shrugged off his James Bond role to play a supergrass on the run, masquerading as a Spanish playboy in the **Lynda La Plante** drama *Framed*. His distinguished co-stars included **Timothy West**, starring as a detective chief inspector, **David Morrissey**, as an ambitious detective sergeant, and **Annabelle Apsion**, as the sergeant's wife.

Before attaining the dizzy heights of Hollywood fame, **Ralph Fiennes** starred in Anglia's *A Dangerous Man – Lawrence After Arabia* as the legendary hero **T.E. Lawrence**. The epic drama, executive produced by **David Puttnam**, portrayed the fierce political battle which followed Lawrence's historic coup over the Turks. It was screened on ITV in 1992 to great acclaim, and scooped an International Emmy Award for the top drama. Fiennes went on to fame and fortune starring in *Heathcliffe*, followed by *Schindler's List* and *The English Patient*.

Joss Ackland and Sarah Winman in *A Quiet Conspiracy*, **1989**.

Ralph Fiennes in *Lawrence After Arabia*, **1992**.

It's explosive...

Leading from the front... Tim Piggott-Smith as *The Chief.*

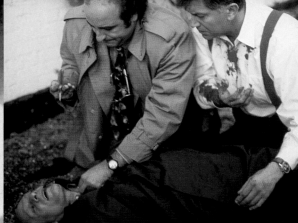
Blood on his hands... Martin Shaw who took over the title role in *The Chief.*

TIM PIGGOTT-SMITH, who starred as the malevolent Captain Merrick in the internationally-acclaimed *The Jewel in the Crown*, played an outspoken chief constable in *The Chief*, Anglia's drama focusing on the politics and power struggles of police life. The series bravely tackled the controversial issues facing Britain's forces and was praised for its realistic portrayal of policing in the 1990s. **Tim Piggott-Smith** bowed out after two series to concentrate on his theatre company. **Martin Shaw** shook off his *Professionals* image to become the new chief in charge of the fictitious force of Eastland, bringing a more charismatic and suave image to the character. Both chiefs had expert advice from a former real-life chief constable for Devon and Cornwall – **John Alderson**.

Explosive scene from *The Chief.*

Marcus Gilbert in lustful action in *Riders*.

It's salacious...

JILLY COOPER'S salacious saga of lust and rivalry in the ritzy world of international showjumping came to the screen in *Riders*. The rapacious Rupert Campbell-Black was played by **Marcus Gilbert**, while *Robin of Sherwood* and *Dynasty* star **Michael Praed** was gipsy Jake Lovell. The drama also starred **Stephanie Beacham**, who found fame in *Dynasty* and *The Colbys*. Norfolk schoolgirl **Sienna Guillory** made her television debut in the drama as her daughter.

And the raunchy romps in **Jilly Cooper's** book *The Man Who Made Husbands Jealous* was brought to ITV by Anglia. Newcomer **Stephen Billington** landed the title role to woo neglected wives and enrage their husbands. He went on to achieve greater television stardom as the wicked Greg Kelly, who beat Sally Webster in *Coronation Street*.

Iain Glen, as a Vietnam war photographer, in *Frankie's House*.

It's harrowing...

AWARD-WINNING actor **Iain Glen** played the gregarious young British war photographer Tim Page in *Frankie's House*, the poignant story of Page's harrowing experiences in war-torn Vietnam. Page became the war's most celebrated photographer and teamed up with American movie idol Sean Flynn, son of errol, who was on a 'playboy goes to war' assignment for *Paris-Match*.

Flynn – played in the four-part series by **Kevin Dillon** – and Page found escapism from the horrors of battle in the high life of a sex, drugs and music culture centred on Frankie's House in downtown Saigon. Page was wounded five times and eventually decided to return to Britain while Flynn pursued the war into Cambodia. He has not been seen since setting out on his motor-cycle in April, 1970, and is still listed as missing in action.

It's devilish...

SPANDAU BALLET star-turned-actor **Martin Kemp** played the Devil in disguise in *Growing Rich,* a six-part serial written for Anglia by best-selling author **Fay Weldon.** It is the story of three young girls, played by **Caroline Harker, Rosalind Bennett** and **Claire Hackett,** who are desperate to escape their rural rut. But their destinies are in the hands of the Devil, who masquerades as a suave chauffeur to a wealthy businessman, played by distinguished actor **John Stride.** **Martin Kemp** went on to play nightclub owner Steve Owen in *EastEnders*.

Martin Kemp, as the Devil, in *Growing Rich*.

Outrageous...

AMERICAN actress **Lynn Whitfield** starred as the legendary Josephine Baker in the rags-to-riches story of the outrageous black American entertainer in Anglia's award-winning film *The Josephine Baker Story*.

David Puttnam and **Robert Halmi** were the executive producers of this musical drama, which portrayed how Baker's wild and daring performances took Paris of the Roaring Twenties by storm and led to her being hailed as 'The Black Venus'. The drama scooped top Emmy awards for Whitfield and her director husband **Brian Gibson**.

King of the horror movies, **Christopher Lee** and *Dempsey and Makepeace* star **Michael Brandon** were caught up in the sinister world of international terrorism and political intrigue in Anglia's adaptation of **Eric Ambler's** best-selling novel *The Care Of Time*. The screening of the film, which depicted a Gulf ruler threatening to use chemical warfare, became a political hot potato itself. ITV delayed transmission when the Gulf crisis broke out in 1990, saying it was inappropriate to screen the story during the conflict.

There was a tough new look for screen heart-throb **Robson Green** when he took on the role of a dedicated detective in a crack murder squad in Anglia's thriller series *Touching Evil*. A cruel scar on his forehead and furrowed brow replaced the cheeky charm, which wooed female fans, as he played Detective Inspector Dave Creegan, a man driven by his determination to put serial killers behind bars. But he won a whole new set of fans as the series rocketed to the top drama slot with more than 12 million viewers. Created by acclaimed writer **Paul Abbott**, who penned *Cracker* and *Reckless*, the series was rated number three in *Broadcast* magazine's annual appraisal of the UK's most popular new shows in 1997. A third series was being filmed in 1999.

Two of television's most celebrated and best-loved performers, **Pam Ferris** and **Sarah Lancashire**, starred in Anglia's big drama hit *Where The Heart Is*. The heart-warming drama about the lives and loves of two community nurses in a small Yorkshire town stormed straight to the number one spot in the programme top ten with more than 12 million viewers. It also won the accolade of top new series in *Broadcast* magazine's annual appraisal in 1997.

Acclaimed actors **Tony Haygarth** and **Thomas Craig** play Pam and Sarah's husbands, while **Marsha Thomason** is a feisty new nurse who shakes up Skelthwaite and steals the heart of Pam's screen son, played by rising star **Jason Done**. The third series of 14 episodes was filmed in West Yorkshire in 1999.

Modern Anglia dramas, such as *Touching Evil* and *Where The Heart Is*, are part of the output of United Productions, the television production arm of the United News and Media group of which Anglia and its sister ITV companies, Meridian and HTV, became part after a series of mergers in the 1990s. The guiding hand as controller of drama at United Productions and executive producer of both these hit series is **Michele Buck**, whose previous career in television production included successful series such as *Gems* (at Thames Television), *Boon* and *Peak Practice* (with Central) and *Unknown Soldier* (at Carlton).

Lynn Whitfield stars as the outrageous entertainer *Josephine Baker.*

Robson Green and Nicola Walker in *Touching Evil*.

Michael Brandon, Yolanda Vazquez and Christopher Lee in *The Care Of Time*.

Pam Ferris and Sarah Lancashire, stars of *Where The Heart Is*.

The right time and the right place...

DAYTIME television was one of the fastest growing new programme areas in British broadcasting in the 1990s, with Anglia firmly in the vanguard.

By the end of the decade, the company was established as the major provider of ITV's daytime factual shows, thanks to its success in establishing the talk shows *Vanessa* and *Trisha* as ratings winners, as well as developing a range of allied programmes for ITV and other broadcasters in Britain and overseas.

Twenty years ago, daytime television was regarded by TV schedulers as a rather nebulous prefix to children's programmes. It was largely the province of educational programmes, magazine shows, quizzes and matinee movies.

Then, in the early 1980s, the arrival of *Breakfast TV* breathed new life into the daytime schedule by delivering an audience in the post 9 am period. A large proportion of that audience were women, at home on their own, with limited opportunity for conversation. And what many wanted was lively, challenging and watchable chat delivered into their living rooms.

The Time... The Place..., introduced by ITV in 1987, fitted the bill. It was one of a new breed of topical talk shows more in keeping with a daily newspaper than a weekly magazine. It presented a national debating forum with a regional identity by travelling around the ITV companies ...Glasgow, Bristol, Nottingham and Norwich were among the regular ports of call, as well as London.

Granada Television's former programme controller, **Mike Scott**, was the show's first host, later sharing the role with former *Newsnight* and TV-am reporter **John Stapleton**. It was a show very much in tune with the thinking of Anglia's controller of current affairs, **Malcolm Allsop**, who also developed the audience participation talk show regionally, in political forums and late evening entertainment shows such as *Anglia Live* and *Frontline*.

In 1992, Thames Television, which ran the unit responsible for *The Time... The Place...*, lost its ITV franchise, and Anglia stepped in to take over the role. **Allsop**, who became the programme's executive producer, pledged to maintain the successful formula which had brought audiences of up to 2.5 million – double that of BBC rival **Kilroy**. "It's popular because it tackles the issues that ordinary people are concerned and talk about," he said.

By the time the 1,000th programme was broadcast in February, 1993, presenters **Scott** and **Stapleton** had travelled the equivalent of ten times around the world on their journeys round the British Isles. They also visited the United States, Australia, Russia, Germany and the Middle East for special programmes.

The two men's recollections of defining moments on the programme reflect the way it tackled emotive subjects that touched ordinary people's lives. **Stapleton** nominated a discussion on childhood meningitis. "I was almost moved to tears. It was one of the hardest programmes I have ever done. To hear parents talking about normal, happy children who had been killed by the disease in a matter of a few hours – it was all I could do to carry on with the show."

Mike Scott with John Stapleton in *The Time... The Place...*

Travelling man John Stapleton arriving in Norwich.

John Stapleton on the set.

Scott remembered being close to tears in a programme about glue-sniffing. "I went to two parents in the audience who said their son had never been a glue-sniffer until school friends persuaded him to try it just once. That first time killed him. Everyone was knocked sideways by their story, including me."

After Scott's retirement, **Stapleton** continued as the main presenter. To allow for his demanding schedule, the travelling was reduced so that Monday and Friday programmes were always in London, where he lives with his wife, **Lynn Faulds Wood**, a consumer journalist, and their son, **Nicholas**. The three midweek programmes were usually from one regional centre, which varied week by week.

In the autumn of 1994, he also managed to find time for a Friday evening dash to Norwich to present a regional discussion show, *John Stapleton Tonight*. Earlier in that year, Anglia announced it was linking with leading American talk show producer Multimedia — producers of the *Phil Donahue Show* — to launch a new afternoon programme on ITV hosted by journalist and broadcaster **Vanessa Feltz**.

An edition of *The Time... The Place...* with Mike Scott presenting.

The queen is dead... long live the queen

THE first commission for the *Vanessa* show was for a 12-week series, and its larger-than-life host was soon setting out her stall. **Vanessa Feltz** said her aim was to breathe new life into the talk show: "We're not interested in giving free publicity to boring celebrities peddling their latest book or film. We'll be talking to real people about real issues."

The show would be "alarming, disturbing, upsetting, heart-warming and embrace the whole gamut of human emotions," she said.

"I'm so excited I'm on intravenous Mars bars!"

Feltz had visited the States and met up with **Phil Donahue** and Multimedia executives who were impressed with her style. **Malcolm Allsop** predicted that she was destined to become "a major new talent for ITV in the Nineties".

And how right he was. In its afternoon slot, two years later, the *Vanessa* show was on screen three times a week and pulling in audiences of around three million – unprecedented for a daytime programme. By 1998, competition in daytime television was seriously hotting up. In the autumn, Anglia began making a four-days-a-week show called *Guilty*, for Sky One, presented by *Sunday Mirror* columnist **Carole Malone**.

ITV, meanwhile, was determined to build on the success of its *Vanessa* show. In March it was announced that *Vanessa* would be switching to the big battleground of the morning schedule and would transmit five days a week after the decision to end *The Time... The Place...* after more than ten years.

Vanessa with Phil Donahue.

Vanessa with Elvis impersonators.

Vanessa Feltz in the studio.

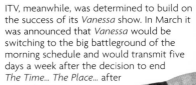
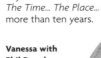

It was a tough new challenge for the woman dubbed Britain's 'Queen of Chat', but Feltz indicated she was ready to meet it. She said: "I 'm thrilled that all of the team's hard work has been rewarded. This is a great opportunity for me and the show and I am looking forward to the challenge.

"I hope we can make the programme essential morning viewing and continue to bring to ITV the most interesting subjects."

A few months later, however, and just days before the new autumn series started, it emerged she was in dispute with Anglia over her contract. The company claimed she had asked for a big hike in salary and other 'unrealistic' demands which they had refused to meet.

Vanessa Feltz had strutted the Anglia studio for the last time.

The newspapers had a field day. "Vanessa ditched on spot for demanding £2.75m deal", announced the *Daily Mail*, while *The Independent* referred to "The £2.75 million kiss off". The *Daily Star*, rather more crudely, headed its story "Fat's it for Vanessa".

The star, who was on holiday in Tuscany when the rumpus became public knowledge, denied making excessive wage demands, and spoke of the pain and distress her abrupt departure from Anglia had caused her. She claimed ITV had tried to set out conditions which would have restricted her broadcasting opportunities.

At the same time the BBC announced they had signed up Feltz in a two-year 'dream deal', reportedly worth around £1 million a year.

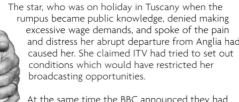

Carole Malone, presenter of *Gui*

Trisha meeting Jerry Springer in the U.S.

Trisha Goddard – ready in the wings.

Anglia, however, was not unduly troubled. It had a ready-made replacement in the wings. Top Australian TV host **Trisha Goddard**, 41, had been having talks with Anglia about other programme ideas and was ready to return to Britain where she had been born and lived for much of her first 27 years.

When Goddard emigrated to Australia she quickly established herself in television as Australia's first black anchor-woman. She became presenter of the prime-time 7.30 *Reports* show produced by the Australian Broadcasting Corporation, and also presented and produced *Live It Up*, an issue-based discussion show.

There were other reasons why she was an ideal choice for the ITV show that frequently aired people's problems. She is a trained counsellor and mental health expert and has suffered more than her own share of personal agonies during her time in Australia.

Twice divorced, her first marriage lasted only three months when she discovered her husband was gay. After his death, she learned he had AIDS, and she took an HIV test which, thankfully, proved negative. Back home in Britain, her youngest sister committed suicide. Then Goddard's second marriage, to a TV colleague, ended after she discovered, during pregnancy with their second child, that he was having an affair. And the baby, her daughter **Madison**, was taken seriously ill with breathing problems at ten weeks, and was rushed into intensive care.

The strain proved too much for Goddard, who had continued with her high-profile TV career throughout. She had even broadcast from a Sydney hospital two hours after giving birth to her first child, **Billie**. After Madison recovered, Goddard collapsed. She took an

overdose and spent four weeks in a psychiatric hospital, suffering from clinical depression.

She admits that when she was scaling the TV heights in Australia, she became 'a career-driven monster'. But all that changed after her illness. She vowed to devote more time to her children and, after marrying her husband, Peter, she has settled into an idyllic family life, with a built-in safety valve – her husband and children tell her when she is overdoing it.

Anglia had no doubt that Trisha Goddard was the ideal presenter to take over their show. But those first few weeks were still a nail-biting time. By the end of the first month, however, she was already trouncing the BBC opposition, including *Kilroy*. In December, 1998, came the announcement everyone was expecting. The BBC was pitching its new *Vanessa* show against *Trisha*. And the deposed 'Queen of Chat' was predicting a big comeback.

"She's no competition. I'm certainly not worried – no sweat," Feltz was reported as saying about her rival. She even joked that she had spent the previous four months sitting at home, pelting the television with tomatoes and eggs whenever *Trisha* appeared.

But it was Goddard, with a three-year Anglia contract under her arm, who came out on top. On the first day, Feltz's show was watched by under a million viewers, while *Trisha* pulled in almost a million and half.

Feltz admitted to *The Mirror*, "I feel wretched". But, two weeks later, there were worse headlines in *The Mirror* when the paper alleged on its front page that some guests on her BBC show had been recruited as fakes. Goddard's show did not escape the paper's

attentions either. But it was accepted that the *Trisha* guests had lied about their identity and tricked their way on to the show.

Anglia, which pointed out that only six out of more than 1,500 guests had lied their way on to its shows, further tightened its research procedures and threatened to sue any future pretenders. The serious allegations about Feltz's show, however, dealt it a mortal blow, and a few months later, it was axed by the BBC.

Staging shows on a daily basis involving dozens of disparate people from all over Britain is always going to present hazards for any broadcaster – both in terms of the participants' honesty and the way people's problems are dealt with by the show. But, as the relatively low number of complaints over the past six years bears out, Anglia has always striven to be both factual and fair with guests and viewers alike.

Goddard said in a recent interview: "We are very careful about the way we deal with people and their problems. I will not trash someone. I find it difficult to abandon my ten-year background in mental health. I do it because I care."

And on another occasion, she said: "I'm very concerned that we go through guests' notes very carefully and make sure we know in what ways they might be vulnerable. No one is left high and dry."

Continuing popularity suggests the age of the talk show will extend well into the 21st century – and Anglia will be leading it there – with **Jerry Springer** the latest addition to the stable. In late 1999, the popular American chat host was signed up to work with Anglia on a British version of his top-rated *Stateside* show.

Trisha on the set.

A star is born...

TRISHA GODDARD may be Anglia's Queen of Daytime TV in 1999, but 40 years earlier the company introduced a sparkling princess to its daytime screens who blossomed into a regal star of TV and film.

Susan Hampshire appeared on Anglia TV's opening day, previewing her role as a regular singer and presenter on *The Midday Show*, which was to be the new station's main regional news and entertainment programme.

Transmitted at two minutes past one each weekday, the show made its debut on the second day of broadcasting, October 28, 1959. And Hampshire, then aged just 17, was very much the glamour girl.

She recalls: "The format was the forerunner of what are now the very popular morning magazine programmes. Roger Gage and myself were the resident presenters, doing interviews, singing and dancing live every day.

"There was no pre-recording, not even of the songs. I wasn't very good, but good-natured and bright. But Roger had a wonderful singing voice and the small band and terrific pianist (Peter Fenn) never let us down."

Even before she went on air, Hampshire was already an ambassador for the new station. She and Roger Gage were out on the road taking part in what was described as the 'Conversion Campaign'. They travelled round the villages with an outside broadcast unit, persuading people to turn their aerials from the BBC to the new Anglia TV.

Every day the *Midday Show* welcomed to the studio a party of visitors from a town in the area – the first was from Haverhill, in Suffolk. The programme included interviews – sometimes with stars of stage and screen who were visiting Norwich – and, on different days of the week, items on records, books, films, motoring, gardening, shopping and pets, many of them introduced by the producer, Philip Bray.

In May, 1960, the show went out of the studio for the first time as an outside broadcast live from the Theatre Royal, Lowestoft. Later that year, Susan Hampshire left to pursue her film career and took on her first major role in *During One Night*, a 1961 X-rated wartime love story, starring alongside Don Borisenko. *The Lowestoft Journal* reported in December, 1961: "It will surprise

some to see Susan in this role. Parts of the story may be designed to shock and the underlying influence of sex will either attract or repel, but there are many films – some pleading 'sophistication' – such as this which can only be judged after viewing."

Susan Hampshire has, of course, gone on to become one of Britain's best known and most popular actresses, with appearances in dozens of plays, television series including *The Forsyte Saga* and *The Pallisters*, and more than 30 films.

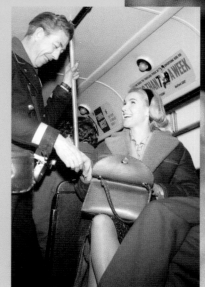

Bright young Anglia star Susan Hampshire preparing for *The Midday Show* **– at home, on the bus, in make-up and on the studio set.**

Susan's singing partner at Anglia, Roger Gage, went on to a successful career as a TV director. On a return visit to Norwich in the summer of 1999, he recalled that he was initially booked for three weeks, but the contract stretched to over a year. He was hired at £30 a show which was "a fabulous amount of money", and found Susan Hampshire "charming" to work with. He said: "Five live shows a week was extremely hard work, but the atmosphere was so exciting. Everyone was so young and enthusiastic to get the new station on air. "They were happy days and I am delighted Anglia has been so successful in its 40 years as a broadcaster."

Life after the Midday Show...

AFTER the *Midday Show* ended and regional news and features switched to *About Anglia* in the early evening, the afternoon schedule for much of the next 20 years was dominated by magazine shows catering mainly for women and retired people, and programmes for children.

The first Anglia programme especially for women, *Monday Date*, began in October, 1962. It was introduced by **Shaw Taylor** and had a 1.35 pm slot. *Woman and Beauty*, in 1967, dealt with clothes, jewellery and make-up and included interviews with leading photographers and models by presenters **John McGregor** and **Pamela Donald**. *At Home*, which followed a year later, included items for children and older people.

In the 1970s, *About Women*, presented by **Ellis Hill**, changed the emphasis to appeal more to career-minded women. Programmes dealing with social issues became popular in the afternoons, and Anglia specialised in these. For example, when equal opportunities legislation came into force in 1975, the company screened *Time to Work*, a series giving information and advice to women starting or returning to work.

Arthur Askey.

And in 1976, designated Age Action Year, **Andrew Cruickshank** – Dr Cameron in TV's original *Dr Finlay's Casebook* – and former *What's My Line* panellist **Polly Elwes** presented a new networked series, *A Ripe Old Age*, six lifestyle programmes aimed at the older generation. Guests included evergreen comedian **Arthur Askey**, round-the-world yachtsman **Sir Alec Rose** and the woman who produced best-selling books about life 'below stairs', **Margaret Powell**.

It aimed to make people positive about old age, with the first programme presenting the statutory retirement age as an artificial watershed. Other programmes dealt with money, part-time work, safety and comfort at home and holidays for older people. *A Ripe Old Age* returned for a second series two years later, with **Cliff Michelmore** as presenter.

Agony Aunt **Claire Rayner** was the presenter of a 1979 series for ITV called *Divorce and After*. Prompted by the increasing degree of marriage breakdown in Britain – then running at 150,000 a year – the series offered practical advice for people facing marital stress, the trauma of divorce, or its often equally difficult aftermath. Anglia also produced a book to accompany the series.

Claire Rayner.

Rayner hoped the programmes would prevent some marriages ending on the rocks by making people think again about their situation. One of the main problems was failure to communicate, she said. "Couples share a home and a bed but seldom share what is going on in their heads. If either partner has a problem, they are both involved and should talk to each other about it."

The Child Wants a Home, another networked series, dealt with adoption and fostering. It was screened in 1977 at a time when the number of babies available for adoption had fallen due to improved contraception, easier access to abortion and increasing acceptance of unmarried mothers. The six programmes, illustrating the joys and pitfalls of adoption, were presented by MP **Philip Whitehead**, himself adopted, and actress **Carole Mowlam**, who had two adopted children.

Anglia returned to the parenting theme in 1998 with an eight-week regional daytime series called *Bringing Up Baby*. Presented by **Denise Waterman**, the programmes aimed to help parents get the most from their children's precious pre-school years. Parents discussed common problems with child experts and shared ideas and experiences in a colourful studio, created to look like different 'rooms' of a real house.

Mother of two **Denise**, married to record producer **Pete Waterman**, enjoyed a career as a dancer and singer (including a stint as a *Benny Hill* girl) before finding her way into other areas of television. She had been a co-presenter of

Actress Carole Mowlam with her own adopted children on the set of *The Child Wants a Home*.

the home-orientated BBC series *Room for Improvement*, and presented a cookery show for satellite TV – although she acknowledged she was neither a DIY enthusiast nor an expert cook.

Parenting, however, was something she did not have to mug up on. "Been there, got the T-shirt!" she said. "It is so nice to think I am not going to be searching for questions. I have got a genuine interest in the subject – I actually know about it!"

And it is an area she thought television should pay more attention to. "There ought to be as many parenting programmes as cookery programmes" she said.

Denise Waterman.

Why I feel so much at home in Norwich...

TRISHA GODDARD writes about her experience of travelling from the other side of the world to Anglia's Norwich studios to take over one of Britain's most high-profile talk shows:

❝ ANGLIA TV was nothing like I thought it would be. Not only did it look totally different to any TV station I'd seen, housed as it is in a series of historic buildings joined together with airy concrete and glass additions, but the people are so different.

To put you in the picture, I'd spent the past 12 years of my television career in Australian TV studios. Anglia staff are far less aggressive than my Sydney TV colleagues. Mind you, I suspect that they are more laid back than their London mates. You see, although you get the high pressure in the studio, the minute you leave the building you're in cosy, cobbled-streeted, downtown Norwich. There are no 'star' hangouts and everyone knows everyone. Norwich folk make sure you stay very ordinary and you automatically change down a couple of gears the minute you get in the street.

Then there's my show *Trisha*. Well, actually, how dare I call it my show? There are no stars in the show I do. I'm the front person, that's all. I love to get in there and mix it with the rest of the team. I'm a trained producer, and love the atmosphere of a production office, so I help write scripts and come up with ideas for the show and I even have my own desk.

My arrival at Anglia was swift and unconventional. **Malcolm Allsop** tracked me down in Australia on the strength of a four-year-old tape and convinced me to up sticks and move to Norwich. I'm glad he did, because I wanted to live here and Anglia's heart really is Norwich. It's been mainly through Malcolm's vision (with managing director **Graham Creelman**'s support) that Anglia has developed and sustained, and is continually improving, its expertise in the talk show genre.

My feet didn't touch the ground after arriving in England. Within a week of landing I had made five shows. Even so, I still signed a three-year exclusivity contract with Anglia. And, despite leaving my house, job and friends on the other side of the world, I've finally found my TV home. ❞

Trisha Goddard with Malcolm Allsop on her first day at Anglia's studios.

Many Happy Returns...

Stephen Fry
Actor and writer who grew up in Norfolk

"Romper bomper stomper boo, tell me magic mirror do. I see Graham Bell, I see Michael Hunt, I see Nicholas Parsons, I see Miss Rosalyn and I see you. Happy Birthday."

Baroness James of Holland Park, OBE
Better known as award-winning crime writer P D James

"I am happy to send warm congratulations to Anglia Television on their 40th anniversary. It was Anglia who, over the years, produced the television series of my Dalgliesh novels, and I have happy memories of visiting the sets and seeing the care and sympathy with which the novels were adapted for the small screen. As a lover of East Anglia, I particularly welcome the contribution that Anglia Television has made to this unique region of England."

Anton Rodgers
Actor

"I was fortunate enough to do several plays for Anglia from early on in my career and I always looked forward to doing them, mainly because I had such a good time and I knew the production standards would be superb. In the days that we did single plays they were certainly one of the forerunners of a very high standard. At the time I was working with some of the best directors in television and most of them seemed to work for Anglia. I wish everyone a wonderful 40th anniversary and hope that the standard that you initiated will continue for many, many years. Good luck – and thanks for the booking!"

Anna Massey
Actress

"Over the years I have had the pleasure of working many times for Anglia Television. The experience was always enjoyable and rewarding – a television company producing excellence. My very best wishes to them on their 40th Birthday."

Tim Pigott-Smith
Star of the first series of The Chief

"There was a time before I worked at Anglia, when it was a company kindly, but jokingly referred to as 'Nineteenth Century Fox'. When we created the first series of *The Chief*, I came to value the company for those old-fashioned values that gave rise to the joke.

"My birthday wish for Anglia is that they will put the clock back to the good old days of TV drama. People are crying out for it.

"I was made extremely welcome by the crew, and we enjoyed a great sense of family. Some eight or nine years after, I am still in touch with friends, resident in Norwich, made on the series. I miss you. Congratulations and best wishes to all of you."

Martin Jarvis
Actor

"I have much enjoyed my association with Anglia Television as actor, narrator, panellist and ardent viewer. It's a company that has even widened my education. My physical education was given a proud boost when I learnt how to abseil down a cliff for my part as the mysterious Wilfred Anstey in PD James's *The Black Tower*. What did it matter that the cliff in question was actually in Swanage – most of the rest of the series was shot in Cromer, happily masquerading as Dorset.

"My natural history education has been enhanced by the many *Survival* commentaries I have enjoyed recording over the years. People stop me in the street, assuming I am a world expert on the migration of the wildebeest and the mating habits of every kind of mammal from the Arctic to the Equator. Occasionally I can even answer their questions correctly.

"I owe the distinct improvement in my maths education to the popular *Sale of the Century*. Not because I was directly involved in that programme, but it was required viewing for me and my children in the late Seventies. We used to count the number of times Nicholas Parsons made a mistake or fluffed some part of the information. Sometimes the errors and their corrections ran into many complex figures. It was hard work but we loved totting them all up. And we awarded ourselves bonus points if, after the commercial break, he had to correct something he had told us earlier. Both children, after this early training, always did well in mental arithmetic at school.

"But perhaps my most treasured memory of Anglia was the enjoyable day I spent as judge of the *Miss Anglia* contest. When I asked a particularly nubile young lady what her hobbies were, she replied: 'Reading.' And what sort of books did she like, I inquired? 'Well, all sorts' she answered, and then with a flutter of her eyelashes, and a sexy smile, she added, 'But I especially love friction.' There's never been any friction, as far as I am concerned, at Anglia. Just a great atmosphere and always some new adventure. Happy 40th."

T P McKenna
Actor

"I appeared as a regular in *The Chief*, first with Tim Pigott-Smith and then with Martin Shaw. I have happy memories of working in Norwich and have always found the Anglia company generous and supportive. I wish them a happy 40th anniversary and send my congratulations."

John Shrapnel
Actor

"The first pay-cheque I ever got was from Anglia. I was bussed over from Cambridge (where I was an undergraduate) to read some pieces by my tutor, the poet Francis Warner, for an arts programme. Anglia would have been a teenager at the time. It was a long while before I returned (to play a crazed evangelist in *The Chief*) but by that time I'd fallen in love with the area, and moved in. The cheque sorted out a tricky college bar bill. So Many Happy Returns, Anglia. And... cheers!

Pam St Clement
EastEnders *actress and presenter of Anglia's* Whipsnade *series*

"I have loved being part of the wonderful heritage of wildlife and animal programmes on Anglia Television. Happy anniversary from myself and all the furred, feathered and scaly friends at Whipsnade."

Ian Holm
Actor

"I have been closely associated with *Survival* over a number of years and am very proud to be a small part of your 40th anniversary."

TALES OF THE UNEXPECTED, launched in 1979 and sold to more than 70 countries, topped anything Anglia had ever done in popular drama.

The £1.5 million initial contract to produce a collection of twist-in-the-tail stories by master of the macabre, Roald Dahl, resulted from a chance meeting at a Christmas party in 1976 between the author and Sir John Woolf, the distinguished British film producer who was also Anglia's drama supremo.

For years, film and television producers had been falling over themselves to get rights to Dahl's stories – without success.

Sir John grasped the opportunity after Dahl casually asked him: "How would you like to make a television series of my stories?"

The 25 stories adapted for television were selected from two of the writer's collections – *Kiss, Kiss* and *Someone Like You* – and were a mixture of suspense, horror and black comedy.

Originally, it was intended to have Peter Ustinov presenting some of the stories, but in the event Dahl himself introduced each episode, sitting in front of a blazing fire in his drawing room...

in reality, a specially-designed set in a studio at Anglia House.

The first one made was *A Dip in the Pool*, starring American character actor Jack Weston. It was shot on the cruise liner Navarino in the Aegean. Although the first filmed, it was the eighth of nine transmitted in the first run. The second in order of filming, *The Man from the South*, shot on location in Jamaica, was chosen to launch the series on ITV on March 24, 1979.

Dahl's introductory words to that first televised *Tale* were: "Do you know what keeps haunting me with just about every paragraph I write when I'm doing a story? It's the thought that the reader's interest is easily lost. That's why, as a kind of insurance, I often try to create severe tension among the characters... so that, hopefully, every reader will be compelled to go on reading or the viewer to go on viewing. The one coming up now

is a tension story, and if any of you switch it off before it's over you'll be punching me right on the nose. I hope you won't do that."

In fact, there was no danger of Dahl's nose being put out of joint by viewer rejection. The series was an instant ratings winner, with more than half of that first Saturday night's TV audience tuning in to *The Man from the South*. There was a blip the next week, when *Mrs Bixby and the Colonel's Coat* managed only a 30 per cent audience share thanks to the Eurovision Song Contest on BBC1, but thereafter the series was regularly in the Top Ten ratings.

The BBC's *Match of the Day* certainly met its match. On May 12, *A Dip in the Pool* swamped the FA Cup final highlights, attracting more than 11 million viewers – a 63 per cent audience share.

Anglia was moved to issue a Press release announcing:

"Television's top-rated Saturday night soccer programme has been toppled from its long-standing No.1 spot in the ratings by Anglia's new £1.5 million thriller series."

Roald Dahl camera side.

The Man from the South set the standard in every way for Tales...

On the beach... Pamela Stephenson (right) and Jose Ferrer (above) in *The Man from the South.*

THE MAN FROM THE SOUTH set the standard in every way for *Tales*. It was a lavish, expensive production, with a cast headed by a major international star, in this case **Jose Ferrer**, once acclaimed as the Olivier of American acting for his roles in films such as *Moulin Rouge* and *Cyrano de Bergerac*. Also appearing in that first *Tale* was an unknown young Australian actress called **Pamela Stephenson.**

Ferrer played a flamboyant stranger who goaded a young sailor (another American actor, **Michael Ontkean**) into making a frightening bet while on holiday in Jamaica. The stakes were high – he could win an expensive car or lose a finger. The action took place around the swimming pool of a Montego Bay hotel.

From the outset, **Sir John Woolf** had his sights firmly on the American market. By using big-name stars, top directors (**Herbert Wise** among them) and evocative locations, he knew *Tales* would prove irresistible to TV executives there. And so it proved, with Anglia announcing, even before the British launch, the sale of the first series to US networks for £1 million, followed a few months later with a £1.25 million deal for a second batch of shows.

Sir John Gielgud and Joan Collins in *Neck.*

Wendy Hiller makes friends with a contrary cat as Joseph Cotten watches in *Edward the Conqueror*.

The galaxy of star names was like a 'who's who' of film and television on both sides of the Atlantic – and the pairing of co-stars was eye-catching. **Joan Collins** and **John Gielgud** teamed up in *Neck* – Collins as the seductive Lady Turton and Gielgud as a disapproving butler. Filming took place at Somerleyton Hall in Suffolk, one of many East Anglian locations used for the dramas.

American actor **Joseph Cotten**, who had made his screen debut in *Citizen Kane*, joined top English theatrical Dame, **Wendy Hiller**, in *Edward the Conqueror*, the story of a couple whose relationship was put under strain by the woman's obsession with a strange cat.

Susan George, fresh from a string of successes in Hollywood glamour roles, returned to British television for the first time in five years in *Lamb to the Slaughter*, playing a housewife who beat her husband to death with a frozen joint of meat. She said: "Believe me, making *Lamb to the Slaughter* is the best time I've had on a production for five years. I told them: 'I don't know what I've been doing in Los Angeles because this is what life is all about. This is acting.' "

She took another memorable lead role as a mother in *Royal Jelly*, the tale that launched the second series on ITV in 1980, teaming up with **Timothy West** in a creepy story about bees and a baby that would not put on weight.

One piece of casting that caught the public imagination brought together **Joan** and **Pauline Collins** in *A Girl Can't Always Have Everything*. Joan also co-starred with Pauline's husband **John Alderton** in *Georgy Porgy*, a saucy tale about a vicar and his wife.

Joan's record of appearing in three *Tales* was matched by **John Mills**, who starred in *Galloping Foxley*, *The Umbrella Man* and *Operation Safecracker*. Among those notching two apiece were **John Gielgud, Jack Weston, Susan George, Julie Harris, Pauline Collins, John Alderton, Derek Jacobi, Amanda Redman** and **Andrew Ray**.

Timothy West and Susan George, *Royal Jelly*.

John Mills, *The Umbrella Man*.

Other luminaries of British stage and screen to grace the credits of a Dahl story were **Bernard Miles, Michael Hordern, Ron Moody, Roland Culver** and **Cyril Cusack**. And there was a liberal sprinkling of star names from across The Pond, such as **Elaine Stritch, Rod Taylor** and **Gloria Grahame**.

The girls... Pauline and Joan Collins, *A Girl Can't Always Have Everything*.

The galaxy of star names was like a 'who's who' of film and television on both sides of the Atlantic

The first post-Dahl series still had a very British feel...

SIR JOHN WOOLF would have liked a third series of Dahl stories, but there were not enough available and Anglia turned to other writers to sustain the series. With the standard set, the American appetite proved undiminished, so much so that some of the later *Tales* were made in the States, with all-American casts, an inevitable development but one with which Sir John was less than enamoured.

The first post-Dahl series still had a very British feel, however, with **Denis Quilley, Simon Cadell, Suzanne Danielle** and **Sean Barrett** cast as an airline crew in *Hijack* and pop star **Toyah Willcox** starring with **Ralph Bates** in *Blue Marigold*. It was quite a departure for the 23-year-old 'High Priestess of Punk' – she played a successful model who ruined her career with drink, greed and jealousy. Willcox declared that she was heeding the warning of her character. "I recognise this is a dangerous business and I have no plans to fail in it," she told the *Daily Express*. She has remained true to her word.

Robert Morley turned up playing a businessman in an episode called *The Party*, and revealed that he started work as a vacuum cleaner salesman. "I don't often play businessmen, but when I do I always sympathise with them. I was very lucky to get into something else," he said.

The following year **Michael Craig**, who had featured in Anglia's opening programme in October, 1959 – via clips from Ipswich-shot scenes of *The Angry Silence*, in which he was starring – played a man suspected by his wife (**Dorothy Tutin**) of having an affair in *The Eavesdropper*.

And waifish Gigi star **Leslie Caron** sought revenge as the long-suffering wife of a bullying French husband in *Run Rabbit, Run*.

Derek Jacobi mesmerised a community with his clown-like antics in *Stranger in Town*. Jacobi, no stranger to elaborate make-up and costumes, as viewers of *I, Claudius* will recall, had to put in plenty of preparation time for his hirsute and bizarrely-dressed character in this production – and even more for his role as a tattooist in *Skin*. In the latter, much of which was filmed in Paris, he played the character both young and old, and needed four-hour make-up sessions. While the make-up girls worked at making his face young or old, artist Tom Taylor painted a huge facsimile tattoo on his back.

Toya Willcox in *Blue Marigold.*

Derek Jacobi gets in step in *Stranger in Town.*

Anna Neagle, Sheila Burrell and Phyllis Calvert in *The Tribute.*

Robert Morley gets in the mood, *The Party.*

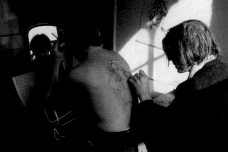
Derek Jacobi suffers four hours of make-up in *Skin.*

Harry H. Corbett, Bill Owen and Fulton Mackay, *The Moles.*

Steptoe and Son star **Harry H. Corbett**, who died from a heart attack in March, 1982, took his final television role alongside **Fulton Mackay**, from *Porridge*, and *Last of the Summer Wine's* **Bill Owen** as a businessman turned bank robber in *The Moles*. Hitchcock's *Psycho* shower victim, **Janet Leigh**, starred alongside **Frank Sinatra Jnr** in *Light Fingers* during the same run.

The following year's offerings included *A Sad Loss* in which actress **Hayley Mills** found herself stepping outside the law – just as her father had done in two earlier *Tales*, when he portrayed a safe-blower and an umbrella thief.

Former teen heart-throb **David Cassidy** took on two of the most challenging roles of his career – by playing identical twins in *Heir Presumptous* – while fellow American **Van Johnson**, an idol from another era, played an ex-airman on a nostalgic return visit to England in *Down Among the Sheltering Palms*.

Peter Cushing temporarily turned his back on horror to take a leading role in *The Vorpal Blade* while **Anna Neagle** starred in *The Tribute*, her first television drama for 20 years. By coincidence, it was with Anglia

that she made her TV drama debut in 1960 – playing the head of a South-East Asian convent captured by Communists in *A Letter from the General*.

Other American stars were also seen in editions of *Tales* during the year and the one that followed. **Sharon Gless**, from *Cagney and Lacey*, played against **Dick Smothers** – one half of the **Smothers Brothers** comedy duo – in *Youth from Vienna*.

Gayle Hunnicutt adopted her real-life role as an American living in London for *The Luncheon*, based on a short-story by **Jeffrey Archer**, and movie star **Richard Basehart** starred as a criminal expert and lawyer aiming to commit the perfect crime in *Turn of the Tide*.

International stars **George Peppard** and **Kevin Dobson** – *A-Team* leader and Crocker in *Kojak* – played Vietnam war veterans renewing a mutual dislike in civilian life in *Dirty Detail*, which led off the next series. And comedy entertainer **Tom Smothers** followed in his brother's footsteps by making an appearance as a faithful chauffeur who saved his tycoon boss and two friends from an impending scandal.

The run also featured famous TV law enforcers from both sides of the Atlantic in unusual characterisations. Britain's **Roy Marsden** took time out from his *Dalgliesh* role in Anglia's **P.D. James** serials to play a Government minister in *The Mugger*, while **Don Johnson**, from *Miami Vice*, was cast as a fast-living romantic novelist in *People Don't Do Such Things*.

Two 1988 series featured such stars as **Charles Dance, Zoe Wannamaker, Pauline Collins, Joss Ackland, Richard Briers, Patricia Routledge, John Alderton, Peter Davison, Liza Goddard, Glynis Barber, Nicholas Ball, Michael Brandon, David Suchet** and **Topol**.

Tales continued, via repeats, through to December, 1990 – ending with a second showing of the Dahl story *Vengeance is Mine Inc*, as a tribute to the author who had died the previous month.

Before the programme, **Roy Marsden** paid a personal tribute to Dahl.

More of the unexpected...

Paul Spurrier and John Mills in *Galloping Foxley*.

John Mills' school days

TRUTH was as strange as fiction for actor-knight **John Mills** when he took the lead in *Galloping Foxley*.

He played a man haunted by memories of bullying and brutality at a public school – a plot that bore an uncanny resemblance to the miserable time he spent at a school in Norfolk 60 years earlier.

Scenes for *Galloping Foxley* were also shot in Norfolk, just a few miles from the scene of his boyhood trauma.

"This is my story," said Sir John. "I wanted to do it because it applied to me. I had a hideous time during my first year at the school."

He recalled how he was made to stand holding a jug of icy cold water over his head. "The bullies would stand around and when your arms sagged they would whip you with wet towels."

Those unexpected tales...

THERE were a few tales of the unexpected associated with the filming of the prestigious series.

Arranging a drama shoot on location is always a nightmare of logistics, and, occasionally, everything that can go wrong, will.

Probably the worst moment in the *Tales* operation came when it was decided to create a little piece of Jamaica at Saunton Sands, in North Devon, for the filming of *The Boy Who Talked With Animals*.

Artificial palm trees and grassy sunshades were ordered from a London scenery firm. But on the journey to Devon some were damaged when a lorry caught fire. Eventually everything was in place — apart from the English weather. Un-Jamaica-like leaden skies were augmented by a wind of almost Caribbean hurricane proportions that wrecked the set.

The crew arrived one morning to find the artificial palms shredded along the beach. To make matters worse, the location was accessible only via the seashore, and the soft sands of Saunton proved impossible terrain for some vehicles which got bogged down hundreds of yards from the action. The whole shoot over-ran and some sequences had to be filmed later on the Norfolk coast.

The Boy Who Talked With Animals was Anglia's most expensive *Tale*, eclipsing *The Man from the South* which was shot in Jamaica itself!

Despite the most careful planning, stunts sometimes have their unexpected moments, too. One which went spectacularly wrong involved a staged car crash in Norfolk in 1981 during filming for *Death Can Add*. A remote-controlled Mercedes was set up to hit a ramp, crash through a barrier, take off over a steep embankment and burst into flames in mid-air. But the car veered off course, narrowly missing one camera team and careered down the embankment straight towards another camera position where the crew had to jump for their lives. The camera was destroyed and two people were taken to hospital with minor burns.

Tales of the unknown...

STAR-STUDDED and lavish *Tales of the Unexpected* may have been, but it also gave some 'unknowns' a taste of fame. Best remembered was the dancer who performed for the opening title sequence, dubbed by one newspaper as "the sexiest dance on television".

Karen Standley, a 27-year-old secretary and housewife from Berkshire, took a day-off to record the sequence at the request of a friend.

She was seen only in silhouette on screen and for the recording had to wear a white body stocking and tights, with white greasepaint on her arms and legs to achieve the desired effect.

"The greasepaint kept melting under the hot studio lights," she said. "It was horrible and uncomfortable and it took three baths to wash it all off. But it gave me some money — nothing staggering, but I got a new outfit out of it." Standley was quite self-critical of her performance. "I think I could have danced better," she said.

Tales was a twice-in-a-lifetime experience for Suffolk boy **Paul Spurrier**. As a 12-year-old child actor, Paul, who lived at Oulton Broad, near Lowestoft, and attended Norwich School, was chosen to appear alongside **John Mills** and **Anthony Steel** in *Galloping Foxley* – a story of a man haunted by memories of public school bullying

He then had an even bigger role as *The Boy Who Talked With Animals*, partnering American actor **Stuart Whitman** in the story of a lad who found animals better company than people.

The ironic thing about the latter role was that he was actually allergic to animals because of asthma. "I can't even keep birds," he said. "The dust on their feathers makes me ill."

Paul had a number of other television roles as a teenager, but did not have ambitions to make acting his life. "The profession is far too precarious," he said in 1981, favouring a career as a film director. "I would dearly love to get behind a real film camera. That's much more interesting than hanging around for hours and having to study lines."

At 18 Paul stopped performing and now runs his own film and TV production company in Battersea. In 1998 he made his first film.

The *Tales* link also brought unexpected success for a 54-year-old widow **Aileen Wheeler**, from Gravesend, Kent, who won a *TV Times* competition to write a short story. She received a £200 prize, beating more than 11,000 other entries. And when she went to receive her prize from Anglia's executive producer **Sir John Woolf**, she learned that her story was to be used in the series. It was called *Blue Marigold*, and **Toyah Willcox** was cast in the lead role as a self-destructive model. Wheeler admitted it was only the competition that had spurred her into writing the tale. "My head is always full of ideas for plays and stories, but I never get round to putting them on paper," she said.

I had devoted over thirty years to writing short stories and during all that
time I had rejected many offers from television people, especially in America.
I did sell a few to Hitchcock in the very early days because I needed the money, but
apart from that, I had been carefully hoarding them in the hope of finding the right
person - a person I could rely upon to make a big series of the highest quality.

So I plunged with Woolf.

And Woolf plunged with me.

I am tremendously pleased with what has been done so far. I have never before
seen a series of television plays made with such meticulous care. The stories are
being dramatised faithfully and with great skill. I have no complaints whatsoever,
which is a rare thing for a writer to say these days when he sees his work
being adapted for television.

Roald Dahl

Tails of the unexpected...

ANIMALS also had a part to play in *Tales of the Unexpected*.

In *Edward the Conqueror*, starring **Wendy Hiller** and **Joseph Cotten**, a cat was central to the plot. A wonderful two-year-old British cream with the somewhat unusual name of Lulu (he was a boy) duly joined the cast, along with his near-identical brother — Katrina — as stand-in.

In the story — which was shot in particularly difficult and wintry conditions in a mill house deep in the Norfolk countryside — a stray cat responds to the wife's piano playing in such a strange way that she becomes convinced that it is a reincarnation of the composer Franz Liszt.

Unfortunately, from the moment the feline star arrived on location, it decided it didn't want to know poor Wendy Hiller, (whom it was supposed to adore) and attached itself instead to Joseph Cotten (whom in the story it was supposed to hate).

Hiller, a cat lover, struggled (quite literally) to achieve the necessary scenes of affectionate closeness with the cat, and was scratched for her pains. Needless to say none of this showed up in the final cut and 'Maestro' emerged a star.

In *The Absence of Emily*, starring **Anthony Valentine** and **Frances Tomelty**, it was a dog which got all the attention. While filming was going on at the Feathers Hotel in Holt, Norfolk, word swiftly got round that the little Jack Russell bitch was in the care of the RSPCA, having been found abandoned, left tied to a tree. Like all good stories there was a happy ending when one of the chambermaids offered the newly-named 'Emily' (what else?) a home.

Sting in the tale...

TIMOTHY WEST discovered hidden talents as a beekeeper while filming *Royal Jelly*. As **Susan George's** apiarist husband in the story, he had to shoot scenes at the beehives unprotected — while everyone else, from the director to the cameraman, was clad in boiler suits and face-nets to guard against stings.

The only precaution **Timothy West** took before he lifted the top from a hive was an anti-histamine injection.

The real beekeeper, **Peter Beckley**, said: "Timothy West was exceptionally good with bees. He has a keen eye and a calm manner and handled them with ease." West felt an affinity with the bees, too. "I might take this up," he said. "I know my wife (Prunella Scales) likes the idea."

And the sting in the tail? Only one person got stung — the company doctor who was standing by in case of injury to the actor.

What the Bishop said to the actresses....

GEORGY PORGY, starring **Joan Collins** and **John Alderton**, ran into unexpected trouble when the **Bishop of Norwich** intervened to stop a saucy scene being shot in one of his churches.

Twelve actresses — including Joan Collins — were due to be filmed sitting in the pews naked from the waist up. The story line was that John Alderton, who played the vicar, fantasised about his female parish-ioners in a state of undress as he delivered his sermon.

But when the bishop found out he withdrew permission for the scene to be filmed. In the end, it was shot in an old crypt converted into a coffee bar in the centre of Norwich. And the actresses were not naked after all — they all wore body stockings. Joan Collins could not be present when the scene was finally filmed. Her place was taken by a stand-in.

A nation at prayer...

ANGLIA'S latest and perhaps most lavish contribution to religious broadcasting is its new, networked *Sunday Morning* series, for which the contract was won against fierce competition.

Launched in January, 1999, this weekly programme hosted by husband and wife team **Michael Nesbitt** and **Linda Bryan**, has delivered a lively mix of topical features, music and human interest stories.

The schedule for its initial run was for 15 hour-long acts of worship on the first Sunday of each month, plus key religious dates, and 37 editions of the magazine programme, including a short act of worship in churches around the country.

A previous version of *Sunday Morning*, again in magazine format with multi-denominational morning worship from around the UK, was commissioned from Anglia by ITV in 1993.

The series of live two-hour programmes, again won against keen competition, was fronted by former ITN and Anglia newsman **Richard Bath** and **Kay Avila**, one of the original presenters of Anglia's *Food Guide* magazine.

It included *A Border Pilgrimage*, which traced the footsteps of Celtic saints, *Chalke Talk*, with youth worker **Steve Chalke**, *The Cooking Canon*, with **John Eley** firing off culinary ideas, *Faith In Action*, featuring former England football manager **Glenn Hoddle**, and *The Good Retreat Guide* with **Rowanne Pascoe**.

In another strand, *A Little Piece Of Heaven*, other personalities returned to places which had special spiritual significance for them. They included actresses **Stephanie Cole**, **Wendy Craig** and **Jean Marsh**, comedians **Don Maclean** and **Frank Carson**, singer **Paul Jones** and veteran *Coronation Street* actor **Bryan Mosley**, who died early in 1999, just three weeks after the fictional death of his shopkeeper character, Alf Roberts.

Finally there was a 'problem page' in which **Canon Martin Shaw**, spiritual adviser to the Anglican Diocese of St Edmundsbury and Ipswich, offered advice on moral, religious and ethical dilemmas.

At the end of 1993 there was a Bible painting competition for children. **Cliff Richard**, one of the judges, presented the top prize of art equipment and a copy of his *Favourite Bible Stories* to eight-year-old winner **Emma Gregory**, of West Hallam, Derbyshire.

During and between the two series there has been regular live coverage of church services throughout Britain with *Morning Worship*. The series was first presented by **Richard Bath** and **Susan Rae** and an early transmission from Southwark Cathedral took the best programme award at Britain's top Christian broadcasting competition – the Christian Broadcasting Council Media Awards. And an outside broadcast on the dedication of Brentwood's Roman Catholic Cathedral, won the Peter Freeman Prize for the best-presented act of worship on ITV in the Sandford St Martin Trust Religious Television Awards. The latter was a fitting success as the late **Canon Peter Freeman** had been Anglia's religious adviser for many years.

Other highlights included a special 1993 Remembrance Sunday edition called *A Cry For Peace*, broadcast live by LWT from Enniskillen in Northern Ireland. Six years earlier a bomb exploded at the town's cenotaph during the Remembrance Day service, killing 11 people and injuring more than 20 others.

Husband and wife team Michael Nesbitt and Linda Bryan who host *Sunday Morning*.

One of the dead was **Marie Wilson**, whose father Gordon, a tireless worker for peace, took part in the programme, assisting in the declaration of a special 'Peace Cairn' – a traditional pyramid landmark of rough stones – which Enniskillen's young people built near where the explosion took place.

There was also a special broadcast from Greenwich in 1997 to mark the 1000-day countdown to the Millennium.

In focus... a cameraman in position for *Morning Worship*.

The Big Question...

ONE religious programme which will linger in many viewers' minds – although it ended well over a decade ago, in 1984 – is *The Big Question.*

Launched in the early Seventies, the series brought together three different characters – the Dean of Norwich and later St Paul's Cathedral **(the Very Rev Alan Webster)**, a United Reformed Church Minister **(the Rev Edmund Banyard)** and a Franciscan monk **(Father Eric Doyle)**.

The programmes became cult viewing – despite their slot at the end of the day's schedule – as the trio wrestled with moral and theological issues. The team stayed together, even after all three moved away from East Anglia, and took pride in the fact that their debates showed three different churches working and thinking together. Tragically, **Eric Doyle** died at the age of 46 shortly after the series came to an end and four episodes were repeated as a tribute.

From its earliest days Anglia showed commitment to religious broadcasting.

One of the first special events was in November, 1961, with *A New Mass*, from St Peter Mancroft Church in Norwich. This was the first performance of a service of Holy Communion set to music written for Anglia by composers **Davis Heneker** and **Lancelot Hankey**.

Two months later, in January, a religious broadcast went far beyond the limits of the region, with six other ITV companies taking Anglia's coverage of the enthronement of the new Bishop of Peterborough.

Line up for the final programme in *The Big Question* series.

At the turn of 1962 there was *The Christmas Story*, an outside broadcast from Peterborough Cathedral of a special presentation written by a Northamptonshire vicar, and *In Our Time*, a monthly series in which churchmen gave their views on current affairs.

Highlights of the ensuing years were coverage of the consecration of the Bishops of Thetford and Lynn from Westminster Abbey, a series of scripture readings for Holy Week by actor **Marius Goring** and outside broadcasts from around the region, including Lincoln Cathedral and the grounds of Raynham Hall in Norfolk.

The Bishop of Norwich featured in two programmes – *The Making Of Maurice Norvic* and *A 20th Century Bishop* – and the lives of men who had influenced Christianity were recalled in *Stories of the Saints*. *Too Many Mansions* examined the dilemma facing ecclesiastical authorities and conservationists as more churches became redundant and fell into decay.

There was also *A Tinker Out Of Bedford*, which told the story of **John Bunyan** – author of *The Pilgrim's Progress* – who was imprisoned for his religious beliefs. The programme was broadcast in 1988 to commemorate the 300th anniversary of Bunyan's death and extracts from the author's work were read by actor **Tim Woodward**.

Regular late-night religious programmes in the first two decades or so of Anglia included *Anthology, At The End of the Day, The Bible for Today, The Living Word, Men Who Matter, Reflections* and *Your Music at Night*.

Anglia also contributed for more than a decade to one of ITV's most popular religious programmes – *Highway* with **Harry Secombe**.

The series was launched in October, 1983, as a co-production with Grampian, HTV (West and Wales), Scottish Television, Tyne Tees and Ulster. In fact, Anglia made both the first and last of the hundreds of *Highway* programmes.

For Secombe it was a very different role from anything he'd done before but the arch-Goon had one assurance for viewers: "I won't be playing a sanctimonious old twit – and that's for sure!"

He added: "Of course it's a bit of a change from my usual approach to entertainment – and you can't be funny in a programme for Remembrance Sunday. But that doesn't mean going around with a face like an old boot – and there will be humour in the series."

The first two Anglia programmes focused on Cambridge and King's Lynn. Guests included trombonist **George Chisholm**, former Archbishop of Canterbury **Lord Coggan** and **Sarah Jones**, widow of Falklands hero, **Colonel 'H' Jones**.

Personalities appearing in later programmes from the region included writer **Kingsley Amis, the Beverley Sisters, Cindy Buxton, Geoff Capes, Bob Champion, Leonard Cheshire** and **Sue Ryder, Leslie Crowther, Billy Dainty, John Dankworth** and **Cleo Laine, Robert**

Cliff Richard appeared in a documentary on the religious rock festival *Greenbelt '88* at Castle Ashby in Northamptonshire, where he topped the bill. He is pictured with reporter Tony Adams.

Dougall, Paul Eddington, Robert Hardy, Edmund Hockeridge, Hammond Innes, Karen Kay, Evelyn Laye, Derek Nimmo, Linda Nolan, Nick Owen, Jimmy Savile, Semprini, Helen Shapiro, The Spinners, Una Stubbs, Donald Swann, Mary Whitehouse and **Bernie Winters**.

Even **John Major**, Prime Minister at the time, and his wife **Norma** took part in the series, which in its early days earned Anglia the *Harry Secombe Spirit of Highway* award for the best programme.

Harry Secombe in Captain Hook costume for *Highway*.

Castle's on the air...

IN the late eighties and early nineties, **Roy Castle** made four network series with a Christian theme.

First there was *Marching As To War*, the story of the Salvation Army. Coinciding with the start of the series, which included the story of **William Booth's** preaching about the evils of the demon drink, Castle admitted in an interview with the *News of the World* that his own earlier life in showbusiness had been tainted by a drink problem. But he had found his own salvation by turning to Christianity.

"Most of my unhappy memories stem from when I'd had a couple of drinks," said Roy. "You can't take those times back. All you can do is get born again and make a fresh start. I'm not teetotal now, but I doubt if I'll ever get drunk again."

Roy Castle's next religious series for Anglia was *The Hymn Makers*, which looked at the lives and music of some of Britain's best-known hymn writers.

The third, *Castle's In Europe*, in 1990, was a travel show with a difference – Castle hosting a five-part holiday series with a religious flavour. In it, he explored the Christian heritage and present-day pageantry of five famous holiday destinations in Italy, France, Germany, Spain and Greece.

Finally came *Castle's Abroad* in 1991, this time looking at the historical, cultural and spiritual backgrounds to places and events during a five-nation tour. Poland was the country which made the biggest impact on Castle – partly because it was home to the Auschwitz gas chambers, but also because of all the other oppression and poverty the country had suffered.

Roy Castle meets a Lapp reindeer farmer in *Castle's Abroad*.

Roy Castle marches out for *The Hymn Makers*.

"The poor people of Poland have been up against it for a thousand years," he said. "I would love to see those people get a break. My heart goes out to them."

Castle was due to travel to the United States for his next Anglia series, but, just as he was about to pack his bags, he was diagnosed with advanced lung cancer. His brave public acknowledgement of the illness and his campaigning to raise funds for cancer treatment, and to warn against the dangers of smoking, captured the hearts of people everywhere. When he finally succumbed to the illness, the tributes reflected the deep affection felt by the nation – including many at Anglia who knew him as a colleague and friend.

His place in presenting Anglia's religious series from the USA in 1992 went to **Anne Gregg**. *Annie Across America* took the former BBC *Holiday* programme presenter on a coast-to-coast tour, in search of the soul of modern America through a colourful tapestry of religion, history and culture.

Her journey from Boston to Los Angeles, via New York, New Orleans, Florida, Salt Lake City and Las Vegas also touched on major social issues such as drugs, AIDS and poverty. People she met along the way included a priest who exorcised evil spirits, Mormons and a wedding parlour 'queen' – as well as former Wimbledon tennis champion **Stan Smith** and astronaut **Charles Duke**, both of whom talked about their religious convictions.

The following year Anne Gregg made another series *Package Pilgrims*, exploring destinations with appeal to the growing number of tourists looking for holidays to refresh the soul as well as the body and mind. For each of seven programmes she was accompanied by a preacher who acted as religious guide. She started in Malta before travelling to Rome, to the Holy Land for two programmes, and then to Tuscany, Paris and Assisi.

Gregg had never been to Malta or the Holy Land, where sight-seeing proved a real pain. She got water in her eyes while swimming in the salty Dead Sea and, as she told viewers about its curative powers, she was temporarily blinded.

"It was like having acid thrown in my eyes," she recalled. "The tears streamed out for five minutes and I couldn't see a thing. I thought it was a funny sort of miracle cure," she laughed. "I get into the Dead Sea perfectly all right – and come out blind!"

In a 1990 Anglia regional series, **Richard Collier**, a solicitor and ordained Anglican priest, **Jane Collier**, a Cambridge University economics lecturer, and Roman Catholic priest **Gary Dowsey** lined up as *Devil's Advocates*. They grilled personalities, including Government minister **John Gummer**, GEC chairman **Lord Prior** and cookery guru **Delia Smith** about their Christian beliefs.

The same year an Anglia camera team went to the USSR to film *Father Oleg, Mother Russia*, a documentary about the work and beliefs of a Russian Orthodox priest, which was screened by Channel Four on Christmas Night.

Anne Gregg visits Malta in *Package Pilgrims*.

Another series on the regional front – launched in 1990 – was *Journeys*, which focused on subjects ranging from a community of Anglican nuns to evangelical worship, an aid mission to Romania by East Anglian churches and changing attitudes to miscarriage and stillbirth. It also examined the funny side of religion, the place of ancient rituals in modern Christianity and the story behind the opening of Britain's newest cathedral – at Brentwood in Essex. Actor **Peter Barkworth**, actress **Wendy Craig**, *Coronation Street* star **Bryan Mosley**, singer **Helen Shapiro** and writer **George Target** were among celebrities appearing in later series.

Around the same time, reporter **John Swinfield** made a series of religious documentaries. He started off with *Chaplain Ron*, about the work of a prison chaplain. Then he visited places such as Bolivia, Brazil, El Salvador, Peru, Indonesia, the Philippines and Thailand for a series of films on Catholic priests and a former nun. These went out under the regional title of *Against The Odds* or, on the ITV network, as programmes in the *Encounter* and *Heartland* series.

Coronation Street **actor Bryan Mosley visits Kersey in Suffolk for** *A Little Piece of Heaven*.

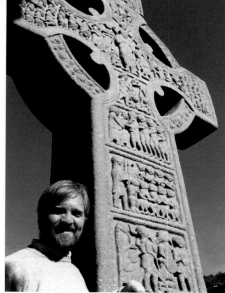

Canon Martin Shaw in *Island Soldiers*.

Halfway To Heaven **presenter Richard Collier with Derek Nimmo.**

One of the documentaries, *Beggars In Paradise* – shown in the *Heartland* series – won the Sandford St Martin Trust award for the outstanding religious programme on British television during the previous three years.

The film was described by the judges as "a compelling portrait" of **Father Chris Conroy's** work among poverty-stricken peasants in the Peruvian Andes – and "the most glorious, flowing 55 minutes of television."

In *Halfway To Heaven*, screened in 1991, celebrities including actor, writer and impresario **Derek Nimmo**, singer **Helen Shapiro** and broadcaster **Sir Jimmy Savile** talked to presenter **Richard Collier** about their faith and things they found important.

Curate's Egg in 1992 examined the lives and work of several new Christian ministers in their first East Anglian posts. *Divided We Stand* the same year looked at the religious life of the Anglia region by focusing on worship, baptism, education, morality, multi-faith and marriage.

Alvin Stardust (right) and Bobby Ball with Gloria Hunniford in *Gloria!*

In 1993, **Gloria Hunniford** toured the Norfolk Broads in a one-off religious music special called *Gloria!* Joining her on the cruise were comic **Bobby Ball** and singer **Alvin Stardust** who, as well as contributing songs, talked about sex, drugs, booze and showbusiness.

Ball revealed how the pressures of showbusiness left him with material assets galore but a hollow feeling inside. "I was a bad husband," he confessed. "I drank a bottle of whisky a day, I fought and I went with a lot of women."

Alvin Stardust recalled the lows in his life as a rock star and admitted: "I have had a few times when I have been drinking too much and taking drugs and everything – like people did in my era".

Both stars described how, since those bad old days, they had found inner peace through faith.

In 1994, presenter **Jayne Evans** set out on a tour of six very different East of England parishes for *Heaven And Home*. During the series she found out how communities were supporting each other and their churches. The same year, **Steve Chalke**, the Baptist

minister and GMTV regular who featured in the first series of *Sunday Morning*, returned to Anglia to present *Seven Deadly Sins* in which he took a close look at the hit parade of temptations drawn up by monks in the Middle Ages – gluttony, anger, lust, sloth, pride and, finally, greed and envy.

He went out into the region to find out whether this ancient list of sins still had something to say about motives, behaviour and attitudes in the Nineties. He also returned to Anglia screens for the opposite side of the coin – *Seven Deadly Virtues* in 1995 – as well as both *Chalke Talk* and *Love Chronicles* in 1996.

In *Seven Deadly Virtues* Chalke examined the value of hope and fortitude, prudence, justice, chastity, temperance and charity with such personalities as Norwich goalkeeper **Bryan Gunn**, whose daughter died of leukaemia in 1992, former jockey **Bob Champion**, *Troubleshooter* **Sir John Harvey-Jones** and speedway riders **Mark Loram** and **Mike Lanham**.

A new version of *Chalke Talk* was an eight-week Sunday talk show with people in the news, presented from the scene of one of the week's big stories. And in the six-part *Love Chronicles*, Chalke sought out the elusive emotion in its many forms.

Island Soldiers was a widely-acclaimed six-part series in 1995. In it **Canon Martin Shaw**, who had also featured two years earlier in *Sunday Morning*, followed in the footsteps of the Celtic saints of the fifth to seventh centuries. He explored their lives and examined the legacy of prayer, meditation and music.

Canon Shaw started the series by joining 30,000 hardy souls on the annual pilgrimage up Ireland's holy mountain and continued his travels to the mystical Hebridean island of Iona and to Lindisfarne (Holy Island) off the Northumberland coast. In the other three programmes he joined pilgrims on the trail of St Patrick in Donegal, visited Britain's smallest city – St David's on the west coast of Wales – and toured the great Celtic monasteries of Ireland.

Actor **Nigel Havers** returned to Norwich, a city with which he had close associations through relatives and friends, to present a one-off religious programme in 1996. In *Norwich Cathedral – History In The Making* he looked at the work of some of the unsung heroes whose work ensured the future of a magnificent Norman building which was celebrating its 900th anniversary.

Signs And Wonders, in 1997, delved into the role of the supernatural in the Christian Church, examining controversial areas like faith healing, visions, prophecy, ghosts and the power of the devil. Balancing the rise of a charismatic movement with more traditional attitudes in the church, each programme probed an area of faith where unexplained phenomena play a significant role.

On the road . . . John Timpson's tour of country churches.

Timpson's Country Churches was effectively given Royal approval when it was launched in 1995. **Prince Charles** featured in the opening programme, emphasising the importance of preserving what, he said, were often the last public buildings left in rural communities. The series brought former Radio Four favourite **John Timpson** back to the small screen after a lengthy absence. During this popular three-year run Timpson went in search of curiosities and oddities among the region's churches and extended his search to other parts of the country for one of the series.

In some locations there were special guests – such as former hostages **Terry Waite** and **John McCarthy** at Great Braxted Church in Essex. Events from the history of one or two churches were even re-enacted. At Upton, near Acle, in Norfolk, for instance, church records revealed how two men burst in during evening prayers on Christmas Day, 1612, carrying a whalebone from which they had suspended a dead wren and a robin. According to the Archdeacon's damning report the pair were considerably the worse for drink and "went staggering and reeling to and fro in a scoffing and wild profane manner."

The crew threw themselves into their roles with outstanding enthusiasm when recalling this shocking tale – but, sadly, are still awaiting a call from Hollywood's casting agents...

Nigel Havers visits Norwich Cathedral to celebrate its 900th anniversary.

Recipe for success...

TELEVISION without cookery shows these days would be like roast beef without Yorkshire pudding. Yet, despite the plethora of programmes covering everything from 'back to basics' egg-boiling to exotic dishes in far-flung locations, the TV focus on food preparation is, in most cases, a fairly recent phenomenon.

Anglia, however, has been serving up regular helpings of tasty fare for most of its 40 years. And if it hasn't quite managed the entire A to Z of British cookery, it has certainly covered a good chunk of the alphabet.

There were regular food spots as early as October, 1959, when *The Midday Show* took to the air.

There were also regular features on food production, right from the start of *Farming Diary*, originally presented by **Dick Joice**, in November, 1959. By 1962, he was presenting the programme from America, where he spent ten days studying American farm mechanisation methods.

One of Anglia's earliest programmes dedicated to the culinary arts was *Cookery With Mrs Daines*, a popular *About Anglia* item which was promoted to a full

Sunday afternoon series of its own in January, 1964. A different angle on food was provided in 1971 by *Roast Beef And Plum Pudding*, a dramatised documentary in which **Dick Joice** – as **Parson Woodforde** – recaptured the rich flavour of life in eighteenth century England.

Although not a cookery programme as such, *Hintlesham Hall And Me*, in 1973, was again firmly set in the culinary world, with **Robert Carrier** offering a step-by-step recipe for success at his famous restaurant. And the produce of the grape was not forgotten either, with *Full, Round And Fruity* examining the aristocrats of wine later in the same year.

There was also a topical look at the industry providing the basic ingredients for cookery in *Food File*, a 28-part series which ran from April, 1975, to March, 1976, and was introduced by **Suzanne Hall**. A spin-off from that came in the form of several Anglia contributions to the ITV network series *Regional Flavour*. Presented by **Jane Probyn** and cookery expert **Zena Skinner**, they involved excursions to various parts of the East of England to seek out traditional dishes.

These were but a flash in the pan, however, compared with *Patrick's Pantry*. The series began as a segment of

About Anglia in 1977 after presenter and former chef **Patrick Anthony**, who started his culinary career as a management trainee with the **Joe Lyons** organisation, persuaded his TV bosses to let him demonstrate how to make Irish coffee.

From this small beginning was born a regular cooking spot which was to last almost 20 years. Anthony reckoned he'd chopped up more than 2,500 bunches of his trademark parsley by the time he reached that milestone.

Going green in the kitchen... Patrick Anthony and trademark parsley.

Dick Joice, as Parson Woodforde, gets carving in *Roast Beef and Plum Pudding.*

The cameras focus on Robert Carrier in *Hintlesham Hall And Me* **in 1973.**

Zena Skinner out and about in *Regional Flavour.*

Brian Turner brings a regional flavour to his
Out to Lunch series, such as on a visit to
Donny Cole's Lowestoft herring smokehouse.

It also acted as a springboard for success on TV-am and shows like *Ready, Steady, Cook* as well as a regular column in the *Daily Star* and, not least, Anglia's 30-minute *Food Guide* series.

In this series, which hit the screen for the first time in 1991, **Patrick Anthony** was joined initially by one of Britain's leading restaurant and food writers, **Denis Curtis**, and Channel Four's *Take Six Cooks* presenter **Kay Avila** from whom **Susan Rae** took over three years later.

Although Anthony still cooked up a recipe idea in each programme, the series took a fresh approach to television food shows. It looked at a wide range of subjects, including the revival in classic English cooking, the spread of American-style fast food, fish and high-fibre diets. The second series, which started in November the next year, included the launch of a 'Host of '93' competition, in which viewers were challenged to come up with a dinner party theme and create an appropriate menu.

Another competition, to find viewers' favourite family recipes, featured in the final *Food Guide* series, in 1995. **Denis Curtis** bravely completed the series despite fighting a losing battle against cancer, which resulted in his death in September of that year.

By now, however, you could say that Anglia had got cookery programmes off to a 'T' – and 1996 seemed a good time to introduce a leading chef called Turner to regional viewers.

Despite his experience with such programmes as *Ready, Steady, Cook* and *This Morning*, the new series *Out To Lunch With Brian Turner* brought this Yorkshire-born owner of a fashionable Chelsea restaurant his first experience of TV cooking outside the studio.

"Its a departure for me – and I'm really enjoying it," said the 50-year-old who left his native county for London more than 30 years ago but still retains the Yorkshire accent, humour and no-nonsense approach to life.

Brian Turner learned his culinary craft at some of London's most prestigious hotels and restaurants, such as Claridges and the Savoy Grill, as well as Simpsons, in the Strand. His career also included a two-year spell at the Beau Rivage Palace in Lausanne, Switzerland, where he built up his knowledge of classical cuisine.

It was on November 5, appropriately, that Turner lit up Anglia screens for the first time and he soon became a firm favourite with regional viewers. His approach to presenting the series was simple: "I like to think old Aunt Edith's out there watching and I'm telling her how to do something," he said.

"My little bit is to show people things, give them ideas and encourage them to have a go themselves."

Turner's own willingness to have a go nearly ended in tragedy on one filming trip. Producer **Paul Freeman** recalls that "he got stuck in as usual" on a Southwold fishing boat and was about to help haul in the nets when a metal bar broke loose and swung round, hitting the presenter on the back of the head. "He was absolutely pole-axed and out cold. We thought he was dead." Thankfully Turner came round and was wrapped up while the catch of sole was hauled in. After a trip to hospital for repairs to his head wound he insisted on completing the day's filming, but looked rather pale as he cooked up a recipe on the causeway.

The inimitable **Nosh Brothers** – Mick and Nick – brought their 'in yer face' style to solving the problems of calamitous cooks around the region in a six-part series called *Save Your Bacon*. Among the challenges

Recipe For Disaster... **Brian Turner (left), Katrina Buchanan and James Martin.**

they faced were feeding body-builders who wanted to pep up their tastebuds while they pumped their muscles, devising a menu for firemen fed up with long watches during the night and sorting out a sumptuous meal for a secretary desperate to make an impression on her new boss.

The heavyweight pair are not actually brothers and neither was formally trained as a chef, although Mick (he's the one without the beard) served what he described as "a gruelling apprenticeship" in the film location catering industry.

They met, inevitably, at a dinner party, where Nick was doing the cooking as a favour for a friend. But the day job intervened when Nick was called away from the stove to take an important telephone call involving a film deal and Mick took over to finish the cooking. Friendship blossomed and a professional partnership followed as the pair, who ran their own restaurant for a time, began catering for celebrity parties.

Among their books was one called simply *Entertaining* which not only provided plenty of ideas for delicious dishes but also threw in, for good measure, the Nosh guide to etiquette.

One suggestion was to put dinner guests who can't drink because they are driving in a separate room with a Diet Coke and a game of Monopoly. Fortunately, another essential piece of advice, on what to do if someone dies at the table – throw a cloth over him or her – wasn't needed during the recording of *Save Your Bacon*

The Nosh Brothers, Nick (left) and Mick, ready for action in *Save Your Bacon*.

The celebrity quiz-and-cookery show *Recipe For Disaster* featured two faces familiar to Anglia viewers – **Patrick Anthony** and **Brian Turner** – as well as fellow top cooks **James Martin** and **Mark Wogan**. The idea was to pair two of the cooks with celebrity partners who bid for ingredients by answering general knowledge questions. The teams then faced the challenge of coming up with a tasty dish, with a good helping of banter along the way.

Celebrity guests included **Liza Goddard**, broadcaster **Paul Ross**, Anglia personalities **Tim Curtis**, **Helen McDermott** and **Caroline Oldrey**, churchman **Terry Waite**, cricketers **Mark Ilott** and **Rob Bailey**, MPs **Ian Gibson** and **Keith Simpson** and 'Agony Aunts' **Christine Webber** and **Anne Atkins**.

Leading contender for the title 'Teller of the Sickest Joke' during the series was, surprisingly, **Terry Waite**, who described the worst meal he was served up as a Beirut hostage. It was, he recalled, a sheep's head, complete with eyes, which he reckoned was enough "to see him through the week!"

The 13-part first series was hosted by comedienne **Katrina Buchanan**. A verdict on the food cooked up in the series was delivered by **Madge the Dinner Lady**, alias Roly Poly and Jelly Rolls actress **June Allum**.

Most recently, **Brian Turner** has appeared with more mouth-watering dishes, which are both quick to prepare and healthy, in the revived *About Anglia* magazine format.

More 'out to tea' than 'out to lunch' for Brian Turner at a village cricket match.

Bangers galore... Denis Curtis meets a Norfolk butcher Bryan Pickering.

It's all Greek to Denis Curtis as *Food Guide* visits a Norfolk restaurant.

They didn't think it was all over then...

Nick Hancock *Swot or Wot?*

Fiona McInnes who chaired *Top of the Class.*

Bob Wellings as quizmaster in *Challenge Trophy.*

WHEN **Nick Hancock** came to the end of a 13-part children's series *Swot or Wot?* on Anglia in December, 1993, they didn't think it was all over.

For the irreverent sports quiz *(They Think It's All Over)* which later brought him national fame as he baited **Gary Lineker, Lee Hurst, Rory McGrath** and company, had yet to hit the screens. And *Swot Or Wot?*, an inter-schools quiz, had been a success.

In fact, the last edition of that year's *Swot or Wot?* series proved to be Hancock's swan-song – with *Gamesmaster* host **Dominik Diamond** taking over the hot seat the next year.

Former teacher Hancock certainly showed his class while he was in charge, displaying the no-nonsense style which was to stand him in good stead later. The 26 teachers who joined their pupils in the firing line for three of the six rounds in each week's contest were put down in typical Hancock style.

"I think they were frightened they might make fools of themselves – and, pleasingly, most of them did," reported the man whose credits at that point of his career included appearances in *Room 101* on Radio 5 and television shows *Mr Bean, Have I Got News For You* and *The Mary Whitehouse Experience.*

The quiz contained both Swot questions – on academic subjects or general knowledge – and Wot questions to test 'street cred' when it came to comics, computer games, films, football, music and television.

"Some of the teachers showed themselves to have very little knowledge of what's going on in the world – and I think most of their musical knowledge stopped around 1976," added their former colleague.

"Many would probably think Duran Duran were a very hip new group – but, on the other hand, it made you feel depressingly old when the kids didn't know who the Rolling Stones were. It was a microcosm of the way the generation gap works."

Hancock denied showing any favouritism towards one of the teams – Haverhill's Castle Manor School – where he taught drama and P.E. in the mid-Eighties.

But he did say that his own pupils at the school were charming and well-behaved: "They were impeccable – because I was such a good teacher!"

Child's play or kid's stuff?

ANGLIA children's programming dates back to 1960 when *Afternoon Club* was introduced by **Valerie Oldfield** – the company's first woman announcer. It was screened five days a week and had regulars such as **Hugh Gee** (Uncle Gee) showing puppets made from conkers and **Sandy Sandford** telling stories and devising secret recognition signs for small children.

John Seymour would show how to make a garden swing, a model aircraft or a sledge and art teacher **Cavendish Morton** organised painting competitions. Regular features included a film series about children in other countries and an inter-schools' quiz.

In 1963 the series developed into *The Junior Angle Club* with **Sandy Sandford.** There was music, a junior news bulletin and **Kingsley Amis** gave tips on story-writing.

Another popular series was *Top of the Class*, a children's general knowledge contest launched by chairman **Peggy Wright** in March, 1962, and then presented by **Colin Bower** and **Fiona McInnes.**

Later came *Challenge Trophy* in which sixth-formers competed in a general knowledge quiz. This ran for four years under quizmasters **Peter Tuddenham** and **Bob Wellings.** There was also, in March, 1965, *Better Than Magic* – a series in which **Arthur Garratt** explored the world of science with young friends.

Hugh Gee produces a mouse from a paper bag in *Afternoon Club.*

Romper Bomper Stomper do, tell me, tell me, tell me do...

Esther Rantzen failing her audition for presenter of Anglia's *Romper Room*.

WAS there ever a children's show to rival the impact that *The Romper Room* had on the region's consciousness? Even today – 22 years after the series finally ended – stories about it still crop up and viewers recall their memories.

The show was an often-chaotic live television kindergarten designed to help children aged between three and six adjust to group play. The idea and title originated in America in 1953. **Bert Claster**, a producer in Baltimore, installed his wife, Nancy, a former nursery school teacher, as the original hostess. Other television stations in America were allowed to copy the programme only on condition that the original format was adhered to and every company's 'Miss Romper Room' was sent to them for training.

When Anglia decided to adapt the programme they advertised for a presenter and received 40 applications – among them one from a **Miss Esther Rantzen**, who made it to the final shortlist of six.

Eventually, they gave the job to 26-year-old former children's nurse **Rosalyn Thompson**, from Attlebridge in Norfolk. She was dispatched to Baltimore for a fortnight's training, leaving **Esther Rantzen** to go on to other things.

The show went on air in 1964 and was a runaway success – proving incredibly popular with small children and mothers who sent in 200 letters a week. For each edition local children travelled to the studio where 'Miss Rosalyn' supervised as they ran, jumped, shouted, painted and banged wood with hammers. She also told them about washing, teeth-brushing and safety both in the streets and at home with the aid of two puppet bees – 'Mr Do Bee' and 'Mr Don't Bee'.

'Miss Rosalyn' continued in the role for more than 2,000 programmes before marrying the Anglia series director, **David Kenten**, and retiring in 1976. **Biddy Massen** became the new 'Miss Romper Room' but the series lasted only another year.

Hello, goodbye... 'Miss Rosalyn' says farewell as Biddy Massen takes over as *Romper Room* presenter.

A galaxy of stage and TV stars added their voice to 'Alice in Wonderland'...

Alice (Giselle Andrews) and friends.

Paul Eddington... his voice was used for the White Rabbit.

A later success was Anglia's five-part adaptation of the **Lewis Carroll** classic *Alice in Wonderland*, which combined a live Alice with puppets and electronic special effects, including multi-image projection. The production, one of the most ambitious children's television projects undertaken, was shown on the ITV network from March, 1985. It starred **Giselle Andrews**, a 13-year-old pupil at Yarmouth High School in Norfolk, as Alice.

A galaxy of British stage and TV stars recorded the voices of the puppet characters, which were based on the celebrated book illustrations of **Sir John Tenniel** and came from an original production staged by the Da Silva company at Norwich Puppet Theatre. They included ex-Goon **Michael Bentine** (March Hare), **Eleanor Bron** (Duchess), *Carry On* star **Bernard Cribbins** (Mock Turtle), **Leslie Crowther** (Cheshire Cat), **Windsor Davies** (Gryphon), **Paul Eddington** (White Rabbit), **Leonard Rossiter** (King of Hearts), **Joan Sanderson** (Queen of Hearts) and **Eric Sykes** (Mad Hatter).

Giselle Andrews with Bernard Cribbins, Leslie Crowther and Windsor Davies in *Alice in Wonderland*.

Just a minute...

IN April, 1977, **Chris Kelly** presented *Chatterbox*, a new public-speaking contest between teams from comprehensive schools. Competitors, aged 13 to 16, had to talk for a minute on subjects of their own choice, then speak for another 30 seconds on a 'mystery object'. They were judged on their clarity of speech, fluency, confidence and timing by a panel including a teacher of speech and drama, an experienced after-dinner speaker and a guest celebrity.

Chris Kelly presents *Chatterbox*.

The answer was blowin' in the wind...

FROM 1970 onwards Anglia produced several more innovative series for younger viewers. One stemmed from **Paul Honeyman**, Anglia's head of features at the time, who believed — despite widespread opinion to the contrary — that there was a place for story-telling on television.

A chance meeting in a Newcastle pub with **John Worsley**, a portrait painter whose sitters included **Viscount Montgomery** and **Edward Heath**, led to the production of a format. During the war, Worsley had been the official Royal Naval artist who covered the Allied landings at Reggio and Salerno, He was later captured and, while a P.O.W. in Germany, devoted his artistic and sculpting talents to creating the famous escape dummy, Albert R.N. His link with child audiences began in the Fifties, when he regularly churned out drawings for the weekly *PC 49* strip in the *Eagle* comic.

Worsley and **Honeyman** obtained rights to the **Kenneth Grahame** classic, *The Wind in the Willows* and the artist painted 700 wash illustrations featuring the characters of Toad, Rat and Mole. Worsley often started work in his Putney studio at 4 a.m. to get finished in time and would drive up to Norwich in Moby II, a twin-screwed, amphibious car complete with an anchor rack on the bonnet, a fog-horn and picnic-cum-cocktail trays which clipped on to the doors when dining afloat.

Holidaymakers on the Norfolk Broads would rub their eyes in disbelief as they rounded a remote bend in the river to find the former Navy lieutenant sitting on the bonnet of the strange craft, sketching.

Worsley would often take his amphicar — Red Ensign and burgee of the Royal Naval Association aloft — out for a relaxing day's cruise.

"I know people think I'm slightly mad but I enjoy messing about in boats," said the man who once accidentally 'parked' on a mudbank near Tower Bridge, left a door slightly open when he got out to enjoy a gin and a sandwich and found his car partially flooded on his return.

It was the river trips, however, which inspired his drawings of the loveable characters from *Wind in the Willows*.

"I always regarded Henley as Toad's home — he was a hell of a snob," said Worsley. "Ratty, of course, lived much further downstream."

Worsley's paintings for *Wind in the Willows* were filmed with a rostrum camera, which homed in on various details in keeping with the accompanying narration recorded by Honeyman himself and augmented with music and effects. The series was an instant success and Honeyman and Worsley followed it up with *The Winter of Enchantment, A Christmas Carol, Treasure Island* and *Baldmoney, Sneezeworth, Dodder and Cloudberry* — by which time Worsley had produced 2,000 paintings in six years.

The pair's last series together was *The Whisper of Glocken* but, sadly, Honeyman died before it was completed. He was just 41. Honeyman's illness also prevented him from recording the narration for the

last three episodes, which were spoken instead by **John Hedges**, familiar to *Survival* viewers for his wildlife commentaries.

"There was a huge sense of disappointment that Paul was unable to finish the series and all of us at Anglia were determined to complete it for his sake," said **Harry Aldous**, a colleague and friend who directed the series and worked with Honeyman on *Baldmoney*.

John Worsley at work in his studio.

Award-winning Knightmares...

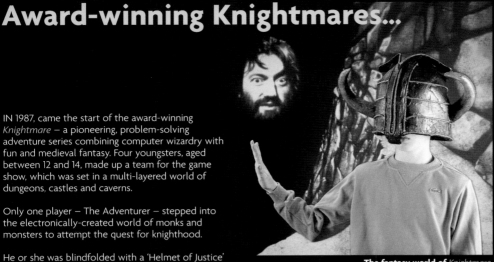

IN 1987, came the start of the award-winning *Knightmare* – a pioneering, problem-solving adventure series combining computer wizardry with fun and medieval fantasy. Four youngsters, aged between 12 and 14, made up a team for the game show, which was set in a multi-layered world of dungeons, castles and caverns.

Only one player – The Adventurer – stepped into the electronically-created world of monks and monsters to attempt the quest for knighthood.

He or she was blindfolded with a 'Helmet of Justice' and had to negotiate perils and puzzles against the clock to move through the medieval maze. The other three team members stayed behind in a conventional studio to act as guides and advisers with the help of the guardian of the dungeon, Treguard (played by actor **Hugo Myatt**).

Actors played the monsters, warriors and other apparitions encountered by the youngsters in their quest. The dungeon scenes were created by the use of sophisticated 'colour separation overlay' – an electronic process in which images can be combined. The system had been successful in television fantasy drama but had never been tried in an unrehearsed game show.

Knightmare was the brainchild of former Anglia News journalist **Tim Child** and was produced by his company Broadsword. It ran on ITV for eight series – it was still being shown on the Sci Fi channel recently – and only three teams managed to conquer the dungeon in more than 120 programmes.

The fantasy world of *Knightmare.*

Virtually Impossible was another Broadsword network children's programme which followed up on the success of *Knightmare*. There was definitely something fishy about the 10-part series, which was shown at the end of 1994 and the beginning of 1995 – for the series was hosted by a computer-animated fish called Codsby. The voice was that of alternative comedian **Logan Murray** from London's *Comedy Store*.

The programme claimed the distinction of being television's first virtual reality game for children. Teams of four battled their way through a fiendish collection of 3-D computer games as they tried to liberate software from the clutches of the wicked 'Ice Woman'.

Dedham teenager Kathryn Gregory meets Jason Donovan on the *Ghost Train* **set.**

Matthew Collins with sixth-formers in *Paperchase.*

Paperchase, screened for the first time in July, 1990, was a series which tested sixth-formers from the East of England on their local, as well as general, knowledge. It was hosted by **Matthew Collins**, normally seen on TV jetting all over the world as *The Travel Show's* independent traveller.

The idea was for three teams of two to answer questions in the opening rounds about towns, villages or places of interest along a route from their home base to a common destination. Each correct answer moved them another stop along the way. The first two teams to complete their journey then had to make stops along the route to each other's home town or city. One team from each programme went through to the semi-finals with three finalists battling it out to win a Mediterranean trip.

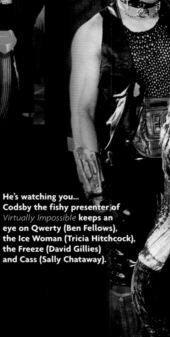

He's watching you...
Codsby the fishy presenter of
Virtually Impossible **keeps an**
eye on Qwerty (Ben Fellows),
the Ice Woman (Tricia Hitchcock),
the Freeze (David Gillies)
and Cass (Sally Chataway).

Anglia also made editions of ITV Saturday morning children's magazine shows like *Ghost Train, Get Fresh* and *Get Mucky*. One of the Ghost Train's journeys – to the Norfolk Broads – featured a special interview with **Jason Donovan** as well as a guest appearance by **Michelle Collins**, alias *EastEnders'* **Cindy Beale**.

Another series for sixth-formers – in which they made their own television documentaries – came to Anglia in April, 1991. Each edition of *Sixth Sense*, hosted first by former stand-up comedian and *Playschool* presenter **Johnny Ball** and later by top youth presenter **Andy Crane**, featured two regional teams presenting a report on a controversial issue from their locality.

A picture editor and professional camera crew were on hand to offer guidance. The students then faced an examination of their work – by Ball or Crane and professional broadcasters including **Richard Kershaw, Sue Robbie** and **Gareth** (Gaz Top) **Jones** as well as representatives of both sides of the featured topic. Prizes consisted of trophies and cheques for school funds.

Sue Robbie, Andy Crane and Gareth Jones in *Sixth Sense*.

Patrick Anthony and Frankie Howerd *The Next Week Show*.

The Next Week Show, which began in 1978, represented another effort to move on from conventional children's programmes. The idea was to alert children to exciting and interesting events in the coming week and suggest ideas for things they could make and do. Presented by **Patrick Anthony** and **Katie Glass**, it included film coverage, a TV guide, pop music guests and celebrities who were appearing in the region.

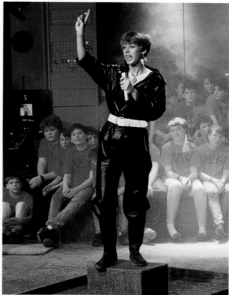

Charlotte Hindle in *Get Fresh.*

What a scream... Rosemary Leach as 'Nursie' in If You Meet a Fairy, one of the tales in *Frighteners.*

The naming of BC... Helen McDermott presents prizes to the winners of the 1980 Birthday Club puppet-naming competition Siobhan Russell (13), from Hellesdon, Norfolk, and Ciara Flood (9), from Denton, Northamptonshire.

Still going strong... with his latest 'assistant', Sarah Burrell.

Vince Henderson with contestants in *Cross Combat.*

A very different kind of energy was demanded of youngsters in *Cross Combat*, a regional series introduced by **Vince Henderson**, from the *Dear Mr Barker* and *Heartland* TV series, in 1996. Each programme featured two teams of four, aged between 11 and 13, in a game combining the strategy and simplicity of noughts and crosses with the energy and excitement of an assault course and the mental stimulus of a quiz.

A telling venture by Anglia into the realms of children's drama came with *Frighteners*, a series of four chilling, twist-in-the-tail stories of the supernatural for Children's ITV in 1997. The dramas were aimed chiefly at children from 11 upwards and were shot on location in Suffolk by independent Myrddin Productions. The producer was former Suffolk primary school head Charles Buchanan, who wrote two of the plays himself, with the others coming from established children's writers Malorie Blackman and Jan Mark.

Derek Benfield, Patricia Routledge's husband in the *Hetty Wainthrop* detective series, starred in one of the dramas. Other leading roles were taken by **Nathan Constance** and **Hannah Lawrence** (Luke and Jules from BBC children's drama *The Biz*) and character actress **Rosemary Leach**.

Cat is out of the bag...

ONE of the most frequently-seen faces in Anglia's programming for children, however, has been that of a lively leopard cub – **BC**. His remarkable career started nearly two decades ago, in 1980, when – encouraged by presenter **Helen McDermott**, who had a similar friend at her previous TV station in Plymouth – he strayed into the Anglia studios and was given the job of sorting out the cards for younger viewers in *Birthday Club*.

He became BC after a children's competition to find a name and his popularity soon sparked a strong demand for promotional T-shirts, badges and puppets. BC even had a book written about him by **Michael Speake** – one of his many co-presenters over the years – and boasted a purpose-built BC-mobile (registration number BC 4U) to take him to his public appearances around the region.

All down to a fine art...

UNTIL *Folio*, a 13-part regional magazine series launched in 1980, the regional arts scene was covered largely in local news items or one-off feature programmes and documentaries.

As early as 1960 there was *The Final Curtain*, an inquiry into the future of live theatre in East Anglia, with **Anthony Wedgwood Benn** and **Kenneth Robinson** as well as **Ian Emerson**, of the Maddermarket Theatre in Norwich. The next year there was a ballet, written for Anglia by dancer **Leonard Boucher** and performed by him, his wife and daughter.

The Quest Of Terence Gray, in 1962, looked at how the Cambridge Festival Theatre, under its manager and owner, became the country's leading venue for experimental theatre. There was also a programme, narrated by **Chris Kelly**, in which modern jazz composer and musician **Johnny Scott** looked at East Anglia in musical terms, and another celebrating the centenary of Kipling's birth, starring **Nigel Stock**.

In 1970 came *Arts For Everyone*, a feature on the work in Lincolnshire of one of the oldest regional arts associations, and *John Constable*, a documentary in which **Roy Dotrice** spoke the painter's words. The

Constable profile was subsequently screened at the Edinburgh Festival, at exhibitions of British painting in Tokyo and Paris and again, much later, in 1991 at the Tate Gallery to mark the artist's work.

At the end of the Seventies and beginning of the Eighties there were two diverse documentaries looking at the stars of two very different art forms. In *Morecambe And Stone* Eric left Ernie behind to team up with a new partner, **Richard Stone**, a Colchester postman's son whose meteoric rise saw him become, at 27, Britain's youngest Royal portrait painter. He had a drawing of **The Queen** and an oil of **The Queen Mother** to his credit.

Morecambe was persuaded to sit for the rising star of the art world and the session was filmed as an amusing study of the interaction between artist and subject.

Steps, Notes And Squeaks, on the other hand, gave viewers the chance to see the incomparable **Svetlana Beriosova** in action. The production, devised by prima ballerina **Maina Gielgud**, took a behind-the-scenes look at the world of ballet.

Anne Gregg in *Folio*.

You've been framed . . . Eric Morecambe alongside his portrait painted by Richard Stone.

With a growth of interest in the arts, however, Anglia decided to tackle the subject on a more regular basis. A fresh approach was adopted, giving artists the chance to speak about their work, encouraging initiatives and even commissioning new work.

And so *Folio* was born. First presented by **Chris Kelly** and later by **Paul Barnes** and **Anne Gregg**, it quickly established an enthusiastic audience and a reputation for taking the stuffiness out of the arts. **Hammond Innes** was the first guest and other writers followed, including **Kingsley Amis, Malcolm Bradbury, Alan Sillitoe, Rose Tremaine, Keith Waterhouse, Sir Angus Wilson** and **P.D. James**.

Others featured were actors **Simon MacCorkindale** and **Sir John Mills**, **Sir Frederick Ashton** of the Royal Ballet, comic **Max Wall**, dancer **Wayne Sleep**, designer **Jasper Conran** and pianist **Semprini**. On film there were amusing characters like caricaturists **Peter Fluck** and **Roger Law** (the duo behind the *Spitting Image* puppets) as well as more serious artists such as painter **David Gentleman**, poet **George McBeth** and sculptor **Elisabeth Frink**.

Folio included everything from a focus on a cult, Suffolk-based, rock group to an extract from a play based on the true story of a Victorian gentlewoman who led a permissive life as she travelled the world adding to her butterfly collection.

Welsh boy singer **Aled Jones** made his acting debut when he appeared in an extract from *Now We are Sixty*, a musical play by **Gyles Brandreth** and **Julian Slade** about the life and works of **A.A. Milne**.

Peter Fluck and Roger Law, creators of the *Spitting Image* puppets.

Michael Barrymore and Peter Jay meet up with the Bluebell Girls in a *Folio* **documentary.**

Later series included a programme – with a visit from **Princess Margaret** – on a musical enterprise at the home of singer **Cleo Laine** and her jazz musician husband **John Dankworth** and a profile of Great Yarmouth theatre impressario **Peter Jay**, with an appearance by **Michael Barrymore**.

There was also a film about artist **Dennis Creffield**, who achieved a 40-year ambition to draw all 26 medieval English cathedrals in charcoal, and a contribution from **The Duke of Edinburgh** to the Royal Television Society-nominated *Light Out Of The Sky*, a profile of the painter **Edward Seago**, which also featured actors **Peter Cushing**, **Donald Sinden** and **Michael Denison**.

Sir John Betjeman.

But the arts were by no means confined to just one series in the Eighties and early Nineties. There were still one-offs such as *Fantasy On A String*, a 1981 film about the birth of Norwich Puppet Theatre in a redundant church, and two years later *David Gentleman's Cambridge*, a portrait of the city through the eyes of the distinguished travel book illustrator.

Welsh boy singer Aled Jones in *Now We Are Sixty*.

Susannah York as the central character in the Betjeman poem *Lenten Thoughts Of A High Anglican*.

One network programme which stood out was *Betjeman's Britain* in which the works of poet laureate **Sir John Betjeman** were dramatised on television for the first time. Sir John read seven of his favourite poems from two long-playing records. The poems were set to the original album music of **Jim Parker** and filmed with celebrities including **Eric Morecambe**, **Peter Cook**, **Madeleine Smith** and **Susannah York**.

One poem, *Indoor Games At Newbury*, saw **Eric Morecambe** in his first 'serious' acting role, playing a funny uncle who organised a children's party.

"Today Cricklewood, tomorrow the world!" he exclaimed after his triumphant appearance, in which he was restricted to one speaking line and miming some words.

The other featured poems were *Lenten Thoughts Of A High Anglican* (with **Susannah York**), *Seaside Golf* (**Peter Cook** and **Madeleine Smith**), *Upper Lambourn*, *South London Sketch*, *A. Russell Flint* and *Autumn 1964*.

On the regional front an important programme in 1989 was *The Bottom Line*. Playwright **Arthur Miller** and **Dustin Hoffman** teamed up to warn of the threat of commercialism to the serious theatre. It featured an exclusive interview with Hoffman and Miller was seen working with such stars as **Warren Mitchell**, **Prunella Scales**, **Timothy West** and **Susannah York** preparing for a gala performance at the Theatre Royal, Norwich, of excerpts from the playwright's work.

There were other series, too, such as *First Impressions*, *Movie Memories*, *Moving Art*, *Pictures In The Mind* and *The Video Age*. The first series of *First Impressions* featured ten young regional craftspeople individually and then in a final, presented by **Emma Freud**, in which they competed for two major commissions.

The second was restricted to youth dance and culminated in a televised final featuring six groups selected by Eastern Arts. Each finalist had to create a four-minute piece of work for television in costumes of their own design at a location of their choice. Winners of the £1,000 prize were Peterborough's Figure of Eight.

In 1981 **Roy Hudd** started a relationship with Anglia which was to last five years, as host of film nostalgia series *Movie Memories*. Hudd traced his own love of the movies back to his grandmother, who worked at a Croydon theatre and once met **Rudolph Valentino**. The show, screened nationally, answered viewers' film queries, showed requested clips, homed in on sequences of screen favourites and had a studio guest.

Among those featured were **Robert Beatty, Dora Bryan, Phyllis Calvert, Ian Carmichael, Kenneth Connor, Michael Craig, Diana Dors, Liz Fraser, Richard Greene, Peter Jones, Geoffrey Keen, Victor Maddern, Leslie Phillips, Joan Sims, Anthony Steele, Sylvia Syms, Richard Todd, David Tomlinson, Jack Warner** and **Googie Withers**.

Keen recalled being given the tall order of hitting **Rock Hudson** in a film and failing because he couldn't reach the 6ft 4in Hollywood heart-throb, who was standing above him on a hill. Syms remembered actor Laurence Harvey getting so bored during filming of the Continental version of *Expresso Bongo* – which helped launch **Cliff Richard**'s career – that he walked on set wearing nothing but a jock strap with a rose pinned to the front...

George Melly presenting *Moving Art*.

Sanderson, Anne Stallybrass and **Bill Oddie**. In *Pictures In The Mind*, psychiatrist **Anthony Fry** discussed with guests, including **P. D. James, Fiona Richmond, Hank Wangford** and **Billie Whitelaw**, five pictures significant to their lives.

The Video Age, despite having a network lunch-time slot in 1983, attracted star names as studio guests. **Patrick Stoddart** was the presenter and among his guests to review the video scene were *Bright Eyes* composer **Mike Batt**, singer **Elkie Brooks**, comic **Billy Connolly**, rock star **David Essex**, military expert **Sir John Hackett**, actor **Jeremy Irons**, photographer **Lord Lichfield**, former newsreader **Angela Rippon**, racing expert **Brough Scott**, dancer **Wayne Sleep**, comedian **Kenneth Williams** and film star **Mai Zetterling**.

Marquee took over the more conventional generic arts mantle in 1992 but focused on even more diverse and offbeat aspects of the arts. The first series opened with a look at the part musicians from the Southend area had played in modern popular music history and continued with profiles of writers **L.P. Hartley** and **Dodie Smith** (Essex author of *101 Dalmatians*) and documentaries on allotments, the Fenland landscape and public art.

Billy Connolly with Patrick Stoddart in *The Video Age*.

Moving Art, a roadshow presented by **George Melly**, went out into the region, visiting art galleries in seven towns and cities to see what the East of England's contemporary artists and craftspeople had to offer. At each venue – Ipswich, Milton Keynes, Northampton, Peterborough, Norwich, Southend and St Albans – there were expert judges, including Carmelite nun **Sister Wendy Beckett**. Celebrity guests were **Patrick Cargill, Derek Nimmo, Ruth Madoc, Nicola Pagett, Joan**

The second series featured an RTS award-winning documentary about beach-hut fanatics, a profile of gynaecologist **Sam Hutt** (alias country singer **Hank Wangford**), a dramatisation of the life of *Swallows And Amazons* author **Arthur Ransome**, an amusing look at conservatory owners and a film study, featuring **Harold Pinter**, about the work of prize-winning novelist **Elspeth Barker**. The most recent series looked at subjects including shed enthusiasts, dog fanatics and look-alikes of **Elton John, Marilyn Monroe** and **Cliff Richard**.

The special one-off *A Pleasant Terror*, shown in 1995, was a profile of the Cambridge academic and ghost story writer, **M.R. James**, whose story *A Warning To The Curious* has been the subject of several dramas. Horror star **Christopher Lee**, mystery writer **Ruth Rendell** and stage director **Jonathan Miller** were among those expressing admiration for the supernatural stories of the Suffolk rector's son who delighted in making people feel uncomfortable.

A new pioneering addition to Anglia's arts output in 1992 was its award-winning *First Take* series, launched in association with Eastern Arts. The series of short films, which has continued ever since, provides a showcase for the original and often experimental work of aspiring young film makers in the Anglia region. Subjects have included an animated film about a disturbed teddy bear and documentaries on everything from aerosol art to body-piercing, bikers and a family of *Star Trek* fans.

Celebrities featured in the short films included *Eldorado*'s **Jesse Birdsall, James Bolam** from *The Likely Lads*, **Anita Dobson** and **Leslie Grantham** (*EastEnders*), **James Frain** (*Shadowlands*) and *Boys from the Blackstuff*'s **Bernard Hill, Sue Jameson** and **Steve McGann**.

Billie Whitelaw in *Pictures In The Mind*.

The Jumper, Cambridgeshire director **Mike Barker's** film featuring Bolam and Jameson, won the premier regional award in a competition organised by *Broadcast* magazine. Judges described the film, about a kindly mental hospital assistant and his patient, as "a deeply moving and involving story, original in both concept and execution."

Many of the other young producers and directors have gone on to win work with Anglia or the film and television industry generally.

The Sweet Life in 1997 was an extended, 25-minute *First Take* special shot by **Nick McCann**, who himself won several international awards for his earlier *First Take* short, *The Heart Of Shelley*. It starred **Roy Hudd** as a former variety artist running a seedy seafront hotel. Also featured were *Lovejoy* star **Malcolm Tierney** and former *Dr Who* girl **Mary Tamm**, subsequently cast as **Penny Crosbie** in *Brookside*.

Said Hudd: "If you get a good script and you've had a couple of other good jobs you can afford to do something a bit different and exciting, like this."

The film, which transformed the seaside resort of Gorleston-on-Sea into a film set, won funding from the National Lottery through the Arts Council of England and was shot for both cinema and TV.

Roger Lloyd Pack with Van Gogh's ear.

Head for heights . . . John Redhead climbs Norwich Cathedral in *First Take***.**

Two more recent series of *First Take* have been presented by Radio One film critic **Mark Kermode** and featured more short films made in the East of England with the support of Anglia and the Eastern Arts Board. One of the most striking, perhaps, was *The Wonderful World of Dolly*, with Norwich film-makers **Jonathan Flowers** and **Sara Doyle** telling the story of three people's obsession with American country singer **Dolly Parton**.

In another, artist, poet, street entertainer and dare-devil climber **John Redhead** was filmed as he set out to be the first man to scale the 900-year-old Norwich Cathedral, from the cloisters to the top of the spire. As a bonus, he also climbed Happisburgh lighthouse on the Norfolk coast and a massive dockside silo at Lowestoft as well as demonstrating his talents for art and street theatre.

In the same series, character actor **Roger Lloyd Pack**, best known as Del and Rodney's slow-witted sidekick, **Trigger**, in *Only Fools and Horses*, took on a very different role. He starred in a short drama as a failed artist whose agent gives him a jar containing the pickled ear of Van Gogh in a last-ditch attempt to inspire him to produce something worthwhile.

By contrast, the latest series featured *Millennium Kids*, in which two disadvantaged Ipswich teenagers looked back on their past problems and forward to their hopes for the future.

Millennium hopes – Ipswich youngsters Leon Marshall and Christine Robinson.

In 1997, *Backstage* took over the arts documentary role of forerunners *Folio* and *Marquee*. One of the programmes focused on Essex-born guitarist and **Fleetwood Mac** founder **Pete Green**, ranked by his fans alongside **Eric Clapton** and **Jimi Hendrix**.

Green's Fleetwood hits, like *Black Magic Woman* and *Albatross*, became rock classics and his music outsold that of the **Beatles** and **Stones**. Then it all went wrong. He became a casualty of drugs, stopped playing and lived like a recluse. But, as *Back For Good?* recalled, Green had returned to the music scene with a new band and seemed to be finding playing again a therapeutic experience.

Music fans have also been treated to *Ray Davies – Visions Of England*, featuring the founder of Sixties band **The Kinks**. The programme went behind the scenes with the singer and composer for the world premiere at the 1998 Norfolk and Norwich Festival of *The Flatlands*, his first major work for orchestra and chorus.

John Bly and Jane Probyn in *Heirloom*.

Fleetwood Mac's Pete Green in *Backstage*.

Antiques and collectables enthusiasts were catered for over many years by *Heirloom* with Hertfordshire antique dealer **John Bly**. The programme began as an insert in *About Anglia*, co-presented by Bly and **Jane Probyn**, before expanding to its own regional and network slots. Numerous fine items, many brought in for valuation by viewers, featured over the years. The most expensive was a nineteenth century murderer's masterpiece, belonging to **Sir Andrew Lloyd Webber's** Art Foundation.

The painting – brought specially to Anglia's Norwich studios from the Tate Gallery where it was on loan – was snapped up on Sir Andrew's behalf by guest **David Mason**, the West End art expert, for a record £1.7 million. That was in 1992 and by the time the painting featured on *Heirloom* the value was estimated to have risen to £2.5 million.

The Victorian work *Contradiction – Oberon and Titania* was by artist **Richard Dadd**, known as 'Mad Dadd', who used a razor to murder his father and then, on fleeing to France, to attack a complete stranger. He was returned to England and committed to Bethlem mental hospital in Kent, where he was encouraged to paint and created the masterpiece over a five-year period.

Craven's Collectables, which took over from *Heirloom* in 1998, was hosted by the man whose name was synonymous with *Newsround* for the best part of two decades – **John Craven**. Although he left the series in the early Nineties and had been seen recently presenting the BBC's countryside current affairs programme, *Country File*, Craven was still recognised by fans who grew up with him on children's television. *Craven's Collectables* delved into viewers' fascinating collections of everything from **Beatles** memorabilia to old bicycles and perfume bottles.

Two recent painting series have introduced artists **Alwyn Crawshaw** and **Hazel Soan** to Anglia viewers. In *Crawshaw Paints Constable Country*, six programmes in 1996, the man responsible for teaching thousands of Channel Four viewers how to paint set off in the footsteps of one of his heroes.

Big wheels in Anglia's latest antiques series – presenter John Craven (left) and expert guest Mike Hicks.

He visited locations made famous by the East Suffolk-born landscape artist and depicted some of the scenes as they are today.

A Splash Of Colour viewers met another talented artist, **Hazel Soan**, in 1997. The success of the series led to a network showing on Channel Four in 1998 as well as another six programmes on Anglia. The most recent addition to Anglia's palette of painting programmes was *King and Country*, a series featuring artist **Ian King**.

Alongside Anglia's other arts programmes there have been regular event listings programmes such as *Wideangle*, launched in 1998, *Weekend*, hosted by **Sam Norman**, first with *Breakfast TV* host **Michael Wilson** and later with **Dale Winton**. More recently, *The Ticket* and *Off The Wall*, with newcomer **Kirk England**, have covered the region's popular culture scene.

Weekend **host Dale Winton.**

The history man...

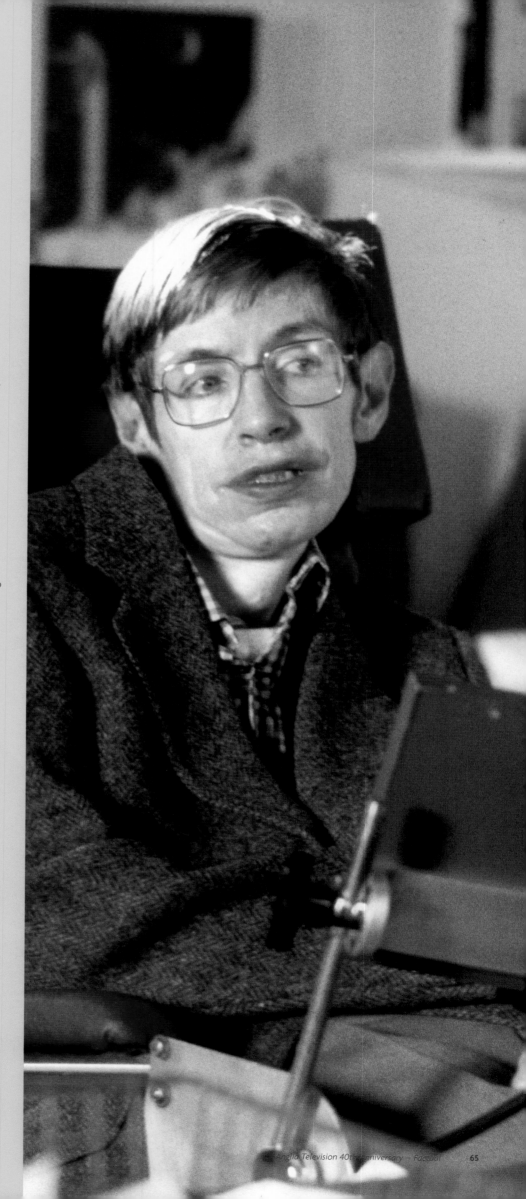

" Which came first, the chicken or the egg? Did the universe have a beginning and, if so, what happened before then? Where did the universe come from and where is it going? **"**

POSSIBLY one of the most challenging questions in the world... but Anglia tackled it by advancing the theories of some of the world's most eminent scientists in 1992.

They came in *A Brief History Of Time*, a highly-distinctive interpretation of **Stephen Hawking's** best-selling exploration of the cosmos.

The £1 million plus feature-length documentary co-production, by American film-maker **Errol Morris**, for Channel Four, examined the theories of Cambridge-based Hawking, who has been hailed as the greatest theological physicist since **Einstein**. It also examined the 50-year-old professor's battle against the debilitating impact of motor neurone disease, which struck him at the age of 21, leaving him first confined to a wheelchair and, from 1985, unable to speak without the aid of a voice-synthesiser.

Contributors to the film, which featured original music by top composer **Philip Glass** and collected several international awards, included such world-renowned physicists as Christopher Isham, Roger Penrose, Kip Thorne and John Wheeler as well as Hawking's mother and sister.

The night before the screening of the production — which involved extensive research in Europe and the United States and filming both at Cambridge and Elstree, where a set of Hawking's Cambridge office was recreated — Channel Four previewed it with a feature on the making of the documentary.

Recalling the effect of his best-selling book, which has been translated into more than 20 languages, Hawking said: "I think *A Brief History Of Time* has been successful for a combination of reasons. One is that people want to understand the universe around them and to know where they come from.

"But I think another reason is that the public loves heroes. They made Einstein a hero and now they are making me a hero — with much less justification. But I fit the part of the disabled genius — at least, I am clearly disabled."

Tackling the issue of where the universe came from and where it is going, the Lucasian Professor of Mathematics said he believed it would come to an end at what he called 'the big crunch'.

"I do, however, have certain advantages over many other prophets of doom. Whatever happens 10 billion years from now, I don't expect to be around to be proved wrong."

Hawking said his greatest desire was that, if a complete theory of the universe was discovered, it should in time be understandable in broad principle by everyone, not just a few scientists.

"Then we shall all, philosophers, scientists and just ordinary people, be able to take part in the discussion of why it is that we and the universe exist. If we find the answer to that, it would be the ultimate triumph of human reason. For then we would know the mind of God."

"People want to understand the Universe and know where they come from" **Professor Stephen Hawking.**

Game show of the century...

SALE OF THE CENTURY will for ever be synonymous with TV game shows. Even 16 years after the last programme was transmitted on ITV, the quiz hosted by fast-talking **Nicholas Parsons** is engrained in the national psyche.

It ran for 12 years, from 1971 to 1983, and was Anglia's most successful light entertainment venture.

When a pilot show was made for a regional series in 1971, no one imagined it would become such a crowd-pleaser. Actor **Nicholas Parsons**, probably best known to TV audiences for his comedy roles – notably as straight man to **Arthur Haynes** – proved an inspired choice as compere. And the secret of the success was largely in the essentially simple format, a fast-moving, general knowledge quiz with the allure of big prizes.

Each programme opened with the famous out-of-vision announcer uttering the words: "Tonight, from Norwich, it's the quiz of the week". That, and the programme's

catchy signature tune *Joyful Pete* led into a quick-fire quiz which quickly became cult viewing.

In full flow, **Parsons** could cram five words into every second and 95 questions in 12 minutes. He admitted he was often criticised for being pompous and abrupt, but insisted: "All I do is try to get in as many questions as possible and give contestants a chance of winning more prizes." Here **Nicholas Parsons** writes about his own personal recollections of the show:

" I have the fondest memories of Anglia Television. My association began in May, 1971, when **Peter Joy**, their senior producer, asked me to front an American quiz show they had planned to present called *Sale Of The Century*. I saw this as an interesting challenge. Peter was a very creative producer and encouraged me to find my way of presenting the programme and not to base my performance on the American version.

As an actor I knew that it was possible to create tension by pacing a show, so I had the idea to build to an exciting finish by rapid-fire delivery of the final questions. To do this, I ignored the rather boring questions sent from America and wrote most of them myself. I realised in retrospect I should have asked a fee for this, but again, as an actor, I took it as part of the job to increase the success of the programme.

Perhaps I would not have been so keen to accept this job had I known that *Sale Of The Century* had already been piloted some time previously by Thames Television with **Wilfred Pickles** as host. It had been a failure. The production I was asked to host was planned as a local show in the Anglia TV area only. It was actually amazing it ever saw the light of day. Everything imaginable went wrong with the pilot recording, chiefly because it was proving impossible to get all the goods for the final sale into the studio as well as the audience.

Al Howard, the creator of the show, had flown over from New York, and after his previous experiences in the country was convinced he was about to see his successful programme fail again. He even phoned Heathrow to see if there was a plane he could take home that night. There were none, so he stayed.

We never actually had a complete run-through of the show. We started the recording not knowing if the final sequence was going to work. Peter and I discussed what should be done and, with the audience in place, we launched into the recording in the hope that our professional experience would carry us through. Somehow it did, and while the technicians and Peter took this in their stride, it was too much for Al. He came rushing on the set, called the audience back and heaped lavish praise as only Americans can on everyone concerned, particularly Peter and myself.

Nicholas Parsons and hostesses Karen Loughlin and Carole Ashby show off the star prize.

The audience were utterly confused and clapped politely, it was so un-British. I was embarrassed. The studio crew just ignored the whole thing and carried on dismantling the set.

Sale Of The Century was an immediate success when it was launched in the autumn of 1971, and other independent companies began to take an interest. There was, luckily, a vacancy on the ITV network for a good new quiz show. (In an attempt to maintain the overall quality of independent television, the IBA had ruled that there could be only two high-reward game shows on the network in any one week, and three in any one region. There was no restriction on other game shows provided big prizes were not involved).

London Weekend Television were the first major company to take *Sale*. By early 1972 a quarter of the network were taking it; but it was not until early 1973 that it was fully networked, and then it became so popular that it ran for nearly a year without a break, which is exceptional for a quiz show.

It first went to number one in the ratings in 1974. In 1976 it was in the top ten for thirty-six weeks and reached number one on Friday, January 23, with viewing figures of 19.5 million. In 1977 it spent thirty-two weeks in the top ten and reached number one on November 18 with viewing figures of 20.6 million. In 1978 the run was shorter, but when it reached number one on December 22, the viewing figure – 21.2 million – was the highest of any show that year.

Thereafter, the programme planners moved the show to different days and times according to the strength of opposition from the BBC. As a result, the programme was regularly in the ratings, but did not have the same consistently high viewing figures that it had achieved when transmitted at the popular time of 7.30pm on Fridays.

Nicholas Parsons on the set of the first series in Anglia House.

When the show became fully networked, **John Jacobs**, then senior producer of drama at Anglia, joined us as executive producer. **Peter Joy** continued to direct, and it was a very happy team. They were worried, however, when they discovered that I was writing most of the questions, because it was against IBA rules. I shared the responsibility for a time with **John Erskine**, who received the credit, and I was rewarded in my overall fee. Later, when **Bill Perry** took over as producer, he decided I should not be involved in the questions and **David Self** was engaged to do this work.

There was a very pleasant working atmosphere at Anglia, particularly during the early years of *Sale*, which was due in part to the attitude of the senior executives. The ones with whom I worked most closely were **John Jacobs**, Canon **Peter Freeman**, and, of course, **Peter Joy**. John was an inspired director who could empathise with actors. He went out of his way to see that we worked in as relaxed and harmonious a way as possible, given the demands of the show.

Canon **Peter Freeman** was Anglia's head of religious broadcasting and much loved by everyone at the studios. Full of energy, he produced five late-night items a week for the region, as well as looking after his parish outside Norwich. He also acted as the adjudicator for the show and I got to know him quite well as a result of our regular meetings. His counsel on any subject was always wise and no problem of whatever kind was ever too small. There were many occasions when members of the staff at Anglia would seek him out for advice or comfort.

When the show had been running a few years an embarrassment occurred over the prizes. The IBA had strict rules about the value of prizes that could be offered in a quiz show; the top prize could not be worth more than £1,000. The top prize on offer each week in *Sale* was usually a car, and when the show first began there were about 20 small cars on the road at under £1,000. Within six or seven years, there were only three cars on the market under this figure, and they were all foreign makes. The IBA refused to change the rules in line with the cost of living, and the programme was taken to task by the Press for being unpatriotic.

One week, to try to ring the changes, we had on offer one of the new Lada cars, which were just coming on to the market. During the rehearsal to time the sale section at the end of the show, I arrived at the car, extolled its virtues, then went to open the door. It came off its hinges. I think jokes about Ladas, now common, started then.

Anglia used the bad press we received to reason with the IBA and the authority relented. As the price of a small British car increased over the years, further adjustments were made. By the time *Sale* finished in 1983, the rules had changed again. It was possible to offer an individual prize of up to £1,750 and a major prize of up to £3,000 to cover the price of a new car, but not every week, and all this was conditional on the total money given away in a four-week period not exceeding £17,500.

The signature tune for the show was composed by **Peter Fenn**, director of music at Anglia, and as a gesture to the director, **Peter Joy**, called it *Joyful Pete*. He played it on his organ at every recording and it was so catchy and distinctive it soon registered with the general public, and even now people will hum it when I make speeches or personal appearances.

We struggled along in the studio at Anglia House for four or five years. The show had now reached a peak, and it was realised that its success warranted a larger studio. This was when Anglia bought the old bowling alley in Magdalen Street and created Studio E. All subsequent recordings were made there. It was sad leaving the old building but it was good to have the space and a larger audience.

When *Sale* began **Peter Marshall** supplied the unseen voice. In 1973, **John Benson** took over and it was he who created and delivered the famous opening line: "From Norwich; it's the quiz of the week". A line that was regularly – and still is – shouted out to me by audiences, as if it was my catch phrase.

In fact, I think thanks to this opening line, a lot of people thought I lived in Norwich. I only visited that lovely city to record the show. I enjoyed my visits there immensely. There was always a very happy atmosphere among the staff and crew, and at times, as often happens in a small company, you felt like part of a professional family. I was sad when the last recordings were made in 1983, but for me it was time to concentrate on my other work. I have, however, discovered that I am still associated with this record-breaking programme, even though it is 16 years since I was last seen in it. **"**

Question time for Parsons...

TABLES were turned on **Nicholas Parsons** when he took part in a celebrity edition of *Sale of the Century* for charity in 1981, pitting his general knowledge against *Name That Tune* host **Tom O'Connor** and *Mr & Mrs* man **Derek Batey**.

Search for a Star presenter **Steve Jones**, who spoke almost as fast as Parsons, averaging four-and-a half words a second, took over the questionmaster role.

As O'Connor pointed out, there was one person who was going to get a hammering if he got any questions wrong. And Parsons admitted: "I'm on a hiding to nothing. I must be crazy to let them put me in the hot seat on my own show."

Despite the fact that he was up against a former deputy headmaster (O'Connor) and a qualified accountant, Parsons disappointed those hoping to see him fall flat on his face – by pipping his rivals at the post.

Some questions for *Sale of the Century* were set by a former schoolteacher, **David Self**. They had to be answered within a four-second limit with correct responses earning a nominal £3 or £5 a time. Self also set questions for Granada's *Square One* and another popular Anglia show, *Gambit*, but admitted there were times when he ran into problems.

Once he set a question asking what the initials 'SOS' stood for and, certain it meant 'Save Our Souls', awarded a contestant his prize money when he gave that answer. Letters poured in telling him he should know better. SOS doesn't stand for anything, in fact. It was invented as a distress signal simply because those letters in Morse Code were distinctive and easily identifiable.

Another question was "What does it mean if a ship runs up a yellow flag?" This time Self checked in two reference books which both said the signal meant there was an infectious or contagious disease on board. Again the letters poured in, from chief petty officers to retired admirals. Apparently a yellow flag stood for quite the opposite: "I have a clean bill of health and require free pratique (clearance)".

Sometimes, though, wrong answers were more fun than the right ones – as in the response to the question "What is a billet doux?" The contestant came up with "It's something you sit on to wash . . . It's a sort of lavatory." Then he stopped, went bright red, and said: "Oh help, no it's not – that's a bidet!"

Sale was also famous for its glamorous hostesses – 15 in all over the years. Several of them, including **Angela Daniels**, **Sneh Gupta** and **Jennifer Cresswell**, were recruited from the ranks of 'Miss Anglia' beauty contest

finalists. Cresswell, a winner, and **Carol Dilworth** were the first two, and the final pairing brought together two blonde Manchester models – **Karen Loughlin** and **Carole Ashby** – for the last three series.

In 1977 the girls were earning up to £70 a show plus expenses – not bad money at the time – and, as producer Bill Perry pointed out, exposure in a peak-time programme which went out to millions of homes usually led to hostesses winning lucrative modelling jobs or film parts.

Former Miss U.K. finalist Loughlin married **Graeme Souness**, the Liverpool FC manager at the time, while Ashby had acting roles in the Bond film *Octopussy*, *Chariots of Fire* and *Yanks*, as well as in the BBC television comedy *'Allo, 'Allo*.

Like all their predecessors – including **Laura Beaumont**, who married former Goodie **Bill Oddie** – they never got to speak on the programme, earning sympathy from Parsons.

"Being a hostess is a very difficult job, especially when you have to work with inanimate objects and can't say a word," he pointed out.

Sale of the Century first went on air in October, 1971, starting as a regional show on Anglia alone, extending to London the next year and then being screened throughout Britain – with the exception of the Scottish region – to 1973.

It was in that same year that **Bill Perry**, who was to produce the show throughout the rest of its life-span, took over the reins — on April Fool's Day: "They must have seen me coming," he joked.

Perry spent three months each year on the road, holding auditions in every ITV region. And he was not jesting when he criticised the standard of would-be contestants. "Only a tiny minority of the people I see have a grasp of general knowledge," he blasted. "It makes you wonder how they have the nerve to put themselves forward – most of them simply haven't got what it takes!"

The show ran to 13 series and was still pulling in between eight and nine million viewers — and some 200 audition applications a week from would-be contestants — when ITV called a halt in 1983 and Anglia's rights to the format were allowed to lapse. Some 500 contestants had appeared on the show and at today's values the prizes won were worth around £1 million.

Nicholas Parsons with five of the 15 hostesses who appeared on the show.

One of the final shows provided Parsons with a champagne send-off – but not the sort he might have imagined. Hostesses Carole Ashby and Karen Loughlin, who had a reputation for impromptu practical jokes, decided to get their revenge on him for having escaped a custard pie attack at an earlier post-programme party.

This time they pounced while the wind-up to the show was being recorded – and gave him a good drenching with bubbly.

"They caught me off my guard," Parsons admitted. "I knew they were planning something for the end of series party later – but I didn't expect them to do anything on the show."

His attackers giggled: "We knew Nicholas liked champagne so we gave him a shampoo. He took it very well."

The girls were not content with just a hairdo for Parsons – they also decided to remove his trousers. Even announcer **John Benson** and musical director **Peter Fenn** joined in, and for once the quizmaster who was never lost for words was speechless...

Tables turned... quizmasters on the spot as Nicholas Parsons, Tom O'Connor and Derek Batey battled it out in a special charity edition with Steve Jones taking over the chair for the day.

MARATHON MAN

NICHOLAS Parsons had verbal staying power as well as speed – as he proved by setting a world, non-stop, after-dinner speaking record of 11 hours in 1978. The previous summer he had broken writer and broadcaster Gyles Brandreth's existing record of four hours by another three.

Parsons and rival Brandreth then met head-to-head in a sponsored charity contest and started their marathons at 8 p.m. before an audience of diners at London's Hyde Park Hotel. They finally dried up and agreed to call it a draw at 7 a.m., raising £10,000 on behalf of Action Research for the Crippled Child.

Can you name the series?

WHAT was the Anglia series that starred **Peter Ustinov**, **William Holden** and **Norman Wisdom**?

The question would probably stump any contestant who has ever appeared on *Telly Addicts*.

Shooting Stars was the long-forgotten programme, hosted by *Daily Mirror* showbusiness writer **Donald Zec** who interviewed some of the screen greats of the time.

Also appearing in the six-part series were **Peter Finch**, **Sylvia Syms**, **Rita Tushingham**, **Robert Stephens**, **Nancy Kwan**, and French star **Nicole Maurey**.

Holden, Kwan and Syms were stars of the movie *The World Of Suzie Wong*, released in 1960, and Maurey appeared in the raunchy (for the time) *Don't Bother To Knock*, a 1961 British farce.

The interviews were recorded on location – at the actor's home in the case of some of the British stars such as Ustinov, Finch and Wisdom, or in London for the convenience of international travellers.

"A penetrating portrait of the top people in entertainment," was how the series was grandly billed in *TV Times*. It was shown in a rather odd slot at six o'clock on a Saturday evening, beginning on September 9, 1961, with **Peter Ustinov**.

On location – An early sixties broadcast crew focuses on actor Peter Finch (extreme left) and interviewer Zec.

Peter Ustinov with Donald Zec.

Sylvia Syms.

Intriguingly, Steve McQueen should also have featured in the series for which this publicity photograph was taken, but for some reason the interview appears not to have been broadcast.

William Holden.

Norman Wisdom.

How Gambit came up trumps...

GAMBIT, based on the card game blackjack or pontoon, was Anglia's other great quiz show success of the 1970s and 80s. Hosted first by **Fred Dinenage** and later by **Tom O'Connor**, it ran for ten years from 1975 and featured **Michelle Lambourne**, another 'Miss Anglia' finalist, as hostess virtually throughout.

Lambourne was probably Anglia's most popular game show hostess. Her girl-next-door appeal brought floods of letters from male admirers asking for signed photos, among them, at the time of the Falklands conflict in 1982, Royal Navy servicemen stationed on Ascension Island to whom she sent a personal message and photographs.

The aspiring actress from Stanford-le-Hope, in Essex, was just 19 when she joined the series for its second year in 1976, and was described as "Anglia's personality find of the year". There was more to Lambourne than the glamour girl card-dealer, however. She organised and ran her own speech and drama classes for children, and had a passion for poetry, particularly Shakespearean sonnets.

She always willed the *Gambit* contestants to do well. It was said she had the most expressive face of any game show hostess, involuntarily registering joy or disappointment according to the fortunes of the players.

Gambit started on air in July, 1975, with Dinenage as compere for seven years until he turned exclusively to sports presenting. **Tom O'Connor** took over in March, 1983, making his debut as what he described as 'a sit-down comedian'.

"It's the first time I have ever appeared on television sitting down," he explained. "It slows me down a bit, but my wife says I'm telling the gags better."

Gambit was right up his street, as he was already a keen, if somewhat cavalier, card player. "I once won 4,000 dollars in a week playing this game in Las Vegas and doing all the wrong things," he recalled. "I twisted on 15 and the Yanks couldn't believe that. They wanted to know why and guys with guns came moving in. It was frightening."

Michelle Lambourne with Fred Dinenage.

Michelle Lambourne signs photographs to send to servicemen in the Falklands.

Gambit was a mixture of skill, nerve and luck. Potentially two major prizes — to the value of a car — could go in one programme.

One contestant, **Phil Hollinshead**, of Weston-super-Mare, was particularly lucky as the result of a birthday-week appearance on the show in 1985, when *Gambit* really turned up trumps. For among the 3.5 million viewers that week were **Stephen Hollinshead**, from Dundee, and **Kenneth Hollinshead**, from Newport Pagnell, who were amazed to spot their long-lost brother on screen.

They managed to trace him through Anglia and were also reunited with another brother and a sister. None of them had seen him since the family was split up and fostered out 28 years previously.

Gambit was briefly revived in 1995, after a break of 10 years, in the hands of rising comedian **Gary T. Thompson**.

Tom O'Connor who took over as host in 1983.

Lucky Ladders **host Lennie Bennett.**

Lucky Ladders joined Anglia's list of quiz successes in the 1980s, becoming Britain's longest-running game show after six extended series and 200 editions.

In the show, two pairs of related contestants attempted to complete a seven-rung 'word ladder' by guessing the five hidden mystery words in between an unrelated pair at the top and bottom.

Lucky Ladders was hosted by former journalist **Lennie Bennett**, who had spent four years with *Lennie and Jerry* on the BBC, five years on the game show *Punchlines* and presented the very first *Blankety Blank*.

The series, produced in association with game show specialists *Action Time*, was launched as a pilot in May, 1987, and started its first five-week network spell the following March on weekday mornings. Contestants could win holiday prizes and cash up to a £1,000 jackpot.

Larry Grayson with *Sweethearts* **guests Barbara Windsor, Wincey Willis and Colin Baker.**

The Zodiac Game appeared in 1984 and was, as its name suggests, based on astrology and predictions. **Tom O'Connor** was the host, with first **Bernard Fitzwalter** and later **Russell Grant** as the show's resident astrologer.

Four teams, each comprising a guest celebrity and a member of the public, were given a choice of answers to set situations aimed at discovering

Russell Grant and Tom O'Connor in *The Zodiac Game.*

whether they would react according to astrological type. The contestant from the winning team went forward to the 'Call a Sign' finale and, in a race against the clock, attempted to identify 12 pictured personalities and match them to their star sign.

Celebrity guests included **Chris Tarrant, Les Dennis, Dana, Nigel Dempster, Graeme Garden, Maureen Lipman, Lynsey de Paul, Wendy Richard, Leslie Phillips, Sylvia Syms** and **Barbara Windsor**.

Another of the stars, comedy actor **Roy Kinnear**, admitted he was somewhat cynical about astrology after living next door to a woman who used Tarot cards to make predictions. "Unfortunately her husband died unexpectedlly," he recalled.

His scepticism was shared by fellow guest, comedian **Duggie Brown**, who recalled a similar experience when visiting a clairvoyant in Blackpool: "The sign outside said 'Closed due to unforeseen circumstances!'".

Sweethearts, a 13-part series devised by the creators of *Bob's Full House* and hosted by **Larry Grayson**, was screened by most regions but in different early evening slots in 1987. It was the veteran camp comic's first presenting role since ending his successful spell in charge of *The Generation Game* four years earlier. It was not a happy comeback, despite the affection in which he was held by colleagues and viewers alike. Grayson struggled with his lines, and sometimes needed help in the form of cards held up

by members of the crew to remind him of his jokes. He felt ITV did not give the show a fair chance by transmitting it simultaneously in all regions. "Some ITV companies even scheduled it against *EastEnders*. What chance have I got against Dirty Den?" he complained in the *News of the World*.

ITV pulled the plug on a second series, and Grayson indicated he was leaving TV for good to look after his step-sister, Fran.

In the show, the man who gave Britain the catch-phrases "Shut that door" and "Seems like a nice boy" interviewed three couples of supposed 'sweethearts' about how they met. The twist was that only one of the couples was genuine and a panel of celebrities, along with viewers at home, had to guess which they were.

It was certainly the era of celebrity guests on game shows. Some of those who appeared on *The Zodiac Game* later found themselves back at the Anglia studios for *Sweethearts* or follow-up games *Show Me*, hosted by Cockney entertainer **Joe Brown**, *Mouthtrap*, which featured the gleaming 'gnashers' of **Don Maclean**, and *Jumble*.

Word association game *Mouthtrap* provided Brummie comedian Maclean with his first chance as TV game show host and he reckoned it was a timely opportunity: "I feel safe to open my mouth like this now the site of the third London airport has been confirmed," he joked.

In each show, fast-talking Maclean — who had his teeth insured for £10,000 and claimed to be the only comedian to contain fluoride — was joined by four contestants and two celebrity guests. The idea was for the contestants to try to predict ten words the celebrities would think of when given a key subject, with a holiday prize each week for the jackpot winners.

Most TV games have a warm-up comic to get the audience in the right frame of mind for the real action to follow. Performing the job on *Mouthtrap* was none other than **Jeremy Beadle**, whose flair for rubbing people up the wrong way produced an extraordinary act of vengeance by some of the studio crew. Fed up at being the butt of Beadle's jokes before every show, they pounced on the comedian one night and imprisoned him — still holding his microphone — in sticky tape from head to toe.

Sally James, Don Maclean and Chris Tarrant in *Mouthtrap.*

Just warming up...

Current couples could earn themselves holidays for notching up more points than the 'ex' – or maybe a blazing row on the way home if the 'old flame' chalked up a bigger score and waltzed off with the prize . . . **Paul Ross** made his Anglia debut in 1997 hosting a new game show devised by his brother **Simon** and sister-in-law **Amanda**, joint managing directors of independent company Cactus TV.

But the fast-moving question-and-answer game called *Upshot* was not planned as a vehicle for Paul. "We hadn't anyone specially in mind to present it," said Amanda. In fact, it was Anglia's executive producer **Jim Brown** who suggested Paul as an ideal host for the show, having known him since working with Paul's wife **Kerry** on a long-running series at LWT.

Paul and Simon – **Jonathan Ross** completes the brotherly triumvirate of TV talent – had never worked together before on a game show. Joked Paul: "Thank goodness it turned out like the *Waltons* and not the *Addams Family*."

Cactus TV produced a new game called *Intuition* for Anglia in 1999, this time with **Amanda Ross** as presenter.

Paul, Amanda and Simon Ross in *Upshot.*

JUMBLE, an afternoon show launched in March, 1991, gave another warm-up artist, London comedian **Jeff Stevenson**, his own game show for the first time.

Stevenson who entertained audiences on top shows including *Brush Strokes, Only Fools and Horses, This is Your Life, What's My Line* and *Wogan*, was joined by more star names who were given cryptic clues and had to unscramble words or phrases.

Included in the first series were **Leslie Crowther, Ulrika Jonsson, Tim Brooke-Taylor** and **Keith Chegwin**. The next year's run featured the likes of **Richard Madeley** and **Judy Finnigan, Gaby Roslin, Frank Bough, Bobby Davro** and **Linda Lusardi**. A face already familiar to quiz game fans from 17 years with *The Krypton Factor* – **Gordon Burns** – was back in the frame for Anglia's 1995 show, *Photo Finish*, a game involving both picture recognition and general knowledge with contestants trying to answer questions matched to picture clues on three giant video screens.

Two series from 1996 were *Hot Gossip* and *Duty Free* – the latter a make-believe travel game hosted by Anglia's then daytime chat show queen **Vanessa Feltz**.

Hot Gossip, presented by **Christopher Biggins**, was a game show scrutinising the secrets of the stars. Teams led by *Sunday Mirror* columnist **Lowri Turner** and **Dillie Keane**, from the satirical group **Fascinating Aida**, engaged in a light-hearted battle to pin down the identity of people who had attracted the attentions of the Press.

Is That It?, launched in 1997, was an anarchic panel game all about relationships and was hosted by American comedy star **Scott Capurro**, with comics **Mandy Knight** and **Matt Welcome** leading an out-and-out battle of the sexes. Two teams had to use their male or female intuition in a range of no-holds-barred rounds designed to sort out the girls from the boys.

Another game which focused on relationships was *Three's A Crowd*, which was hosted by **Andrew O'Connor** and arrived on regional screens in May, 1996. This one featured both the present and past loves of contestants on the show – and the key question was whether the 'old flame' knew more about their former partner than the new love.

From left to right: Dillie Keane, Christopher Biggins and Lowri Turner in *Hot Gossip.*

Radio star Kenneth Horne launched *I Packed My Bag* **in 1961.**

Bags of fun...

ANGLIA'S success with quizzes and game shows dates back to 1961. And the man who started it all was **Kenneth Horne**, whose rich voice and wry humour were already well-known through his long-running radio show *Round the Horne*.

Horne and **Betty Marsden** developed a series called *I Packed My Bag* from a traditional party game in which the challenge was to remember a list of items deposited in an imaginary bag.

One of the most successful contestants was a Colchester nurse whose spectacular powers of recall enabled her to walk away with five prizes, including a radio and a picnic hamper. She was later to prove herself only too human, however, by admitting that the day after her triumph she went out to buy a packet of tea and mistakenly returned home with a bag of sugar.

Two years after *I Packed My Bag* went on air, it was joined by a children's version, *Junior I Packed My Bag*, presented by **Dick Graham**.

The one that got away...

THE game that got away from Anglia was *Mr and Mrs*, the show that **Derek Batey** successfully took over and which helped put little Border Television on the map in the 1970s, and which was revived again by **Julian Clary** in 1999.

Anglia produced the first version in 1969, compered by **Norman Vaughan**, who had enjoyed a meteoric rise to stardom when he succeeded **Bruce Forsyth** as host of *Sunday Night at the London Palladium*. The programme travelled the Anglia region as an outside broadcast, with audiences packing into town halls. The first show was from Hellesdon, near Norwich, in May, but by the time it reached Hull, in September, it was the end of the road for the Anglia version.

But Anglia got one back in no uncertain terms with *Sale of the Century*. Long before **Nicholas Parsons** offered his first 'instant sale', Thames Television had produced a pilot programme with **Wilfred Pickles** as compere . . . but luckily for Anglia it failed to find favour with TV bosses of the time.

The one that got away... Norman Vaughan compered an early version of *Mr and Mrs.*

Champions...

A CROSS-ENGLAND TV challenge, in the style of *It's a Knockout*, was presented by **Nick Owen** and **Penny Smith** in 1993.

Champions, produced for Anglia, Meridian Broadcasting and Westcountry TV, involved 27 teams from the East, South and South-West in activities designed to test their talents and ingenuity.

East of England teams taking part came from Bedford, Cambridge, Clacton, Ipswich, King's Lynn, Milton Keynes, Norwich, Peterborough and Yarmouth.

Penny Smith and Nick Owen in *Champions.*

Meet your match...

A LONGER-RUNNING Sixties game was *Music Match*, a head-to-head, noughts and crosses-style contest of musical knowledge, compered over the years by **Muriel Young**, **David Gell** and **Pete Murray**.

It was some time before an American airman's wife living in Norwich finally cracked the jackpot prize of £100.

Pete Murray with hostesses Carol Dilworth and Jennifer Cresswell, who went on to be the first *Sale Of The Century* **girls.**

Comic capers...

A SEVEN-WEEK laughter series *You Must Be Joking*, launched in 1989, starred two young comedians, **Bradley Walsh** and **Shane Ritchie**, both of whom started their careers as Pontins Bluecoats and have since gone on to become household names.

It offered viewers the chance to put their jokes to the test against professional comics – with cash prizes to be won each time they came out tops. The senders of jokes used on the show each won an immediate £25, with an additional £25 each time any of the week's comics failed to raise more laughs with jokes on the same subject.

Some household names in British comedy – the first line-up brought together **Frank Carson**, **Dave Lee** and **Billy Pearce** – made sure viewers earned their money.

Carson, who must have guested on more game shows than anyone else, reckoned he was harder to turn off than the M1 and claimed to have told 31 jokes to **Bob Monkhouse** as they passed on an escalator. He added: "**Max Bygraves** thought he had gone deaf when we were in the same room and I didn't speak for five minutes."

Shane Ritchie and Bradley Walsh star in *You Must Be Joking*.

It's the way you tell them... Bradley Walsh with a member of the audience in *You Must Be Joking*.

Panel power...

A COMEDY panel game *Bring Me The Head Of Light Entertainment*, devised by bald comic **Lee Hurst** and made by Anglia, established itself as one of the new Channel 5's biggest home-grown successes during the channel's first year on the air in 1997.

Its host, Irish-born comedian **Graham Norton**, was voted best TV newcomer at the British Comedy Awards at the end of that year.

Hurst appeared as a team captain in the first series, but other commitments prevented him returning for the second series. Nonetheless, the programme has continued to enjoy big success, with **Paul Thorne** and **Dominic Holland** as the two team leaders, and it won a Bronze Rose award at the famous Montreux Film Festival in 1999.

Graham Norton has also gone from strength to strength, adding shows like *So Graham Norton* on Channel 4 to his repertoire. He is in no doubt why shows like *Bring Me The Head Of Light Entertainment* are so popular.

"Radio has known about comedy panel games for years, and lately television has re-discovered them," he said. "They're a very good way to use naturally funny people, particularly stand-up comics. Otherwise, there aren't the opportunities for them on TV. And comedians like the shows because they can react to things, which puts less pressure on them and means they don't have to use up their own material."

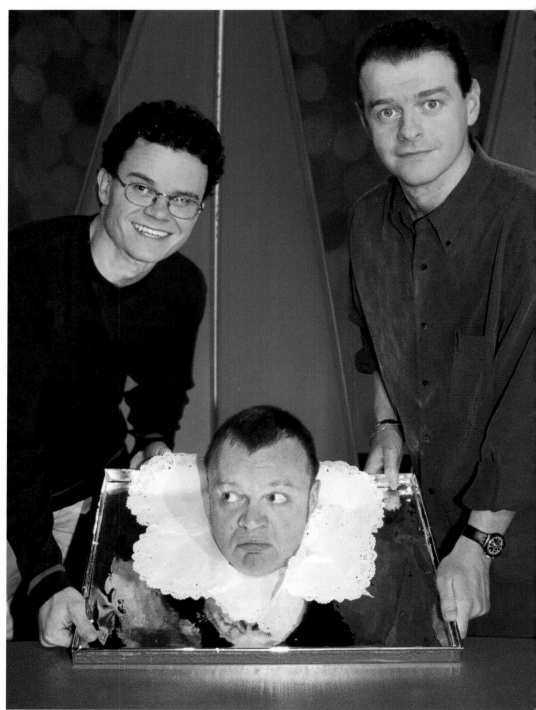

Bring Me The Head Of Light Entertainment...
From left to right: Dominic Holland, Graham Norton and Paul Thorne.

Girls, Girls, Girls...

Nanette Slack... took the
'Miss Anglia' title in 1966.

Beauty competitions were all the rage on TV in the 60s when there was little or no suggestion they might be demeaning to women.

The last seven 'Miss Anglias' with portrait artist Peter Deighan.

The next year, the search for 'Miss Anglia' became a show in its own right under the title *Glamour '62*. The hour-long final was broadcast live from the gymnasium of the United States Air Force Base at Sculthorpe, in Norfolk, and the winner was Scunthorpe's **Joan Ward**, 24, who had been third the previous year.

Beauty competitions were all the rage on TV in the 60s when there was little or no suggestion they might be demeaning to women. Girls from the East of England were also invited to compete for places in a national *Miss TV Times* contest in 1964, the regional heat being televised in a special *About Anglia* programme, introduced by **Chris Kelly**.

Glamour '64 was introduced by **McDonald Hobley**. A year later the presenter was **Pete Murray** and singer **Dennis Lotis** compered the 1966 show when the winner was **Nanette Slack** who went on to win 25 national titles including Miss Variety Club of Great Britain.

The series continued to be known under the *Glamour* title until 1974, when it became *Miss Anglia*. By then it had progressed beyond being simply a beauty parade. From 1969, a contract for a year's employment with the TV company came with the 'Miss Anglia' crown. With **Judy Ball**, and later **Susan Littlemore**, as her manager, the winner became a roving ambassador, travelling the region to open shops and fetes, judge competitions and model for local newspapers. There was also a goodwill visit to troops of the Royal Anglian Regiment's Colchester garrison stationed overseas.

The remuneration improved along with the responsibilities. From a £100 prize in the early days, the 1985 package for the winner had become £1,500, plus a two-week holiday in the United States, a £1,250 dress allowance and a portrait painted by Luton artist **Peter Deighan**.

One winner, however, could not take on the ambassadorial role. In 1977 **Irene Beason**, successful in

The first 'Miss Anglia', Joyce Cooke.

the Milton Keynes heat, went on to glory in the final but had to abdicate her crown to pursue her career as an air stewardess. The title passed to **Sneh Gupta**, a student nurse from Bedford, who went on to become a *Sale of the Century* hostess and then embarked on an acting career.

Sneh was one of a number of 'Miss Anglia' contestants for whom the contest opened up opportunities for TV work. **Jennifer Cresswell**, winner of the 1969 contest and **Angela Daniels**, one of the finalists in 1974, also became *Sale of the Century* hostesses. **Michelle Lambourne**, a 1975 finalist, was for nine years the card dealer on Anglia's quiz show *Gambit*.

BRING on the girls! For 25 years, Anglia held an annual contest with heats around the region and a grand final for the title of 'Miss Anglia'.

The event became immensely popular – one of the highlights of Anglia's regional output. Each year hundreds of young women entered, and more than 30 were selected to take part in a cabaret-style final, where the guests included civic dignitaries from the towns represented.

It all started in 1961 as an insert in the variety series *Showdate*, broadcast that year from the Britannia Pier Theatre, Great Yarmouth. In those days, contestants who lived outside the region were allowed to enter the local heats, but later the contest became strictly regional.

The first 'Miss Anglia' was 24-year-old **Joyce Cooke**, from Brighton, who had been selected as 'Miss Clacton'. She received her trophy and a £100 prize from singer **Marty Wilde**, one of the judges. Runner-up was 'Miss Southend', 22-year-old London model **Anne Simmonds**.

The *East Anglian Daily Times* reported that 1,500 people packed the audience for the final, and the judges included the reigning 'Miss England', **Arlott Dobson**, and comedian **Derek Roy**, complete with his St Bernard dog. There was a romantic sequel to that first contest – one of the finalists, **Jill Edwards** ('Miss Lowestoft'), married Anglia newscaster **Colin Bower**.

Marty Wilde with the first 'Miss Anglia'.

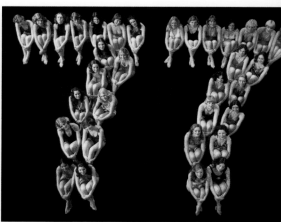

The line-up for 1977.

Dresses were the order of the day in 1982. Toni Johnson was the winner.

Sneh Gupta who took over as 'Miss Anglia'.

Crowning glory for 1984 winner Angela Gouldby.

Last of the 'Miss Anglias'... Elaine Hornett.

In the face of changing public attitudes to beauty contests, Anglia altered the format in the 1980s. There was much less emphasis on swimsuits, for instance. On a visit with 'Miss Anglia' to Peterborough in 1983, **Judy Ball** said: "This isn't a job for a dolly bird in a swimsuit . . . 'Miss Anglia' has got to be versatile. She has got to chat to all kinds of people about all sorts of things. Dress sense is important as is a good sense of humour. And not least she must have plenty of stamina – being 'Miss Anglia' for a year is harder work than most people imagine."

That year's contest, won by **Fiona Miller**, a 20-year-old insurance clerk from Wymondham, in Norfolk, put the emphasis on health as well as beauty, and included the ten finalists working out in the gymnasium at Henlow Grange health farm in Bedfordshire. Producer **Hugh Davies** said: "We're determined to get away from the old idea of beauty contests. Beauty is as much about health and fitness as a pretty face in a swimsuit."

The competition finally came to a close in 1985 with the crowning of the last 'Miss Anglia', **Elaine Hornett** from Harpenden, Hertfordshire. The glittering final was staged at Anglia's studio in Magdalen Street, Norwich, with former Dr Who **Colin Baker** and **Frazer Hines** from *Emmerdale* among the judges. The cabaret star was **Nick Heyward**.

Anglia considered introducing a 'Supergirl' competition to replace *Miss Anglia*, but it was decided it would not have the same viewer appeal. It was not quite the end of the road, however. A year after the final contest, the *About Anglia* programme brought together the last seven 'Miss Anglias' for a special Christmas celebration of the long-running series. Each appeared with her lifesize portrait, and was interviewed by **Christine Webber** about 'life after Miss Anglia'.

Many famous showbusiness names were associated with the *Miss Anglia* programme over the years as both judges and entertainers. During the later years, judges included **Judy Geeson**, **Madeleine Smith**, **Peter Bowles**, **Nigel Havers**, **Lewis Collins**, **Michele Dotrice**, **Anneka Rice** and **Edward Woodward**. And among the cabaret performers were **Barbara Dickson**, **Peter Skellern**, **Dana**, **Guys and Dolls** and **The New Seekers**.

In earlier years, top entertainers were booked for the televised heats as well. **Des O'Connor** teamed up with the **Dorothy Squires Dancers** at the Newmarket heat in 1968. The programme was recorded at the Tattersalls' horse sales arena and drew heavily on the town's racing connections. And at Yarmouth, the band **Dave Dee, Dozy, Beaky, Mick and Titch** performed the cabaret, and that year's final featured singer **Joe Brown**.

The next year, **Georgie Fame** was at the Hull heat, **Tony Blackburn** appeared in Norwich and top of the bill at the final was singer **Vince Hill**.

In 1971, **Semprini** was the guest at Hull, **Tony Hatch** and **Jackie Trent** were at Ipswich, and **Roy Castle** and the group **Marmalade** were the star entertainers at the final. A year later, **Craig Douglas** and **Susan Maugham** were among the music-makers at the heats, while American singing star **Gene Pitney** was special guest for the final. And 1973 saw **Sandie Shaw** appearing in Bedford, **Frank Ifield** and **Kenny Ball** at Boston, and **Anita Harris** at Peterborough. The final was held at Chelmsford where actor **Gerald Harper** and singer **Lena Martell** were among the celebrity guests.

About Anglia personalities **Bob Wellings**, **Graham Bell**, **Christine Webber** and **Patrick Anthony** were among the regular presenters of *Miss Anglia*. Webber and Anthony co-hosted the last five finals and Webber also presented the 1980 contest with **Fred Dinenage**, Anglia's *Gambit* quizmaster.

Christine Webber interviewing 1984 finalists.

Marmalade playing at the 1971 final.

Sitcoms...

Backs To The Land **was filmed in and around the Norfolk village of Heydon in 1976.**

Backs To The Land... **Marilyn Galsworthy, Terri Stevens and Phillipa Howell with real-life brothers David and Michael Troughton.**

BACKS TO THE LAND, Anglia's first situation comedy series, put three girls from London to work on an East Anglian farm in the Women's Land Army during the Second World War. Nick-named 'Mum's Army' when announced in 1975, because of perceived rivalry with Captain Mainwaring's Home Guard on BBC, the series offered starring roles to three TV 'unknowns'.

Marilyn Galsworthy played a dippy debutante, more used to pouring Martinis than milking cows. Previously her biggest screen role had been as the Bond girl eaten by sharks in *The Spy Who Loved Me*.

Terri Stevens, cast as a quick-witted Cockney lass, was 25 and a singer who had appeared on Broadway in the first American version of *Gigi*.

Phillipa Howell, also 25, who played a middle-class Jewish girl, was the best known of the trio through her role as WPC **Betty Arthur** in the popular police series *Softly, Softly* on BBC.

In the story, the girls were assigned to a farmer (**John Stratton**), whose two sons – played by real-life brothers **David** and **Michael Troughton** – were in the Forces. Shooting began on location in and around the Norfolk village of Heydon during the glorious summer of 1976. And the three young actresses played it for real, learning how to muck in (and muck out) with milking, tractor-driving, harvesting, sheep-shearing, hedge-cutting and ditching.

Care was taken to ensure clothes and hairstyles were right for the period.

The producers aimed for authenticity in the East Anglian accents by employing actor **Peter Tuddenham**, who played the pub landlord in the series, in the additional role of adviser on local customs and accents.

Language expert Peter – he also played **Tom Thurston** in the long-running *Waggoners Walk* series on Radio 2 – said: "People often confuse the East Anglian dialect with Somerset. The two are quite different. Norfolk and Suffolk people don't burr their 'rs' or drop their aitches." Care was taken to ensure clothes and hairstyles were right for the period as well, although one former 'Land Girl' viewer got her knickers in a twist over the underwear worn in the programmes. Mrs **Thelma Pennell** complained about the girls sporting 'passion killer' ETB (elastic-top-and-bottom) knickers at a village dance, and lacy all-in-one cami-knickers in another episode. "They're hopelessly out of date," she said. "Panties were the fashion by the 1940s."

But Anglia won support from another former Land Army trooper, Mrs **Joyce Hollocks**, who wrote to the *Sunday People*: "ETBs may have been old-fashioned in the 1940s, but many girls wore them on the farms. I used to wear my father's long johns. In fact, we would wear anything to keep warm in winter, and anything that was comfortable under our breeches."

Backs To The Land was dogged by misfortune even before it started on air. First it was disrupted by a union dispute over sound-dubbing arrangements. Then, when it was eventually slotted in for April, 1977, ITV schedulers could not agree on a simultaneous screening across the country.

London Weekend Television and Anglia showed it on Friday evenings, but other regions gave it Saturday or Sunday slots. The big Midlands-based ATV refused to schedule it at all initially. Such fragmentation made it difficult for the series to become a ratings success or achieve the kind of profile possible with a fully networked show.

There was sympathy for Anglia's dilemma. *The Sun*'s television writer pulled no punches: "Anglia Television recently made their first major comedy series at a cost of £250,000. It is about three pretty girls who became

Land Girls during the war and it is very funny indeed. But not all of you are going to see it. If Thames or ATV had made it, it would probably get a fully networked slot. But Anglia is not one of the big companies so its brave new show is getting the kind of treatment which guarantees it cannot be a hit . . ."

When the series eventually made its debut there were inevitably unfavourable comparisons in the Press with *Dad's Army*, which the nation had, by that time, taken to its hearts. Some critics tempered their remarks by pointing out that the stories of the Warmington-on-Sea Home Guard had taken more than one series to become established as classic comedy, but all in all it was not the start Anglia had wanted for one of its most important ventures.

The company was determined to persevere, however. *Backs To The Land* returned for a second series in November, 1977. **Marilyn Galsworthy** moved on to the Royal Shakespeare Company and was replaced by **Pippa Page**, 22, playing an actress who became a 'Land Girl' after failing a Forces entertainment audition. She was already a familiar TV face as **Terry Scott** and **June Whitfield's** daughter in *Happy Ever After*.

This time more of the ITV regions – nine in total, and including ATV in Birmingham – gave *Backs To The Land* a simultaneous Friday night screening. But four others, including the powerful Yorkshire and Granada companies, still went their separate ways. And it was a similar pattern the next year when the third and final series was screened. The third series was also tainted by stories, which surfaced in a Sunday newspaper, of friction on the set between **Terri Stevens** and **Phillipa Howell**.

The feeling persisted that, as with other drama series produced by Anglia in the 60s and 70s, the programme had not been able to realise its potential because of politicking within the ITV system of the time. *The Times* recalled an earlier Anglia under-achiever in its comment on *Backs To The Land*: "Deserves to succeed – but so did Weavers Green" (the 60s soap that similarly failed to get fully networked). And TV critic **Stafford Hildred** wrote: "The series never really got the recognition it deserved."

Marjorie And Men, Anglia's only other sitcom series, was screened in 1985. It was specially significant for the fact that it provided a first leading role in the genre for **Patricia Routledge** who, of course, followed up with a major success as **Hyacinth Bucket** in the BBC's *Keeping Up Appearances*. It was also a first major series for an up-and-coming 22-year-old actress called **Michelle Collins**, who went on to become **Cindy Beale** in *EastEnders* and, by the end of the 90s, one of television drama's hottest properties.

Marjorie And Men was set in Norwich and centred on **Marjorie Belton**, a middle-aged, divorced bank clerk (Routledge) who lived with her interfering mother and was desperately seeking 'Mr Right'. A strong cast included **Patricia Hayes**, as Mum, and **George Baker** and **Timothy West** among the boyfriends. **Michelle Collins** played the bank junior who gave Marjorie encouragement and tips on such useful skills as disco dancing.

The six-part series was directed by **John Gorrie** with scripts by him and **Philip Spence**, writer of *To The Manor Born*. Gorrie revealed that Marjorie developed from a minor character in a *Tales of the Unexpected* story called '*Down Among the Sheltering Palms*'.

Almost all the filming for the six programmes, produced by Anglia's head of drama **John Rosenberg**, took place in East Anglia. A branch of the Nat West in London Street, Norwich, was used as the fictional bank, and Marjorie and her mother's 'home' was a house on the city outskirts.

Patricia Routledge and Michelle Collins in *Marjorie and Men.*

Patricia Routledge had made a handful of guest appearances in sitcoms – including one as a girlfriend of **Harold Steptoe** – but, before **Marjorie Belton** came along, she had turned down a number of offers to star in her own series because, she said, she was never able to see finished scripts. "I was offered five of the scripts before I said yes to Anglia, and I was terribly impressed with the quality."

Marjorie And Men was generally well received by the critics, with particular admiration for the performances of the two Patricias. **Elizabeth Cowley** wrote in the *Daily Mail*: "This graceful Anglia series... has a new double act that could become a comic cult because the sparring partners are actresses trained to their fingertips, covered with awards – and who know just what to do with a good script."

Patricia Hayes, John Judd and Patricia Routledge in *Marjorie and Men.*

But it was not to be. Despite the excellent acting and high production values, the expected second series of *Marjorie And Men* was not commissioned. Anglia's direct involvement in making sitcoms was effectively laid to rest.

Soaps...

WHEN we think back to the origins of 'soap opera' on ITV, *Coronation Street* and *Crossroads* probably spring to mind. But there were others in the 1960s that were important in the development of the genre. Among them was a twice-weekly serial produced for ITV by Anglia's drama department.

Weavers Green, launched in 1966, was based around a fictional vets' practice in an East Anglian village with a post office and shop, church, pub, railway station and racing stable. Filming took place on location in various Norfolk villages and, as was always the case with Anglia drama productions, there was great attention to authenticity. Vets, farmers, cowmen, agricultural machinery salesmen and even a poacher were among those interviewed before scriptwriter **Peter Lamda** began creating the fictional characters.

Wendy Richard in *Weavers Green.*

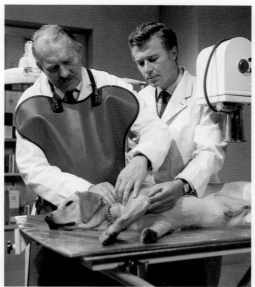

Grant Taylor and Eric Flynn in *Weavers Green.*

Two vets, played by **Grant Taylor** and **Eric Flynn**, were the central characters. And there were also two young actresses in minor roles gaining experience of working on a soap serial that would stand them in good stead for later in their careers – **Wendy Richard**, now of *EastEnders*, and **Kate O'Mara**, who was to join the glamorous cast of *Dynasty*.

In a number of ways, *Weavers Green* was ahead of its time. It was the first such venture by one of the smaller regional ITV companies and it pioneered shooting on location with a mobile videotape unit. Most other soaps used a purpose-built studio set but, in *Weavers Green*, when it rained or snowed in real life, it rained or snowed in the story.

It was also the first truly rural soap, and its vets-and-animals theme was to be successfully exploited over the

Kate O'Mara with Eric Flynn.

next three decades by programmes ranging from *All Creatures Great and Small* to *Vets in Practice*.

Unfortunately for Anglia, TV schedulers of the time did not have the same enthusiasm for vets and pets as their counterparts today, and *Weavers Green* failed to secure two regular weekday slots. One episode was shown on a Thursday, the other at the weekend. The Thursday episode was highly popular, but many viewers missed the follow-up instalment on a Saturday or Sunday – and there were no home video recorders in those days. So, after 50 episodes, Anglia decided the handicap was too great and ended the serial.

Six years later a new countryside soap from Yorkshire Television was given the two weekday slots denied to *Weavers Green*. It was called *Emmerdale Farm*...

Suspense...

MOVIE legend **Orson Welles** signed up with Anglia in 1974 as host and story-teller of a series of 26 half-hour tales of mystery and suspense which was the forerunner of *Tales of the Unexpected* five years later.

Orson Welles' Great Mysteries was a prestigious series in its own right. The cigar-puffing actor-director, clad in cape and wide-brimmed hat to maximise his already powerful presence, set the scene for each episode which included works by masters of suspense such as **Dorothy L. Sayers, Arthur Conan Doyle, Honore de Balzac** and **Wilkie Collins**.

Sir John Woolf and his head of drama, **John Jacobs**, masterminded the venture and brought in international stars such as **Eli Wallach, Don Murray, Donald Pleasence** and **Susannah York** to head the casts. They also engaged **Donald Wilson**, producer of *The Forsyte Saga*, to take charge of story supervision, and **John Barry**, composer of the *Born Free* theme, to write the title music.

The series began transmission in the Anglia region on April 5, 1974, yet surprisingly, despite its high profile and production values, was denied a simultaneous network

Orson Welles.

showing in Britain. Other ITV regions showed the programmes at different times, and it was left to overseas stations, particularly in the United States where it topped the ratings, to cash in on its undoubted appeal. It was shown in more than 60 countries – including Japan, Australia, Chile and South Africa – and won a Hollywood Festival award in 1974 for syndicated drama series.

Memorable casting included **Joan Collins** and **Anton Rodgers** in *The Dinner Party* by **James Michael Ullman**; **Susannah York** and **Peter Cushing** in Balzac's *La Grande Breteche*; **Christopher Lee**, **Jane Seymour** and **Simon Ward** in *The Leather Funnel* by **Conan Doyle**, and **Ian Holm** and **Jennie Linden** in *The Trial For Murder* by **C.A. Collins** and **Charles Dickens**.

Other TV favourites in the cast lists included **Patrick MacNee** (of *Avengers* fame), **Brian Wilde** (Foggy in *Last of the Summer Wine*), **Bill Maynard** (lately of *Heartbeat*), **Pam St Clement** (Pat in *EastEnders*) and **John le Mesurier** (Sgt Wilson in *Dad's Army*).

Joan Collins and Anton Rodgers in *The Dinner Party*.

Peter Cushing and Susannah York in *La Grande Breteche*.

Eli Wallach.

Christopher Lee, Jane Seymour and Simon Ward in *The Leather Funnel*.

DAILY EXPRESS

No. 23,943   Tuesday June 21 1977   Weather : Cloudy   8p

Angry viewers protest after 'War of the Worlds' show

Director Miles

STORM OVER TV'S SPOOF

By Christopher Jones

THOUSANDS of viewers all over the country protested in shock and anger over a science fiction "documentary" put out by ITV last night.

From the moment that "Alternative Three" ended at 10 p.m. irate watchers jammed the switchboards of the Daily Express and ITV companies, to complain.

The hour-long spoof, put out by Anglia Television at peak viewing time, purported to show "evidence" of life on a scientific colony on Mars, and how brain-drain scientists were being shipped to the planet.

'Irresponsible'

The programme was introduced by former newscaster Tim Brinton as a serious investigation into a disturbing trend of scientific discovery.

American and Russian spacemen were seen collaborating to set up the "new colony" on Mars, while viewers were left to suppose that the reason for the exploration was the end of life on earth.

TV advertised the show by saying : "What this programme shows may be considered unethical. . . ."

Viewers taken unawares protested their shock immediately. Others, realising the programme was a spoof complained of ITV's "irresponsibility."

Early today, a spokesman for the Independent Broadcasting Authority said it had thought long and hard before allowing the documentary to be shown.

But Mrs Denise Ball, of Camberley, Surrey, said : "I was scared out of my wits. It was all so real."

And Mr Aidan Jones, a 35-year-old insurance broker from Beckenham, Kent, accused the film makers of irresponsibility.

Programme director Christopher Miles, brother of actress Sarah Miles, was unrepentant.

"This country needs a stir once every five years and I am glad I have done just that," he said.

The programme was planned originally to go out on April Fool's Day—a sort of updated version of the famous hoax by Orson Wells with his "War of the Worlds" radio broadcast in the 1930's.

James Murray : Page 19

Weather Page 2 ● Target Pa

How the *Daily Express* **reported the protests over** *Alternative 3* **in 1977.**

Gregory Munroe... he played investigative reporter Colin Benson in *Alternative 3.*

And spoofs!

ON MONDAY, June 20, 1977, Anglia was responsible for a drama production that has since achieved worldwide cult status among students of both television history and science fiction.

Alternative 3 was sci-fi presented in the guise of an investigative documentary – and it became British television's equivalent of the **Orson Welles** dramatisation on radio of **H.G. Wells's** *War of the Worlds* that panicked America in 1938.

The plot centred on the supposed discovery that top British scientists were vanishing as part of a secret American-Russian conspiracy to colonise Mars because the earth was dying from pollution and global warming. The impression of realism was imparted by the use of actual news footage of natural disasters and droughts (including references to the arid British summer of 1976), and by the involvement of television journalist and former ITN newsreader **Tim Brinton** as presenter.

Originally the spoof had been intended for transmission on April 1 – but no networking time was available until 12 weeks later. Despite a cast list – with some reasonably well-known faces among the actors – and the date of April 1 in the on-screen credits, an amazing number of frightened viewers took it all to be fact, and switchboards of TV companies across Britain were jammed with calls. "I was scared out of my wits, it was all so real," said a typical caller.

Some of the pre-publicity had hinted at the true nature of the programme but most of the TV writers had gone along with Anglia's request not to give the game away completely. One exception was **Elkan Allan** in *The Sunday Times* – possibly in revenge for having himself been fooled by the invitation to the Press screening. "I asked our science correspondent to go to the preview to assess the scientific veracity," he wrote.

By the time the show was transmitted, all of Fleet Street knew the truth, but it did not stop a barrage of sensational headlines the next day. 'TV TERROR' screamed the Scottish *Daily Record* while the *Daily Express* front-page banner proclaimed: 'STORM OVER TV's SPOOF'. The Express followed up next day with an article headed "Will you know if TV is telling the truth tonight?", warning of the power of television to deceive. Generally, the reviewers liked the programme. **Sean Day-Lewis** in the *Daily Telegraph* called it "convincing and imaginative", **Alan Coren** in *The Times*

Alternative 3 **presenter Tim Brinton.**

"deft and engaging", **James Murray** in the *Daily Express* said it had "achieved the rare feat of giving television drama an extra dimension", and **Shaun Usher** in the *Daily Mail* described it as "an ingenious piece of work – one of the best sci-fi offerings since *Quatermass*".

Quoted in the Express, *Alternative 3* writer **David Ambrose** said he was as surprised as anyone that so many people had mistaken fiction for fact. He added: "The answer is, beware of the media. There is an obligation on every viewer to sift the evidence he is being fed and then to make up his own mind if he accepts it. My advice to viewers is 'Keep your wits about you.' ".

The director, **Christopher Miles** (brother of actress Sarah), said: "If the programme has done nothing else it has made people more aware of the threat to the ecology of the world. More, perhaps, than a lot of other earnest documentaries on the subject."

The fact that so many people took it for real was, at least in part, a compliment to the actors. They included **Richard Marner**, who went on to play Nazi officer **Colonel von Strohm** in the comedy series 'Allo 'Allo, and **Shane Rimmer**, a familiar face in *Superman* and Bond films and a number of TV mini-series in the 70s and 80s. But the lead role, that of investigative reporter **Colin Benson**, was taken by a virtual unknown, **Gregory Munroe** who, the following year, appeared in the TV series *Mixed Blessings* and later the film *A Caribbean Mystery*. Sadly he died of a heart condition aged only 44 in 1998.

Alternative 3 was shown in many other countries, although the United States was reluctant to take it, probably because of the earlier furore over *War of the Worlds*. It also generated a best-selling paperback book – reprinted at least seven times – and is still today the subject of magazine articles, calls and e-mails from all over the world to Anglia's offices.

Survival is the name of the game...

WILDLIFE photographers are a breed apart – scarcely less exotic than the animals they film. The story of Anglia TV's *Survival* series is *their* story.

Since the programme's ITV debut on February 1, 1961, the *Survival* team has made close on 1,000 programmes, delighting and amazing television audiences in 112 countries. The contribution of the men and women behind the camera is a chronicle of skill, organisation, courage and determination. There is no job quite like it. What other occupation offers the opportunity of being chased by a grizzly bear, caught up in a hippo fight, charged by a 30-stone gorilla, stalked by an 18-foot crocodile, bitten on the backside by a leopard or woken by a growling lion at the foot of your sleeping bag? And sadly, several *Survival* film-makers have lost their lives on location over the years.

Survival's photographers would be the first to emphasise, however, that conflict with wildlife is not a major problem. The animals only do what comes naturally and are fairly predictable. It's more often humans who cause the real trouble. *Survival* front-liners have been robbed at gunpoint, caught up in wars and held as spies. Add to that the occasional local difficulty caused by earthquakes, hurricanes, floods, avalanches, lightning strikes and volcanic eruptions, or the debilitating effects of tropical diseases like malaria and bilharzia (parasitic worms), and you get an idea of how hazardous life can be.

Yet anybody who goes out to shoot a natural history film will tell you that the greatest enemies are boredom and frustration – and that patience is one of the greatest virtues.

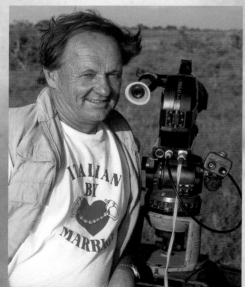

Simon Trevor.

When former Kenya game-park warden **Simon Trevor** decided to make a film about the African honey badger, the key sequence he needed was of badgers raiding a hive of killer bees. It took him three years to get it. "The bees only produce honey once a year, so you only get one crack at it," he explained. "When a badger came along the first year there was a real downpour, the camera got wet and the lights fused. The second year I was defeated by a beetle that got into the hive and ate the honeycombs." Third time round, it worked a treat – apart from the fact that some of the bees vented their wrath and he was badly stung.

It was a similar story when he set out to film a family of ground hornbills raising their single chick in a hollow tree nest. This time it took four years. First year the tree blew down in a gale, the following year's chick was eaten by a predator, the next one choked on its food, and finally junior hornbill number four made it into the big wide world. It's hard to say who was more relieved – Simon Trevor or the hornbill parents.

Filming wildlife is not so much a job, more a way of life. And some of its greatest exponents have devoted their lives to it. Take **Des and Jen Bartlett** the doyens of them all. Des left a bank job in Australia to start filming wildlife in 1952, learning his craft with **Armand** and **Michaela Denis** of *On Safari* fame. Four years later, Jen gave up a promising tennis career to join him, and they have been filming together ever since. Their *Survival* film *Flight of the Snow Geese* won two Emmys and is one of the landmarks of the series.

As the new century dawns, Des and Jen are still out there filming. Their 'home' nowadays borders one of the remotest and least hospitable places on earth, the Namib Desert in south-west Africa. It was there they woke one morning to find a lion growling at them from the foot of their sleeping bag. What on earth do you do when a fully grown lion is standing over your recumbent body before breakfast? Said Des: "We just shouted at the tops of our voices to frighten him off, and when the sun came up we followed his tracks and filmed him among the sand dunes." But of course!

Alan Root, who has filmed for *Survival* since 1963, has had more scrapes than most – and bears the scars to prove it. He lost an index finger to a puff adder bite – allergy to the anti-venom almost cost him his life – had holes ripped in his leg by a hippo and a mountain gorilla, was bitten on the backside by a leopard and has survived more near misses in aircraft than anyone cares to remember.

Though his risks are always calculated, he confesses to being an 'adrenaline freak' and is never afraid to court danger to get the shots. While filming a volcanic eruption, he got so close to the lava flow that part of his camera melted. His scariest moment came when he got caught in the middle of an underwater fight between two hippos. One seized him by the leg and shook him like a rag doll so that his helpless body was flung out of the water several times before the animal released its grip. "There was a hole through my calf large enough to push a Coke bottle through," he said. In hospital he developed gangrene and suffered terrible fevers. "I have had the sheets changed before when I was sweating, but never the mattress. And in between the sweats I needed an electric blanket to keep warm. Three days, 17 pints of saline, eight pints of blood, millions of units of penicillin and several cups of tea later I was declared OK."

Root's visionary skills have resulted in some of *Survival's* most extraordinary programmes. For *Safari By Balloon* and *Year of the Wildebeest* he and his first wife, Joan, used a hot-air balloon for an aerial perspective on wildlife across the African plains. They made the first balloon flight over Africa's highest peak Mt Kilimanjaro for good measure. Root also confounded TV executives by making a film about termites into a ratings winner. The compelling story revealed the insects' highly-organised society and prowess as builders and defenders of their Castles of Clay. It received an Oscar nomination.

In the Central African rain-forest, he tracked down and filmed some of the world's most elusive creatures and made remarkable discoveries about their behaviour. They included a cat-like genet that uses sensitive whiskers to help it locate and catch fish. Until Root came along, no live specimen had been seen by a naturalist. He also filmed the Congo peacock that had been missing, some presumed extinct, for more than 40 years. "The stories of these animals had fascinated me since I was a boy," he said. "It was the film I'd always wanted to make."

Elephant airlift. Drastic action is sometimes needed to save threatened animals. This calf was being transported to a new home in a national park.

Des Bartlett filming crabs on the Skeleton Coast of Namibia.

Alan Root filming a
wildebeest migration.

'Indiana Jones'...

VYING with Root for the title of *Survival's* 'Indiana Jones' is **Nick Gordon**. Originally a chartered surveyor in Lancashire, Gordon decided he wanted to film wildlife after joining a sub-aqua club in Morecambe Bay and being introduced to the wonders of the marine environment. It took a lot of determination to achieve his goal, but for the past ten years he has lived and worked in the Amazon rain-forest, producing a string of fascinating films and tapping into the knowledge and customs of the local Amerindian peoples whose affinity with the forest goes back thousands of years.

Gordon has joined in their weird ceremonies – including banqueting on barbecued tarantula spiders – filmed their special relationships with the forest animals and twice fled for his life when they became hostile. He was also instrumental in discovering a new species of monkey unknown to science.

Though Amazonia is one of the harshest environments on earth in which to work, he never minds going to the office, even if it is a sweaty camera-hide on a scaffolding platform 150 ft up in the treetops. "Back in Britain, when I meet people at a party, they are amazed when I tell them I go to work by canoe, or that if I get up in the night to go to the loo, the first thing I have to do is scan the floor for snakes," he said. "I'm very lucky that the work I do is a passion and I could never tire of it."

Nick Gordon built 150 ft scaffold towers to film in the Amazon forest canopy. His Anglia umbrella served as a useful sunshade.

Nick Gordon filming a Jaguar close-up.

Nick Gordon shows how a cameraman relaxes in the flooded forest.

It's a family affair...

FOR some of *Survival's* film-makers, working with wildlife has been a family affair. **Des** and **Jen Bartlett's** daughter, Julie, accompanied them on all their expeditions until she was 12, being educated by Jen using a correspondence course. **Richard** and **Julia Kemp** took their four-year-old son, Malcolm, when they followed the migration of a million white-eared kob antelope across the Sudan. "Everyone was horrified that we were taking our young son with us, but he came through it all fitter than either of us," said Richard. "He also proved to be a great ambassador in our contact with local tribes."

Ten years later, by which time daughter Emma had made the family up to four, the Kemps were on the trail of wolves in the wilds of Spain.

Mark Deeble and **Victoria Stone** are bringing up their two sons, Freddy and Jacca , in remote regions of Kenya and Tanzania. The couple went to Africa before the boys were born to work with **Alan Root** after their success with underwater films made on the coast of Britain. They got off to a blockbusting start when their first African film *Here Be Dragons,* featuring dramatic footage of the continent's biggest crocodiles, was watched by more than 12 million viewers on ITV in 1992.

Starting a family has been no impediment to Mark and Victoria's day job — in fact, quite the reverse. *A Little Fish in Deep Water,* a film about the marine life of Lake Tanganyika, made during Victoria's pregnancy and Freddy's infancy, won the wildlife film-makers' most coveted award, the Golden Panda at the 1996 Wildscreen film and TV festival.

Said Victoria: "Having the boys with us is wonderful because now, when we stop work, we have something different to stop for. We adore it and have a really good time with them. I love bringing them up in the bush. Seeing a child's natural interest in all that wilderness is fantastic."

Barbara Tyack combines her film-making with looking after her son, Kaya, an African baby she adopted from a Nairobi children's home. Like several of her *Survival* colleagues, she has shown huge fortitude in the face of danger and difficulty. Before she started film-making, she was attacked and mauled by baboons, needing 56 stitches in her wounds. Later she went on to make an award-winning film about the animals. Her young African assistant, Harmen, who saved her life in the baboon attack, later died in a car accident, and in 1998 Tyack was robbed at gunpoint when her camp was attacked and one of her armed guards killed.

Victoria Stone and a passing turtle on the shore of Lake Tanganyika.

A wet life in the great outdoors for Mark Deeble, with (inset) son Freddy.

When nine lives is not enough...

DANGER is part and parcel of the film-maker's life. "You don't dwell on the risks, otherwise you'd never do the job," says **Nick Gordon.** Even so, three *Survival* film-makers have been killed on location, most recently the mercurial German photographer **Dieter Plage**, one of the pillars of the series for more than 25 years. He fell from an airship while filming above the forest canopy in Sumatra in 1993. His death at 56 sent shock waves throughout the wildlife filming community.

Tall and athletic, Plage had been regarded as indestructible. A cameraman with the proverbial nine lives, he had survived a litany of hair-raising incidents and made light of them all. A crocodile once swam straight at him and bit off his camera lens housing; he emerged unscathed from being run over by a charging elephant, and found himself eyeball to eyeball with a tiger which peered into his flimsy hide.

He also suffered skin burns after swimming for hours with pelicans in the corrosive waters of an Ethiopian soda lake. But it was worth it. He had concealed his head and camera inside a dummy pelican to get spectacular close-ups. The disguise was so convincing one young pelican thought Plage was its mother and followed him when he swam back to shore.

Tiger, Tiger was Plage's intimate portrait of the magnificent big cats in India and Nepal, *Orang-utan: Orphans of the Forest* highlighted the plight of these endearing apes — great favourites of his — in Borneo and Sumatra. He had just returned to make a new film about them when he met his death.

Plage was the main cameraman on a four-part *Survival* series shot in the Galapagos Islands in the 1980s. Two of his last films were made with his friend and fellow German, the wildlife artist **Wolfgang Weber,** who led the tributes at a packed memorial service in Norwich.

Perhaps Plage's most challenging assignment, and his greatest achievement, was filming *The Secret World of Bats*. Shot mainly at night using some of wildlife photography's most sophisticated techniques, this remarkable programme was filmed on five continents and revealed for the first time on film the vital ecological role played by bats, which account for almost a quarter of all the world's mammals.

He always said his most dangerous mission was filming the hostile Afar warriors of the Sudan's Danakil Desert. "They traditionally castrate intruders to protect their water and grazing. I never felt fully relaxed while filming them as they regard shooting an enemy in the back as a matter of honour!"

For 16 years his wife, Mary, was his assistant, taking care of the stills photography, organising the camps and sharing the adventures and privations of life in some of the world's wildest and most inhospitable places. They met in England and Mary went to India where he was filming tigers. She soon adapted to life in the jungle, despite the considerable change from her bank job in Bath. They married within months and spent their honeymoon 16,000 feet up Mount Everest in a double sleeping bag, hugging the film camera to stop it freezing up.

In 1975, young American photographer **Lee Lyon**, who had started out as Dieter Plage's assistant in Africa, was the first *Survival* film-maker to lose her life. She was working on her first solo film, covering a round-up of elephant calves in Rwanda, when one of the animals suddenly charged and trampled her. Film she had shot was edited into a moving tribute called *Lee's Story*.

Three years later **John Pearson**, an airline pilot who became an accomplished film-maker in Africa, was shot and killed at a campsite in Tanzania by a guard who opened fire from inside his tent after hearing a noise he mistook for intruders. Pearson's last film, *Hunters of the Plains*, was screened posthumously on ITV in 1979.

Dieter Plage showing a young orang-utan the other side of the camera.

How Survival was put on the map...

IN the summer of 1960 **Aubrey Buxton**, a founder director of Anglia TV and lifelong naturalist, introduced a 15-minute regional nature programme called *Countryman* which proved to be the origin of the world's most famous and enduring television wildlife series.

Within a few months, Buxton saw the opportunity to offer ITV a new natural history strand. As a pilot programme he produced a film about coypus, the South American rodents that had been introduced into the Norfolk Broads where they caused great damage to river banks and vegetation.

The first *Survival* film, broadcast on February 1, 1961, was not much further from home – in fact just over a hundred miles to the south-west. It featured the wildlife of London, and was introduced by Buxton standing beside the lake in St James's Park and on a derelict bomb site in the City.

The London Scene, as it was called, was chosen at the behest of Associated Rediffusion, the London ITV company which had agreed to back *Survival* . . . but was not sold on coypus! A programme about wildlife in London might seem incongruous, but it served a useful purpose. At the time, television viewing was concentrated in urban areas and it was reasoned that if people could be told about wildlife they never suspected was right on their own doorsteps, then *Survival*.would have gone a long way towards establishing the appeal of natural history programmes.

The deputy editor of Rediffussion's current affairs programme *This Week*, **Colin Willock**, was seconded to Anglia for the production of *The London Scene*. Willock, who stayed on and headed Anglia's natural history unit for the next 27 years, recalled in his book *The World of Survival*: "The wildlife content of the programme seems, in retrospect, a bit of a laugh. Apart from a few feral pigeons, some ducks in St James's Park and a fox let out of a laundry basket on a wild night in a quiet street, just off Hampstead Heath, the wildlife scenes had been shot anywhere but in London.

Dieter Plage (left) and Colin Willock on location.

"To be fair, we never suggested that our puffin was standing outside the Thames Embankment entrance to the Savoy Hotel. We merely said that one had been found there and then proceeded to show the bird in its wild state – in Pembrokeshire! If we wanted herons for the well-known breeding colony on an island in one of the Walthamstow reservoirs, we transported them on film from Scotland. The fish we naturally filmed – unnaturally – in tanks."

Willock also revealed that the series could have been called *Tooth and Claw*, which was a front runner for some time in the quest for a title. "Both Aubrey and I objected to it on the grounds that nature was not really like that. In the end we came up with *Survival*.

It was adopted for the reason that most titles are eventually adopted. No one can think of anything better. As it turned out, it was a good and lucky choice."

The second *Survival* programme was made deep in the heart of Anglia territory. It was about the avocet, the rare wading bird that had been brought back to nest in the region. Soon, however, Buxton and Willock were spreading their wings in a big way. The latter was despatched to Uganda to supervise the filming of a programme about the capture and re-location of around 30 white rhino threatened by poaching.

John Buxton, a cousin of Aubrey, went along as cameraman and Willock recruited another lensman, **Chiels Margach**, in Africa. The result was an exciting, fast-moving programme called *SOS Rhino* which was effectively television's first big international conservation story. It was also the programme that really put *Survival* on the map.

Aubrey Buxton produced and introduced many of the early programmes and remained the guiding hand behind the series for more than 30 years. He went on to be chief executive and then chairman of Anglia Television, served on many countryside and wildlife bodies, and was made a life peer in 1978. Today he is honorary life president of *Survival* as well as a much respected father figure of British television.

As *Survival's* executive producer, he gathered around him a talented team of film-makers and showed great foresight, not only in the subjects chosen, but in the way they were presented. Writing in a promotional brochure in 1969, he set out the philosophy that drove the *Survival* team so successfully.

"To entertain was what we purposely set out to do. In order to entertain we resolved to give wildlife filming full feature treatment. We cut at the pace of modern documentary. We went for drama and intimate close-up detail. We invited the most exciting modern composers to score our music. We looked always for the 'nugget', the unique revelation or the previously unglimpsed view. Always we tried to be conscious of the wider drama in which an expanding world confronts a shrinking wilderness."

Chief among the composers referred to was **Johnny Dankworth**, who scored the music for *The London Scene* and many other *Survivals* in the 1960s. It was an innovation that shocked some purists, but demonstrated that wildlife programming was setting out to be more vibrant than anything before.

Survival also had a knack for finding and developing talent, both from far afield and close to home. **Ted Eales**, warden of the Blakeney Point nature reserve in North Norfolk, was recruited as one of the early cameramen. Buxton, who had known him since boyhood, presented Eales with a camera to film terns on the reserve, and was delighted to find that he developed into an accomplished film-maker. It was a similar story in later years with **Chris Knights**, a farmer from West Norfolk, who has made many films about native British wildlife, many of them on his own land. Both Eales and Knights were also presenters of *Countryman* which continued on Anglia screens as a regional insert for more than 30 years.

Peter Scott (left) and Aubrey Buxton.

International cameramen recruited in the 1960s and 70s include a number still associated with the series, including **Alan Root**, **Des Bartlett**, **Simon Trevor** and **Tony Bomford**, while another long-server, **Richard Kemp**, came from the ranks of the dubbing editors.

Survival also called on experienced broadcasting talent. Closely associated with the series from the outset was **Peter Scott**, one of the pioneers of natural history on television through his BBC series *Look*. He had been Aubrey Buxton's first guest on the *Countryman* programmes, and went on to introduce and narrate many *Survival* programmes, as well as acting as a scientific adviser to the series.

His involvement continued until the late 1980s when, as **Sir Peter Scott**, he advised in the making of a major two-hour documentary on Antarctica – the icy wilderness for ever associated with his father's epic and ill-fated expedition at the start of the century. The programme was a celebration of the continent's spectacular wildlife, but also warned of the threats to Antarctica's future from climatic change and human exploitation. Sadly, Sir Peter died within days of its transmission on ITV in September, 1989.

In the 1990s the *Survival* series continued as ITV's premier wildlife strand and has remained one of British television's greatest export achievers. But there have been many changes behind the scenes. The 'base camp' team of production and administrative staff moved to Norwich in 1989 after spending all its earlier career in the slightly incongruous setting of Park Lane, in London, Anglia's former offices in the capital.

Now headed by executive producer **Petra Regent** and production controller **Peter Schofield**, *Survival* approaches its fifth decade as part of one of the largest wildlife programme production business in the world. In 1997 it became linked with Bristol-based programme-maker Partridge Films under an umbrella business called United Wildlife after the acquisition of the HTV Group – owners of Partridge – by Anglia's parent company, United Broadcasting and Entertainment.

Says Petra Regent: "We are making programmes not only about animals, but about animals and people – and the bizarre and extraordinary relationships we have with them.

"As we move into the 21st century it is even more vital that we explore the natural world as it really is – animals live in our homes, cities, and compete for dwindling resources. The natural world is more dependent than ever on our goodwill – environmental and conservation films need not be worthy – they often cover strong stories with high drama, and need only imagination

to catch the public's eye. For the younger generation environmental issues are mainstream concerns, and in the future they may not be so marginalised.

"We are beginning to balance the pure wildlife films which form the bedrock of our output with films which combine wildlife with history or science – even art. New technology exists which enables us to reveal the lives of insects and even smaller forms of life, in the same way that we now film lions or crocodiles. Now we can enter a strange world where we are shrunk to the size where even ants tower above us, their snapping jaws as terrifying as any crocodile".

Ted Eales with his trusty spaniels on the Blakeney marshes.

Into Africa...

OF the hundreds of films produced by *Survival* since 1961, many have broken new ground and set new standards in wildlife filming. In the early days, the most ambitious venture was *SOS Rhino*, the story of the capture by lasso of the last of Uganda's white rhino and their transfer to a game reserve.

The film had an unhappy sequel when the animals were wiped out during Idi Amin's regime, but the programme was hugely significant. Not only was it one of television's first real conservation stories, it also established *Survival* as an international wildlife series, opening the door to East Africa which was then, and remains today, the greatest natural history showcase on earth. Dozens of programmes have been made there since, particularly in Kenya and Tanzania, home of great parks like the Serengeti, Masai Mara, Amboseli and Tsavo

Alan Root has been responsible for many of the most memorable, including the epic *Year of the Wildebeest*, which followed the thundering migration of wildebeest herds across the plains and rivers of the Serengeti, and *Mysterious Castles of Clay*, the intricate story of life in and around the termite mounds that rise like strange monoliths from the bush.

Other landmark films from Africa included **Dieter Plage's** *Forbidden Desert of the Danakil*, made with explorer **Wilfred Thesiger** and retracing his journey 30 years earlier into the heart of Ethiopia's desolate Danakil Desert. It made contact with some of the wildest people on earth, the nomadic Danakil tribe.

Gorilla, another Plage film, shown in 1974, was one of the first to highlight the threat to Africa's unique population of mountain gorillas. It included one of the most dramatic moments recorded in a wildlife programme.

Conservationist **Adrien Deschryver's** attempt to acclimatise an orphaned baby gorilla to its wild cousins took an unexpected turn when a huge silver-back male rushed from the undergrowth, snatched the baby from Deschryver's arms and carried it to his family.

Like **Dian Fossey**, whose work was portrayed in the feature film *Gorillas in the Mist*, Deschryver worked tirelessly to protect the small population of mountain gorillas in the central African region on the borders of Zaire (now the Congo People's Republic), and Rwanda. It was largely through his efforts that Zaire's **President Mobutu** set up Kahuzi-Biega as a national park for the mountain gorillas.

Despite the dedication of conservationists, like Fossey and Deschryver, however, these noble apes remain among the most endangered animals on the planet, their numbers teetering around the 600 mark. *Survival* cameraman **Bruce Davidson** filmed their plight 20 years later in the aftermath of the Rwandan civil war, a massive humanitarian crisis and an upsurge in poaching for a moving 1996 special called *Mountain Gorilla, A Shattered Kingdom.*

For eight years Davidson worked peacefully alongside the gorillas before tragedy struck the communities of giant apes he had come to love like a family.

Within weeks, the stars of his film had been gunned down – casualties of the humanitarian disaster that spilled from war-torn Rwanda into the wildlife haven on the hills of Zaire's Virunga National Park.

Three of the giant silver-back males and one female were killed. Each death pierced Davidson's heart. By the time he helped carry the 28-stone corpse of the third silver-back, Luwawa, off the mountain, he was numb.

"I just couldn't believe it. Within a month all the principal characters of the film were dead," he said.

"It was terrible working with an animal one day and the next day having to bring his body off the mountain. It was almost like having to bring back the body of a friend. There were so many memories wrapped up over the period of time I was working with those animals."

> "I just couldn't believe it. Within a month all the principal characters of the film were dead."
>
> **Bruce Davidson**

Salaama, one of the silver-back male gorillas filmed by Bruce Davidson and subsequently killed by poachers.

Into the lion's den...

LIONS, tigers, leopards and cheetahs have provided dramatic footage over the years. Programmes devoted almost exclusively to the king of the beasts include **Des** and **Jen Bartlett's** much-acclaimed *Lions of Etosha*, while the dominant social role played by lionesses was highlighted in two films, *Queen of the Beasts*, filmed by **Richard Matthews** and screened in 1989, and **Barbara Tyack's** *Lion Queen*, the story of one particular lioness and her struggle to keep her family together, shown in 1999.

Leopards and cheetahs were stunningly featured in **Mark Deeble** and **Victoria Stone's** *Sunlight and Shadow: The Dappled Cats*, screened in 1991, and **John Pearson's** *Hunters of the Plains* 13 years earlier.

India's great wildlife emblem, the tiger, was definitively portrayed by cameramen **Dieter Plage** and

Mike Price in *Tiger, Tiger*, shot in Northern India and Nepal and screened in 1978. It included night filming using an image intensifier, and moments of great suspense as the camera teams encountered tigers almost face to face. At that time *Survival* also highlighted the gathering campaign to try to save the tiger from extinction – a battle which is still being fought today in the face of a continued downward drift in their numbers, as emphasised by **Ashish Chandola's** study of *The Tigers Next Door*, screened in 1996.

And across in South America, **Nick Gordon** crowned ten years of filming in the Amazon rain-forest with the world's most complete film about the most elusive, and arguably most beautiful, big cat of all, the shy and sassy jaguar, called *Jaguar: Eater of Souls*.

Elephant kingdoms...

ELEPHANTS have been among the greatest animal stars of *Survival* films from both Africa and the Indian sub-continent. *The Family That Lives with Elephants* told the story of a young Scottish scientist, **Dr Iain Douglas-Hamilton,** and his family's special project to study the 500 elephant population of Tanzania's Lake Manyara National Park.

Cindy Buxton's 1978 film *Last Kingdom of the Elephants* focused on one of the world's biggest concentrations of elephants, with an estimated 100,000 spread through the Luangwa Valley in Zambia.

Simon Trevor, who lives among elephants in his home on the edge of Tsavo's national park, highlighted the problem of ivory poaching and the parallel controversy over official culling to reduce over-population in two films *Elephants of Tsavo: Love and Betrayal* and *Keepers of the Kingdom*.

And the Indian elephant has also featured, notably in *The Last Round-up,* which showed the final capture by tribesmen in Assam of elephants for logging work in the forests.

Around the world...

A Weddell seal pops
up in Antarctica.

THERE is hardly a corner of the earth that *Survival* has not visited. The Galapagos Islands, whose unique array of creatures has fascinated mankind since it inspired **Charles Darwin** to formulate his evolutionary theories, have been visited a number of times. **Alan Root** first went there to record the story of *The Enchanted Isles* in the 1960s. Fifteen years later a camera team led by **Dieter Plage** produced a mini-series showing the animals of the land, sea and air, and the influence that man has had on this natural paradise.

Mankind's effect on the natural world has been a continual theme for *Survival*. In most cases the influence has been negative, but *Space for Wildlife* showed how the Kennedy Space Centre, in Florida, had produced beneficial spin-offs for the natural environment. Closed-off areas and tight security mean wild creatures can get on with life unmolested. They even got used to the Shuttle blasting off and nesting pelicans and osprey hardly turned a feather at the awesome sight and sound from the launch-pad a mile or so away.

A warning about future human interference was contained in *Antarctica: The Last Frontier* which looked at the threat to the world's last great wilderness posed by a possible breakdown of international treaties prohibiting commercial exploitation and military intrusion. The programme was produced by **Graham Creelman**, who took over as executive producer of *Survival* in 1988, and headed the unit for the next six years.

During this time there were new initiatives to broaden *Survival's* appeal. For example, **Gaby Roslin** presented a series called *Predators* for which she travelled to Africa and North America, sat in a snake pit with around 50 serpents, sailed alongside killer whales and came face to face with a grizzly bear while trekking in Alaska. It proved to be one of ITV's most popular factual series.

In the late 1980s, *Survival* also took advantage of the thaw in the 'Cold War' to negotiate a co-production deal with Soviet broadcasters for the first comprehensive wildlife series from inside the Soviet

Union. Camera teams were dispatched to Siberia, the Volga, the Steppes and the forests and mountains of the Russian far east region to bring back images of stunning landscapes, evocative animals and amazing native peoples in the series titled *The Nature of Russia*.

Among the rarest footage was cameraman **Richard Kemp's** night-time encounter with the elusive Siberian tiger, of which only 200 are thought to be left in the wild.

Young polar bears
sizing each other
up in the Arctic.

Describing the moment the tiger came into his viewfinder as he crouched in a flimsy camera hide, Kemp said: "My heart was pounding like crazy. He looked up with staring eyes that appeared like green saucers in the light of my infra-red lamp. He realised there was something up there he didn't like.

"God, was he big. I just hoped he couldn't hear my heart thumping in the frosty silence and that he wasn't picking up the noise of the camera . . . As he looked towards me I sensed his power. It was something you can't forget."

There was also poignant evidence on that mission of why the Siberian tiger — the biggest of all the world's great cats — is staring extinction in the face. Russian scientists discovered the bodies of two cubs that had starved to death after their mother had been killed by poachers.

The final frontier – British Antarctic survey ship in the world's last great wilderness.

Into the deep...

THE natural world underwater is one few of us get a chance to visit first hand. *Survival* films have proved eye-openers for many, therefore, by revealing the beauty and sometimes the brutality of this alien world. Among the most evocative have been programmes about the great whales, and those most fearsome of marine predators, the sharks.

In the 1970s, *Survival* collaborated with **Peter Benchley**, the author whose story about man-eating sharks had been into the movie *Jaws*, one of the box office sensations of the decade. The result was the real story about the fearsome Great White, showing it as a ferocious and efficient hunter, but not an indiscriminate killer prone to vengeance attacks on people.

Benchley confessed he was unhappy with the image he had created for sharks in *Jaws*. "I had absolutely no idea of what an injustice I was doing to the poor creature," he said. "I just want to explain unsensationally that the shark has a place in nature and should be left alone."

Survival reinforced the theme in 1998 with a film by **Doug Bertran** called *Cuddly Sharks* which took a detailed look at Great White and Tiger sharks. A theory expounded in the film was that sharks may mistake human swimmers for their normal prey – seals in the case of the Great White, or turtles for the Tiger.

Shark attacks on people are very rare. Tens of thousands of bathers take to the waters off California's beaches. Yet in 50 years there have been only 60 recorded attacks and just six of those have been fatal. Even rarer – none has ever been authentically recorded – are attacks on humans by killer whales. Yet as a *Survival* film by **Jeff Foott** in 1987 showed, this highly intelligent ocean predator can be a ruthless and savage hunter, capable of propelling itself up a seashore to grab seals beyond the waterline.

In one of its first films for the new century, *Survival* examines the huge diversity of the shark species and how these great survivors over millions of years have established their niche in the natural world.

Some *Survival* sea stories come from much closer to home than the shark and killer whale films, both shot off the US coast. Cameraman **Tony Bomford**, in his 1997 film *Hunters of the Silver Shoals*, had an awesome encounter with one of the biggest fish in the sea, the whale-shark, swimming just a few miles off the coast of Britain.

Sharks feature in one of *Survival's* first films of the new century.

A little closer to home...

EAST AFRICA has been the source of most *Survival* films but not far behind is the British Isles. Ever since that first programme focusing on the wildlife of London, people have remained fascinated by the creatures that share our islands. That fascination achieved an even greater dimension in 1993 when the **Prince of Wales** invited *Survival* cameras to spend a year filming the wildlife and countryside of his Gloucestershire estate of Highgrove.

Titled *Highgrove – Nature's Kingdom*, the one-hour programme showed how the Prince's organic farming approach and conservation techniques benefit wildlife, including badgers, weasels, barn owls, nuthatches and pond life. The film was made in conjunction with *Highgrove: Portrait of an Estate*, a book written by the Prince and environment journalist **Charles Clover**.

Husband-and-wife *Survival* camera team **Maurice** and **Carroll Tibbles** spent 18 months filming the story through the changing seasons. Maurice, who has lived in the West Country all his life, even admitted he did a bit of poaching as a boy – although not on the Highgrove farms. He is another of *Survival's* long-serving photographers. Many of his 50 or more films have featured native British wildlife, such as the animals that come out to play on golf courses when the golfers retire to the 19th hole; creatures that find a comfortable living within the perimeter fence of the expanded Stansted airport; and a touching tale about Britain's *Badger Woman*, **Eunice Overend**, who has devoted much of her life to researching, caring for and championing one of our most-wronged animals.

Many *Survival* films have explored the intricate world of insects and water-life via the specialist camera techniques of Oxford Scientific Films. Their sophisticated filming equipment enabled them to reveal in fascinating close-up exactly what goes on in the cabbage patch or under the waterlily pad.

Survival has always had a special appeal to young people, and has devoted whole strands of programming to schoolchildren, most notably through the series *Animals in Action*, which ran on British TV for nearly 20 years from the late 1970s. Its first presenter was artist **Keith Shackleton**, followed by one of the *Survival* producers, **Mike Linley**, with each series compiled from *Survival* library footage. The aim was to entertain and inform children about the natural world, and to encourage them to investigate more for themselves.

As with all *Survival* shows, there is an international element to children's programming as well. Through the 1990s, for instance, *Survival* has worked closely with **Jim Henson's** New York-based Muppet production team to produce wildlife shows that feature animal behaviour film introduced by puppet characters in a talk-show format. Effectively the Muppet animals speak for their real-life counterparts so that children – and their parents – can learn more about the variety and richness of the animal world. The *Animal Show* with Stinky and Jake, latterly made at Anglia's Norwich studios, has been sold to broadcasters in Europe and America, and one series was bought by the BBC.

The Prince of Wales inspecting a nestbox at Highgrove.

'Badger Woman' Eunice Overend.

Animal Show **producer Jocelyn Stevenson, chief writer Jim Lewis and Muppet presenters Stinky and Jake.**

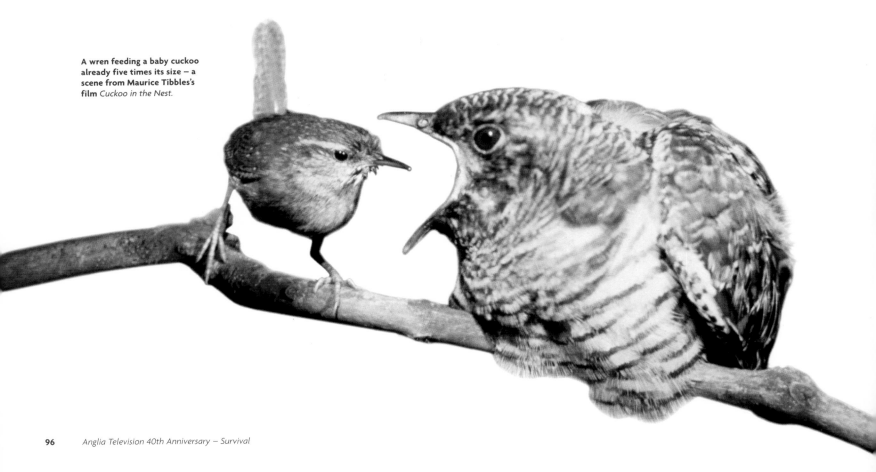
A wren feeding a baby cuckoo already five times its size – a scene from Maurice Tibbles's film *Cuckoo in the Nest.*

How they kept the flag flying in the Falklands...

CINDY BUXTON and **Annie Price** are names that stood alongside the British heroes of the Falklands War in 1982 – even though they never saw any enemy action.

Wildlife film-maker Cindy, daughter of **Lord Buxton**, *Survival's* founder, and her assistant Annie were filming penguins on South Georgia when the Argentines invaded the island. The pair became marooned for almost a month – and became headline news around the world. When nothing was heard from them for a few days fears grew that they had been captured.

In fact, the Argentines never made it to their remote outpost at St Andrew's Bay, and the pair were rescued when Royal Marines recaptured the island. After arriving back in Britain to a heroes' welcome, the girls revealed at a Press conference that they had a couple of catapults and an air rifle to defend themselves, and had been given a pistol by a Royal Navy officer who flew in by helicopter from HMS Endurance. They had been joined at their camp by three scientists from a British Antarctic Survey party who were also stranded.

Cindy said that initially they had expected the Argentinians would pick them up. "We just sat there in the middle of the night and wondered when they would come. After the third day we got a bit bored and began to film again. The main anxiety was that we had put so much hard work into filming the king penguins and elephant seals, and the film would be taken. We thought about hiding it."

For much of the time they flew a Union flag on a makeshift flagpole outside their hut. The 8ft by 4ft flag had been given to Cindy before she left Britain by the landlord and landlady of her local pub at Langham, in Norfolk, **Vic** and **Myrtle Newman**.

Cindy and Annie's Falklands connections endured long after the conflict. They performed the opening of a London pub called The Falkland Arms and modelled a hat which had belonged to the Argentine military governor in Port Stanley and was being auctioned to benefit relatives of British servicemen killed in the conflict. The women produced a book about their adventures, attended the islands' 150th anniversary celebrations, Cindy bought 50 acres of land near Bluff Cove, and a glacier has been named after the Buxton family.

Their film-making partnership continued for another five years before Annie decided she wanted to spend more time at home to be near her family. Cindy continued filming for *Survival* until the mid-1990s. She now lives and works in the United States.

Cindy Buxton (right) and Annie Price filming penguins on South Georgia.

Mow me Kangaroo down...

ROLF HARRIS was singing the praises of his animal friends on TV long before he entered the wards of the *Animal Hospital*.

He was among the first of many celebrities associated with the *Survival* series, and provided both narration and song to accompany the pictures on a number of wildlife programmes of the 1960s and early 1970s.

He adapted one of his best known hits for *Mow Me Kangaroo Down*, a programme detailing the tough existence endured by Australia's animal emblem. In all he wrote three songs for the programme – and even contributed information on Australian native species that were unknown to the production team.

His association with *Survival* went far beyond the bounds of Australia. He provided the commentary and more songs for *All for Their Own Good*, a programme showing how ground-breaking scientific research was helping to promote the understanding of wildlife, and *Ghost Town*, the story of the animals that moved in when the gunfighters moved out of America's Wild West.

In *Birdstrike*, a film about the conflict between birds and jet aircraft at airports, he came up with an hilarious 'talkdown' sequence, giving flying instructions to birds that were in a bit of a flap.

There was more hilarity in *Nothing Going On*, with Rolf Harris describing animal activity to which tourists at Kenya's Tsavo National Park remained oblivious.

In more serious vein, he told the story, again in narrative and song, of an amazing journey by 20 white rhinos from the veldt of South Africa to the rolling pastures of Whipsnade in Bedfordshire.

The white rhino was the biggest focus of conservation concern at the time because, for more than 50 years, it had been hanging on to existence by the skin of its teeth in the face of the twin threats of poaching and disease.

The last surviving animals in an area called Umfolozi were captured and shipped from Durban to Britain as an

Rolf Harris in his *Survival* days.

insurance policy against their extinction in the wild. They formed the basis of the famous white rhinos which are a major attraction at Whipsnade Wild Animal Park today.

Survival's many other celebrity presenters and narrators have included royalty and Hollywood stars – but it is safe to say none has upstaged the animals. Most have been heard but not seen, in line with an early decision to use an out-of-vision narrator on most programmes. The policy has much to do with *Survival's* export potential. It is much easier to sell a film overseas if it does not have someone speaking into the camera in English. A sound-only commentary can easily be re-recorded in any language.

There have, however, been notable exceptions. **David Bellamy** popped up in his own highly visual way in two one-hour programmes, one highlighting the threat to the wetlands of Scotland posed by the planting of pine forests, and the other looking at the environmental row between foresters and conservationists in Washington State, USA, with its focus on the highly endangered northern spotted owl.

Prince Philip appeared on camera to introduce *Survival's* first Galapagos Islands film, *The Enchanted Isles*, in 1967. He had visited the famous Pacific archipelago aboard the Royal Yacht Britannia and, as chairman of the British Appeal of the World Wildlife Fund, was very much aware of the need for preservation and research in the islands.

Survival also went on safari with the Prince to Lake Rudolf, in northern Kenya, during the making of a one-hour programme called *Now or Never* in which he spoke of the dangers to both wildlife and people in the destruction of the natural world. The title was taken from the Prince's opening words. "If we wish to do something to avert total calamity, it's no good saying that we'll do something in ten or twenty years' time, or when we can afford it. It's now or never . . ."

Although much has been achieved in conservation since then, his warning still has an ominous echo 30 years on.

Earlier, the Prince narrated *The New Ark*, another *Survival* about African wildlife which won the series its first international award, the Golden Nymph at the 1963 Monte Carlo film festival.

Actors have been the mainstay of *Survival* out-of-vision commentaries, simply because they tend to be the best people at voice-overs. In the case of some, such as **Anthony Hopkins** or **James Mason**, it was hardly necessary to see them – the voice and delivery was almost as recognisable as the face.

Ian Holm has been one of the most-used voices in recent years, along with **Andrew Sachs**, whose commentary voice bears little resemblance to the zany Spanish waiter he played in *Fawlty Towers*, and **Sean Barrett**, who has particularly rich and resonant tones.

That man of many voices, **Rory Bremner**, recorded his first *Survival* commentary in 1999 – as himself, it should be stressed – while the then James Bond, **Timothy Dalton**, voiced a 1988 series of animal behaviour programmes called *The Survival Factor*.

White rhinos from South Africa grazing at Whipsnade.

Anthony Hopkins and penguin friend.

John Forsythe and Cindy Buxton.

Gaby Roslin filming with *Survival* producer Caroline Brett (left) and Barbara Tyack.

Narrators in earlier times included **Patrick Allen**, rugged star of the Sixties TV adventure series *Crane*, **Henry Fonda**, who told the story of *The World of the Beaver*, TV and radio broadcaster **Bernard Braden** and explorer **Duncan Carse**, who was one of the pioneers of the exploration of Antarctica.

Other stars of stage and screen to have fitted the words to the wildlife over the years include **Orson Welles**, **Robert Hardy**, **Trevor Howard**, **John Hurt**, **David Niven**, **Peter Ustinov**, **Michael Hordern**, **Richard Briers**, **William Franklyn**, **Robert Powell**, **Ian McShane**, **Sean Bean** and **Anthony Valentine**.

There have been far fewer women narrators. The apparent discrimination reflects audience research which has consistently shown that both male and female viewers generally prefer a male voice in commentary. Nonetheless, some notable female voices have graced *Survival*. **Rula Lenska** heads the list as narrator of three one-hour *Specials* (one featured the wildlife of her ancestral Poland and another included an introduction by her partner **Dennis Waterman**). **Toyah Willcox** took over from Timothy Dalton for a second series of *The Survival Factor*, and others have included theatrical dames **Flora Robson** and **Diana Rigg** along with

Stephanie Powers, **Cathy Tyson**, **Anna Massey** and newsreader **Anna Ford**.

The popularity of *Survival* in the United States helped to ensure a liberal sprinkling of famous American voices, such as **Richard Widmark**, **Lloyd Bridges**, **Gene Kelly**, **Leonard Nimoy**, **Stacy Keach**, **John Huston**, **Jason Robards** and astronaut **Neil Armstrong**.

For many years, the *Survival* series on American TV had its own presenter in **John Forsythe**, best known to British audiences as Blake Carrington, head of TV's *Dynasty*. He came to East Anglia to record links for the series in 1980 and met up with film-maker **Cindy Buxton** on the North Norfolk coast.

In Britain, for ten years from the mid-1970s, the voice of BBC radio newsreader **John Hedges** was the most heard on *Survival* films. He holds the record with commentary on 64 shows. In 1996, he was one of a number of narrators who attended a party at London Zoo to celebrate 35 years of *Survival*. Others were **Robert Powell**, **Anthony Valentine**, **Denis Quilley**, **T P McKenna**, **William Franklyn**, **Andrew Sachs**, **Sean Barrett**, **John Shrapnel** and **Alan Dobie**.

Survival **programme narrators celebrate 35 years of the series.**

Many Happy Returns...

Anthea Turner
Presenter of Anything Goes *for Anglia with Paul Barnes*

"I remember my time with Anglia Television with great fondness.
Wishing you all the best for your birthday. Here's to the next 40 years!"

Chris Kelly
Writer and broadcaster

"Who'd have thought the shy young man with the rabbit's
foot charm would turn out to be one of Britain's favourite
entertainers – Tom Jones? Working with dozens of talented
people marked for stardom was a bonus of learning the
business at Anglia. And established names too – Kingsley
Amis, P D James, Angus Wilson. The latter told me a young
girl had passed by while he was in his garden immersed in his
new novel. 'Oh look, Mummy', she said, 'there's an old man
writing. Isn't it nice to see them occupied'. Happy birthday to
you all."

Ruthie Henshall
Actress and musical stage star who grew up near Ipswich

"Although a regular viewer since my early days in Suffolk, it
was not until I played Roxie Hart in *Chicago* that I had close
personal contact with Anglia TV. On a very fraught night, I
was most impressed by the professionalism and the
courteous patience of the team, fronted by Timothy Evans
(reporter of the year, if I recall), who covered my first night at
London's Adelphi Theatre.

"They turned in a very polished piece of film that picked up
the pizazz of the show and the fantastic mood of the evening
– and I know for a fact that it put a lot of extra bottoms on
our seats. Now that I am playing *Chicago*'s other lead role,
Velma Kelly, on Broadway, I suppose it is asking a bit much for
you to nip over to New York and cover that as well! Anyway,
sincere congratulations on your 40th."

Michael Brunson
ITN's political editor

"I spend a good deal of time in Norfolk – in fact, if I'm not in
or around the House of Commons, that's where I'm most
likely to be. And Norfolk isn't Norfolk without Anglia News.
Indeed, I regard Helen McDermott as East Anglia's Trevor
McDonald, if you see what I mean. Congratulations on your
40th anniversary: long may you continue."

Bryan Gunn
Former Norwich City goalkeeper

"I would like to thank Anglia News for all their coverage of
the Bryan Gunn Leukaemia Appeal which helped raise
£500,000. Thanks to your help the appeal was known all over
the Anglia region and I'm sure helped raise a lot of extra
money. I would also like to thank the Anglia sports team,
including Kevin Piper and Steve Aldous, for their help during
my testimonial season and also in the making of my video
Top Gunn. And who'll ever forget that goal I conceded
against Ipswich Town which Anglia covered live on that
fateful Sunday? Here's to the next 40 years".

The Rt. Hon John MacGregor, OBE
Member of Parliament

"Warm congratulations on the 40th anniversary.

"I have observed Anglia's progress over 25 of these 40 years
and have always been glad to contribute both to serious news
and current affairs programmes and also occasionally light
entertainment (some conjuring performances over the years
were always more nerve-racking than political contributions!).

"Anglia has contributed outstanding programmes to both the
national and international networks. But for those of us in the
region, it is its continued and extensive regional coverage
which matters most. Long may it flourish, and always in
Norwich!"

John Timpson
*A veteran of BBC news and current
affairs, who lives in Norfolk and
joined Anglia to present* Timpson's
Country Churches

"Congratulations on your 40th anniversary.
I have worked with a lot of nice people
at Anglia, and enjoyed a lot of good programmes.
Glad you are keeping my former colleagues at
the BBC on their toes!"

A life of leisure...

Premier attraction – *Anything Goes* presenter Anthea Turner in exalted company at the Spitting Image Rubberworks.

Out and about...

I'S hardly surprising, given the company's base in an area so richly endowed with rural treasures, that Anglia has often focused on country and leisure pursuits.

Celebrities who have enjoyed the region's delights in front of the cameras range from 'Mr Pastry', alias **Richard Hearne**, in the early days, to **Fiona Fullerton**, **Liza Goddard** and **Anthea Turner** in more recent times.

Turner, who went on to find wider fame on GMTV and the *National Lottery Show*, arrived at Anglia in 1990 to join **Paul Barnes** for the last two series of *Anything Goes*, which he launched with **Pam Rhodes** in 1985. The networked leisure magazine series offered ideas for days-out, weekend breaks and short holidays in some of Britain's undiscovered corners – as well as popular spots on the tourist trail.

By the time Anthea Turner joined the show, the 28-year-old former amateur actress, AA road traffic reports presenter and Stoke-on-Trent radio record librarian had already worked as a BBC children's television announcer and earned hosting credits for *The Best of Magic*, *Going Live*, *Top of the Pops* and *Up2U*.

But the girl who was already being talked about as one of THE faces of the Nineties almost saw her dreams of fame go up in smoke – literally – the previous year. While working on a live broadcast from the Royal Tournament, a fire flash exploded in her face. Her hair and jacket were ablaze as helpers tried to put out the fire. Turner was rushed to hospital for treatment to serious burns on her face and right hand.

Fortunately, by the time she started work on *Anything Goes*, she had fully recovered and was trying to stick to a New Year resolution to take more care of herself. As part of this resolve she had discovered and publicly launched the Y Plan, a fitness regime devised at the YMCA. But the self-confessed chocoholic couldn't resist some of the sweeter offerings she came across during filming of *Anything Goes*.

She admitted leaving the Chessington World of Adventures attraction feeling sick from eating too many doughnuts and was in ecstasy when the Toffee Shop, in Penrith, and Cadbury World, at Bournville, were locations for filming.

She was also delighted to meet **The Queen**, former Prime Ministers **John Major** and **Margaret Thatcher**, broadcaster **Alastair Burnett** and soccer star **Paul Gascoigne** during the series – even if only at the Spitting Image Rubberworks at London's Covent Garden.

"I couldn't tell the difference between the Paul Gascoigne I met and the real person," she joked. "It was only when I saw a man with his hand up Paul's bottom that I realised it wasn't the genuine article!"

Anthea Turner hugs a rubber Gazza.

Stringing along: 'Pastry-faced' Richard Hearne – complete with sausages – rides into his home city of Norwich for one of Anglia's early leisure programmes.

Back down to earth for Liza Goddard – and a cuddle for Mina.

Changing times for Pam Rhodes and Paul Barnes... in thirties costume.

A Commando assault course drove Liza Goddard up the wall!

Unlike Anthea Turner, who was living in London, actress and TV presenter **Liza Goddard** was well aware of the attractions of the Eastern Counties when she launched *Liza's Country* in 1997. For she and her family had uprooted from Surrey three years earlier to the wilds of North Norfolk, indulging their passion for dogs and horses.

In her Anglia series, Goddard, with pet dog **Mina**, explored the region, trying her hand at activities such as ballooning, taking the helm of a lifeboat, driving a steam engine, bell-ringing and riding a racehorse. She also met celebrities – actors **John Nettles** and **Stephen Fry**, boxer **Frank Bruno**, comedian **Jim Davidson** and former tennis stars **Mark Cox** and **Christine Janes** (nee Truman). She was particularly pleased, during a visit to the King's Lynn Festival, to meet up with **Nettles**, having worked with him for six years in *Bergerac*.

One of Goddard's biggest challenges was tackling a Royal Marine commando assault course during a visit to the Aylsham Show, in Norfolk. It took a timely rearguard action by a Marine to save the day when she got stuck up a 30 ft wall.

"There was one chap on the ground pulling me up via a rope and pulley, and another beside me on the wall, but I couldn't get my foot up and go either up or down," she said.

"Fortunately, the chap on the wall managed to move my foot for me. He actually pushed my bum up, too! I was glad to get to the top, I can tell you." She described the assault course as "absolutely terrifying" but was determined to complete it – right down to the death slide at the end.

"I did it very slowly, egged on by a crowd who picked up on some jeering started by my daughter, **Sophie**, who had really only gone along to look at the Marines, anyway!"

In Anglia's latest country pursuits series, launched in January, 1999, presenter **Fiona Fullerton** went *Off The Beaten Track* for ten weeks. Each time she met two sets of couples, families or friends eager to sample an interesting and unusual two-day country break in the region.

The twist was that those taking part – their interests and abilities had been thoroughly researched – did not know what they would be doing until Fullerton gave them the good, or bad, news. Afterwards, they had to assess the accommodation and pursuits on offer, awarding marks out of 10 for the 'three As' – activities, area and accommodation. Activities included basket-weaving on the Broads, baking bread in Bedfordshire and cleaning out a river in Northamptonshire.

Fullerton, whose roles have included those in the Bond movie *A View to a Kill* and TV hits like *The Charmer*, *Angels* and Anglia's own P D James thriller, *A Taste of Death*, said *Off The Beaten Track* was right up her street.

She added that anyone who saw her as some kind of glamorous, urban socialite couldn't be further from the mark. "I love rural pursuits and green wellies – I'm a country girl at heart!"

Fiona Fullerton.

Back to nature...

SOMEONE else demonstrating a love of rural pursuits was naturalist **Roger Tabor**, who presented a green guide to the wilder, nature-rich corners of the Anglia region around the same time. In a series of short, occasional programmes called *Going Wild*, the chairman of the British Naturalists' Association took a closer look at the flora and fauna, linking the wildlife to the history of landscapes, ranging from Breckland to Broadland and fenland to forest.

Tabor became famous for his behavioural studies of both domestic and wild cats, having started his television career with **Johnny Morris** 25 years earlier. He can trace his own ancestry through several generations of Brightlingsea oystermen and now lives in Essex, in an ancient water mill which he is restoring.

An earlier look at the region's flora and fauna came in 1988, with *Wildwatch*. Conservationists **Chris Probert** and **Simon Hooton** demonstrated, with a series of step-by-step projects, how everyone could do their bit for nature. The programme spawned a series of wildlife gardening surgeries and evening classes as well as a competition to inspire conservation action in the East of England. The winning project – a rubbish dump turned into a nature reserve, complete with nature trails and schools' study centre, was at a seven-acre Frinton-on-Sea oak wood.

The wood's owner and manager, Mrs **Pamela Garrad**, received the prize money and a special carved elm plaque from *Survival* chairman and founder **Lord Buxton**, who urged people to "think big and act small".

He advised would-be conservationists to consider global problems, like the depletion of the ozone layer

Going Wild... **Roger Tabor.**

and destruction of the rainforest, but to make a practical contribution to their own community. "The two are complementary," he said.

By this time, Anglia was well into its stride with country and leisure programmes from around the region. Some of the earliest came in a 1960 series called *Angles*, which consisted of documentaries about life in East Anglia. Subjects included windmills, the church bells under the sea at Dunwich, holiday resorts and missile bases.

A series of outdoor events were covered by **Dick Graham**, **Dick Joice**, **John McGregor** and **Bob Wellings** in *Summertime*, in 1961.

Watching the wild... Chris Probert and youngsters.

Mr Fry's Very Grand Tour...

IN 1995, *Mr Fry's Very Grand Tour*, was a one-off documentary featuring **Stephen Fry's** personal and typically idiosyncratic look at the work of the National Trust in the East of England. At the time of the screening, Fry was 'on the run', having walked out of a West End play and fled to a mystery refuge, hotly pursued by the Press. Anglia viewers were able to see his last stage appearance before his dramatic walk-out.

For his visit to the Theatre Royal, in Bury St Edmunds, Fry, who grew up near the National Trust's Blickling Hall, in Norfolk, and worked as a barman at the neighbouring Buckinghamshire Arms, posed as an 18th century fop.

Ironically, he mused before going on: "Oh I can hear the audience warming up. I really hate the theatre and yet I love it — and that makes me hate it. I mean, I love it, I hate it. I hate it and love it.

"Oh, I don't know what it is about the theatre — it is my mistress, my father, my mother, my sergeant major, my one-night stand all rolled into one. Ah, the agony and the... agony!"

Local lad... Stephen Fry (seen with Merlin Waterson of The National Trust) grew up near Blickling Hall in Norfolk.

Wellings goes on a pub crawl...

Tavern Talk and *Mild And Bitter*, the latter introduced by **Rene Cutforth** and Bob Wellings, were two series which visited pubs in the region and featured topical subjects hotly debated over a pint.

An intervening run of programmes, *Tavern Topics*, took place in a studio-set pub with legendary newspaperman **Arthur Christiansen** chairing the discussions. Sadly, the former *Daily Express* editor collapsed and died in the studio during one of the recordings.

About the same time, **Kenneth Horne**, who had chaired several early game shows on Anglia as well as the cult radio series *Round the Horne*, hosted *Ken's Column*, an off-beat look at life in East Anglia.

Bob Wellings in search of pub pundits for *Mild and Bitter.*

Lullaby or no lullaby...?

ANOTHER celebrity who developed an on-screen link with the rural scene was 'Mr Pastry' who, for *Country Fayre* back in 1963, joined **Dick Joice** to watch preparations for the *Norfolk County Fayre*. Shortly afterwards, came the start of *Portrait Of A Village*, presented first by **John McGregor**, then by **Graham Bell** and later by **Paul Barnes**. A relaxed look at East of England villages and their personalities, the series continued with a minimal change of title for more than 25 years, ending as *The Village Show*. Another early country series was *Craftsmen*, which looked at the work of a miller, a slater and a thatcher.

There was also *Man Between Three Rivers*, a regional Royal Television Society award-winning profile of Lincolnshire countryman **Ernie James** by **Ted Eales**, the Blakeney Point nature reserve warden and talented wildlife cameraman. Around the same time various parts of the regional countryside were featured in Anglia's early contributions to the long-running networked *About Britain* series.

In one of these **Paul Honeyman**, whose career was cut tragically short by illness and death at the age of 41, looked at the Norfolk Broads in *Lullaby For Broadland*.

The same picturesque waterscape has featured on Anglia screens many times since – most notably in **Geoffrey Weaver's** controversial *No Lullaby For Broadland*. This provocative documentary, which won a special regional Royal Television Society award for outstanding contribution to local television, challenged the popular concept that all was well with the Broads, highlighting overcrowding and pollution.

Ted Eales puts countryman Ernie James in the frame.

More recently, in 1988, *Aboard The Broads*, took a wry look at the hardy, water-borne species which gathers in its thousands each summer and casts off without knowing its bows from its bilges. The off-beat documentary followed members of the species – the Norfolk Broads holidaymakers – as they donned souvenir skipper's cap . . . and steered straight into the nearest bridge. Lifting the lid on what the naughty navigators got up to were two great Broadland characters, Potter Heigham boat cleaners **Dot** and **Babs**.

There was a more serious look at the Broads – and a profile of a champion of both them and the countryside generally – in *A Man For All Seasons*, shown on both

Anglia and the ITV network in 1984. The film focused on the late **Ted Ellis**, the self-taught, slightly eccentric but highly-respected Norfolk conservationist.

Despite 28 years as naturalist at Norwich Castle Museum, he readily conceded he had never been qualified by ordinary standards and had pursued 'the amateur's way'. Modestly, he insisted: "I am a link man really. I just like to use the ordinary English language to convey my joy at looking into a world of wonders. Otherwise, people can go very wrong in their attitude to living things through sheer ignorance – and it is partly the fault of the scientist who has not bothered to tell them about it."

Provocative... *No Lullaby For Broadland.*

Ted Ellis.

Working the land...

COUNTRY PEOPLE, in 1982, was a series of six profiles presented by **David Richardson** and featuring rural people working on the land. The first focused on **Roger** and **Cherry Clarke** who were dedicated to preserving four-legged horse power, using heavy horses for every job on their 30 acres at Stoke-by-Nayland, in Suffolk.

Wildlife was in focus again in 1986 when Anglia celebrated the diamond jubilee of the Norfolk Naturalists' Trust with a visit to some of the 36 reserves then under its control. A few months later historical writer **Russell Chamberlin** acted as guide to some of the region's most interesting reminders of the past in *Heritage In The East*.

The Fens featured again in 1988 in *The Dutch Adventure*, a documentary which marked the 300th anniversary of a prince from the Low Countries becoming King of England. Narrator **Tim Woodward** looked first at repercussions in the East of England of the invasion of **William of Orange** and the flight of **James II**. Secondly, the film recalled the work of Dutch engineers who drained the Fens in the 17th century and left them as a living monument.

But such work may not have found favour with wildlife conservationist and artist **Sir Peter Scott**, who featured in *A World Of Sky*, a networked *About Britain* documentary focusing on The Wash a few years earlier. Sir Peter recalled how his career was inspired by living on the edge of The Wash, in an old lighthouse lapped by

the sea. By the time of the film it had receded half a mile. The dramatic change in sea level had been brought about by land reclamation for farming and Sir Peter came down firmly against such schemes, unless there was a proven need.

The plethora of gardening programmes on television these days might suggest that the subject had only just been discovered. By the early Seventies, however, Anglia was already sowing the seeds with 33 editions of *Gardening Diary*. Since then, it has travelled extensively with **Alan Mason**, who, with green-fingered friends from around the region, compared British methods, styles and traditions with those of France, Italy, Spain, Portugal and Holland in *Gardens Without Borders*.

He was joined by former nurseryman and writer **Martin Fish** and one-time fashion model **Ali Ward** for *Great Little Gardens*. In this six-part series the trio peered over the hedge to admire the work of dedicated amateurs and celebrate some of the finest small gardens in the East of England.

Another gardening programme, in 1987, was *On Mr Repton's Advice* which looked at the work of the 18th century landscape gardener whose designs grace some of the finest country houses in the East of England. Woburn Abbey is, perhaps, the most famous house to have benefited from the handiwork of **Humphrey Repton**. Other regional examples of the work of the Bury St Edmunds-born

designer featured in the film included those at Sheringham Hall, in Norfolk, Wimpole Hall, near Cambridge, and Shrublands Health Clinic, near Ipswich.

More recently, in 1996, **Clare Bradley**, gardener on BBC's *Blue Peter*, hosted a series on Anglia. In *Jungle On Your Doorstep* she broadened her scope to look at the unseen wildlife to be found under our noses in the houses and gardens of South-East England.

In 1999 *Home Grown* gave gardeners practical and topical advice in a 12-part series which ran through the growing season. Presenter **Lucy Summers** visited some of the regions most beautiful gardens for inspiration and got her hands dirty on regular visits to the *Home Grown* allotment.

The Clarkes with their favoured form of horsepower.

Inspired by The Wash... Sir Peter Scott.

Lucy Summers (centre) admires some *Home Grown* produce.

Clare Bradley finds a contributor hogging the limelight.

Words of warning...

IN 1991, **David Bellamy**, television's favourite botanist, returned to the place where he learned to sail to present a major three-part series looking at the region's wetlands. Bellamy, who first got to know East Anglia when he was evacuated from London with his brother, was back to spend his honeymoon in the area and pledged to continue to return as long as he lives.

"I had experienced nothing like the Broads when I first set eyes on them," he recalled. 'I did everything that was in **Arthur Ransome's** *The Coot Club*, the first book about conservation I ever read.'

The botanist was quick to point out the huge importance of wetlands to the environment — as one of the main control valves for the 'greenhouse effect' — and to condemn the way drainage had devastated them.

He warned: "Some of the richest farmlands in the world are disappearing. Unless we do something, large slabs of East Anglia are going to return to clay within 30 years. You won't even be able to grow spuds!"

Secrets revealed...

Martin Smith and producer Jacinth O'Donnell in a Norfolk wood.

AMONG Anglia's most recent countryside programmes have been two from the *Survival* stable — *Wensum Year* and *Secrets Of A Norfolk Wood*. Both were filmed by cameraman **Martin Smith**. *Wensum Year* started with Smith's idea for a film about little grebes and grew into a picture of life on, in and around the river over 12 months. *Secrets Of A Norfolk Wood* featured badgers and foxes raising their families as Smith went undercover for a rare insight into nature's real-life woodland tales.

For one particular sequence, Smith swooped, Tarzan-like, through the trees. He used an aerial runway, designed by a Cambridge aeronautical engineer, to capture an owl's eye-view of the woodland floor during a hunt for voles and mice.

For peat's sake... David Bellamy has a dig at drainage methods in *Wetlands*.

A green day out...

A GREEN DAY OUT, Anglia's guide to some of the region's best outdoor attractions, was launched in 1991. In the 12-week series, top TV naturalist and author **Tony Soper** explored a dozen of his favourite places in the region, from the wild open spaces of the Norfolk coast to the tranquil waters of the Grand Union Canal in Northamptonshire.

The series also featured co-presenter **Janet Trewin** with a weekly report from 'The Great Outdoors' and a regular item in which a celebrity guest did his or her favourite things in the countryside. TV presenter and wildlife photographer **Chris Packham** was first in the frame and chose to hike along Peddars Way, the ancient 50-mile footpath running from Knettishall in Suffolk to Holme-next-the-Sea on the North Norfolk coast.

Celebrities in subsequent programmes included actors **Bernard Cribbins** and **Liza Goddard** as well as **Gaby Roslin**, cartoonist **Bill Tidy**, former newsreader **Peter Woods** and 'Green Goddess' **Diana Moran**, from breakfast TV's keep-fit spot.

'Green Goddess' Diana Moran rides round Rutland.

Janet Trewin and Tony Soper at Stoke Bruerne on the Grand Union Canal.

Bodyworks...

Keeping fit. . . Lesley Waters and David Fitzgerald.

Getting and keeping fit was the entire point of *Bodyworks*, a 12-week series in 1994. Presenters **Lesley Waters** and **David Fitzgerald** toured the region, looking at facilities for improving body and mind through exercise, diet and specialist techniques.

Rural works...

By hook or by crook, it's Robin Page with his 13-year-old Norfolk lurcher/Bedlington terrier cross, Bramble.

Countrywide champions – Trish Williamson, Michael Jordan, Janet Trewin and Bryan McNerney.

JANET TREWIN, from *A Green Day Out*, was back on Anglia screens in 1992 with *Countrywide* in which she and co-presenter **Michael Jordan**, along with **Anne Leuchars**, focused on rural life, work and leisure.

They were joined the next year by television historian **Bryan McNerney**, who presented job profiles and tackled country walks, and former TV-am weather girl **Trish Williamson**, who reported on the region's wildlife.

Farmer's son **Bill Dod** and 'action girl' **Jayne Evans** followed in 1994 and just before the series ended Trewin and Dod were joined by action girl **Sally Faber** – the former TV weather presenter – and *One Man and his Dog* host, **Robin Page**.

Talking of dogs... Sally Faber would certainly – on the basis of one *Countrywide* shoot, at least – endorse the advice: "Never work with children or animals."

For she was asked to introduce an item on dog sledding by crouching alongside one of the huskies in the team.

Alas, sex reared its ugly head – and Faber found herself the subject of amorous advances of the canine kind.

To add insult to discomfort, not only did the offending animal manage to thwart all Faber's attempts to

continue in a professional manner – it also relieved itself on the camera for good measure.

On another occasion a film crew arrived on location for a rendezvous with Page only to be halted in their tracks and enchanted by the melodious – if totally unexpected, given the location – tones of a wood warbler.

The spell was cruelly broken, however, when the presenter switched off the tape of bird song to which he had been listening and strode forward to see what was causing the delay.

Countrywide was followed, in 1998, by *A Place In The Country*, presented by Page again and this time **Joanna Pinnock**. The eight-part series took a closer look at some typical rural pursuits, events and pastimes and offered a country-lover's guide to what rustic living is all about.

Road works...

Scooting around for *The Road Show* – Nick Knowles.

MOTORING is another leisure pursuit which Anglia has covered extensively over the years. One of the early programmes was *You're Driving Me Crazy* in December, 1961, with **Dick Joice** taking a light-hearted look at the effects cars could have on the personalities of their owners.

Anglia's first "exciting and instructive motoring series", *Steering Column*, followed in 1966 with the aim of teaching viewers "how to drive on the road and stay alive." **Barbara Castle**, Minister of Transport at the time, appeared in the first programme.

Maths expert **Carol Vorderman**, star of *Countdown*, had the chance to turn in some impressive figures of her own at the start of *The Road Show*, which first hit Anglia and Meridian screens in 1996. She made a special guest appearance behind the wheel of a 220 mph Jaguar XJ220 Supercar, priced at £400,000 when it first went on sale five years earlier.

One of the presenters in early runs of the series – visiting, among locations, the scooter mecca of Clacton to report on a revival of the traditional form of 'Mod' transport – was **Nick Knowles**.

Knowles has been seen recently with Vorderman in ITV's *Find a Fortune* and also co-hosting *Holidaymaker* – the network series produced by Anglia's sister company, Meridian Broadcasting – with **Anna Walker** and **Stuart Miles**.

Carol Vorderman figured in *The Road Show*.

Film crews weather the storm...

ADDITIONAL leisure time in the Nineties has been accompanied by an increasing number of programmes devoted to it.

At the turn of the decade there was *A Place In The Sun*, a networked Anglia series featuring Britons from all over the country who had taken the plunge and bought their foreign dream home.

The launch programme featured three couples who had bought holiday homes in Florida. But while this proved idyllic for them – and for most Britons filmed for the six-part series in Greece, Portugal, Spain, France and Italy – it was anything but for producer/director **Ron Trickett** and his crew.

Warm work – Anglia postman Ron Mace (right) delivers yet another sackful of mail to 'Rain Man' Ron Trickett and his team.

They were plagued by bad weather and misfortune almost throughout the filming. Trickett even earned the nickname 'Rain Man'. In Florida, the weather was fine but the Anglia team missed their connecting flight from Miami to Orlando after US customs and immigration officials detained them to check papers. The Anglia crew had to drive instead.

In Greece, bad weather took over, stranding the crew on Corfu for 48 hours, with only two fine days in 12. Portugal was trouble-free and sunny. But the gremlins got to work again in Spain. This time the crew watched as their gear was impounded by the authorities. They then had bags stolen and found there were no rooms at the hotel where they had booked.

In France, there was a camera breakdown, hire cars were at the wrong airport and a 40-mile traffic jam extended a journey to the Alps by six hours. Just to round things off, it rained again in Tuscany.

"It certainly wasn't the sunshine life for us," sighed the exasperated director. "But the people we filmed loved every minute of living abroad – and that's what it's all about!"

That fact came over so well that Anglia was swamped with requests for information packs. The first programme prompted 15,000 viewers' letters within a week. And it was no holiday for Anglia postman **Ron Mace** and his colleagues, who had to heave 25 sackfuls of mail up four floors to the programme production office in Norwich. A team of temporary helpers was taken on to deal with the flood of inquiries: "The response to the programme has been phenomenal," said Trickett.

Such was the success that ITV quickly commissioned another series of six programmes. It opened with an exclusive look at the hideaway paradise of **Princess Diana**, **Steven Spielberg** and **Robert de Niro** as Virgin boss **Richard Branson** allowed TV cameras onto his private Caribbean island of Necker for the first time.

Other programmes in the second series featured Britons with holiday homes in Cyprus, Switzerland, the Canary Islands and France.

A Place In The Sun **for Virgin boss Richard Branson.**

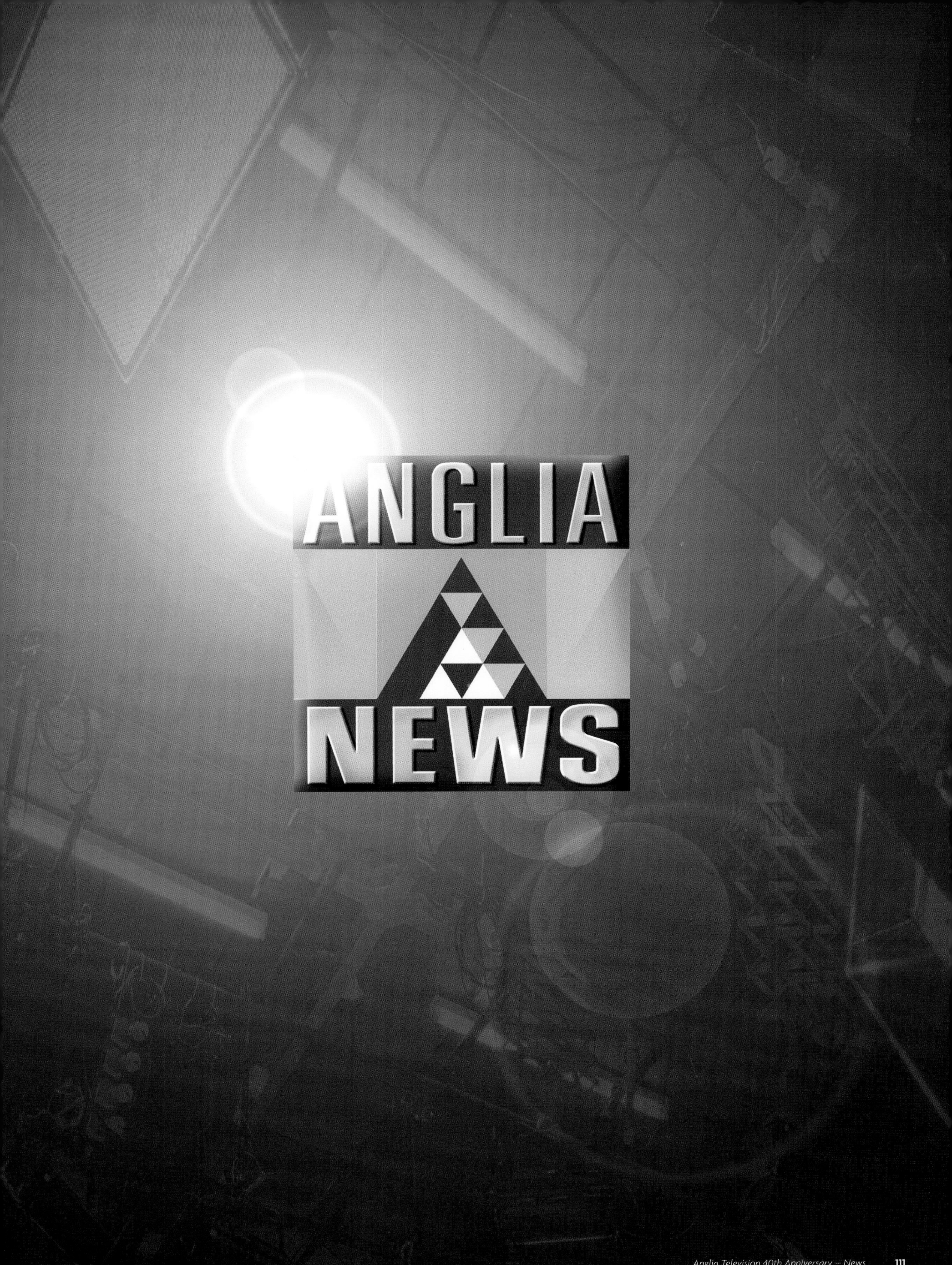
ANGLIA
NEWS

All the news that's fit to screen...

GETTING the latest news on to the television screen is a constant battle to beat the clock.

At least today's state-of-the-art technology has removed some of the pitfalls of earlier days when getting a story back to the studio in time for transmission was fraught with hazards over which the reporter had little control.

Accidents were waiting to happen in the days when a spool of film containing vital pictures had to be physically transported to the Norwich studios – by road, rail or even plane – before it could be processed. For example, the film 'unspooling', or getting lost in transit (typically on Ely rail station, where film from the west of the region would have to be taken off one train and put on another).

And even when film did arrive safely there was still a danger it could disintegrate during processing – an event known as 'going up in the bath'.

Anglia News West producer **Greg Barnes** worked at Hull as a reporter in the 1970s when Anglia also had an office at Grimsby (areas now covered by Yorkshire Television).

"We shared an electrician, so we'd do a film and he'd take it in his car and catch the paddle steamer ferry across the River Humber, work with the Grimsby crew, and then drive both films to Norwich," said Barnes.

"Sometimes, he'd come across on the ferry and we'd have to meet him on our side of the river with our story. On more than one occasion we got there too late and the paddle steamer would already be leaving, with him aboard. We had to lob the can of film to him from the dockside. Luckily, it never missed."

Another way of getting film to Norwich was by air. "There was a daily plane from Brough, a little airport just outside Hull," said Barnes. "We'd give the pilot the film and he'd fly it to Norwich airport where a dispatch driver would be waiting."

"On location when the cameraman had to change film he would do it inside a light-proof, black bag. I can remember helping one day when the middle fell out and the film unspiralled. The whole bag had to go down to the darkroom before it could be opened and rewound."

Recording commentary out in the field could also be a nightmare. "Many's the time I've sat in the back of the

crew car and we'd have to stop because of the noise of the rain on the roof. It has been known for us to knock on someone's door and ask if we could come in to record a commentary."

The time it took to get film and commentary back for processing and editing in the old days meant much earlier deadlines than Anglia News enjoys today.

"Often we'd be sending a story one day for transmission the next, or we'd be out early in the morning working to a lunchtime deadline," said Barnes. "If we didn't get it away by then it didn't get on air that night."

This all changed when video tape replaced film in the 1980s. Tape did not have to be developed, and this brought immediate savings in time. At first, these new tapes (slightly larger than the average VHS) still had to be sent off to Norwich, but then came the facility to play the rushes electronically down the line from Anglia's regional offices direct to the play-out or editing machines at the other end. This meant later deadlines all round – and more up-to-the minute news for the viewer.

Today, Anglia's news centres around the region are all linked to Norwich by a special digital fibre optic cable.

This means tape can simply be fed in at one end and prepared for transmission at the other.

Similarly, reporters can sit in front of a microphone at the nearest news centre and speak the commentary "down the line". Each regional news centre can link up live to Norwich.

And if a camera operator and reporter want to stay with a story live on location (for example at the scene of a big fire, or awaiting a verdict outside a court building) the words and pictures can be beamed to Norwich via satellite – a journey approaching 50,000 miles into space and back.

In the old days, a reporter would not be able to cover a story without the full accompanying triumvirate of camera operator, sound engineer and lighting technician (also known as the electrician or "spark"). The kit required was much more cumbersome, and lights in particular took up a lot of space. Depending on the job, a camera crew would sometimes need two cars to ferry everything around.

The first video cameras used for news were actually heavier than the film versions they replaced, and the recorder, which was linked by cable to the camera, had to be carried separately by the soundman. The next generation of combined cameras and recorders brought more improvements, and lightened the load.

The standard camera used by Anglia News today is lighter still, weighing about a third of the version in use 10 years ago, making it easier to manoeuvre, and reducing the risk of the operator developing a bad back. These digital models offer greater sensitivity in poor light, which often suits the less-than-perfect conditions news pictures have to be shot in.

Today's news camera operators can operate on their own, carrying any additional equipment they need with them. What is recorded goes on to pocket-sized digital tapes, no bigger than the average audiocassette.

Looking to the future, the advent of video journalism means news reporters with cameras will be able to cover some sorts of stories. Anglia News West already employs journalists with this type of skill and training. New portable equipment is also beginning to let camera operators and journalists edit material wherever they are.

A fully-integrated newsroom system, enabling moving pictures to be edited and transmitted via computer, without tape of any kind, is the next likely step. Since its move to a new state-of-the-art newsroom in Norwich, Anglia has the necessary infrastructure in place, in readiness for the new millennium.

Today, the demand for the very latest news is still pushing at deadlines. Last-minute editing can still be going on while Anglia News is on the air, and late-breaking stories can be updated live from the newsroom. Things can still go wrong, of course, and more bulletins and more live satellite links mean new pressures have undoubtedly replaced the old. But at least no one has to worry about missing cans of film on Ely station...

Abreast of the news...

NEWSCASTER **John Bacon** had some memorable moments while reading more than 16,000 bulletins on Anglia. Some involved major news stories . . . others included little things like a bluebottle settling on his nose.

But one he will never forget is the day a topless dancer almost brought the programme to a standstill.

In the late 1960s, a troupe of dancers from Senegal were performing at the Theatre Royal, in Norwich, and Anglia booked them to appear on its programme. "Both male and female dancers performed naked from the waist up," said Bacon. "A wonderful set was designed with palm trees and flaming braziers so that the cameras could tastefully shoot their bodies through trees and smoke.

"We opened the programme with an introduction of them dancing, and cut to presenter **Bob Wellings** who explained they would be performing for us again later – 'But first the news with John Bacon . . .'

"I was sitting in front of a background of news pictures and had just started to tell the story of a pile-up on the M1 when the most well-developed girl in the whole dance troupe decided to walk behind me in full camera view. I could see what was happening on my monitor but it was too late to do anything about it."

Programme editor **Jim Wilson** also recalls the incident as one of the most bizarre during his 30 years in charge of the programme. "The letters we received showed

John Bacon and Caroline Raison.

how much that programme was appreciated," he said. John Bacon's slicked-back, silver hair and impeccable delivery marked him as one of the personalities viewers most associated with the news on Anglia. He joined the company from the BBC in 1964, left for a time in the 70s during which he became a marketing executive with a Middle East company based in Norwich, and returned in 1977 until retiring in 1992.

Bacon also bought a pig farm – a move which caused a fair bit of mirth among his colleagues. "With a name like mine you expect a few cracks," he said. "Once, when a lorry arrived with a load of pig food, the driver thought the name on the invoice was a joke."

Up to the 1990s, the main evening *About Anglia* programme used a newsreader in addition to two presenters, whereas nowadays the roles on the 6 o'clock *Anglia News* are combined. For some years, from 1977, Bacon shared the newsreading duties with **Caroline Raison**. Their immediate predecessor was **David Geary**, who left to return to radio where he had begun his broadcasting career.

About Anglia began in May, 1960, as a twice-weekly news magazine which took some of the features previously carried by the *Midday Show*. Its original presenter was **Dick Joice**. In September of that year it extended to four nights a week, and a few months later achieved the nap hand.

The regional news service started on the very first day, however, with a bulletin at 6.05 pm read by **'Sandy' Newman Sanders**, who had also at one time been a pig farmer as well as a lecturer at the London Planetarium. Later, he went on to become Anglia's education officer.

His colleagues at the newsdesk were a colourful Scotsman called **Drew Russell** and **Colin Bower**, who was a presenter of the first *Miss Anglia* contest in 1961 and subsequently married one of the finalists – the 'Miss Lowestoft', **Jill Edwards**.

The first big story covered by *Anglia News* was on the second day of transmission when two men were rescued by the Aldeburgh lifeboat. It was the first of many dramatic sea rescues reported by Anglia over the years.

Other newsreaders from the early 1960s included **Chris Kelly** and **Anne Gregg**, both of whom went on to achieve national television fame. Gregg, who arrived at Anglia in 1962 from her native Belfast, recalls the fun that went hand in hand with the serious side of producing the early *About Anglia*. **Dick Joice** was usually in the thick of the action. "I remember cavorting about on a horse one day in one of Dick's strange little plays he used to engineer within the programme when we were all being silly people," she said.

Dick Joice and Bob Wellings "larking about".

Anne Gregg: enjoyable times.

"That sort of programme at that time was so different from today. There was more entertainment and less hard news and there was a lot of larking about, which was quite enjoyable. And it was all live stuff, of course."

Joice had a few more party tricks that came in handy on *About Anglia*, not least the occasion when he filled in time by talking about a misshapen potato – the incident he credited with starting the *Bygones* series. Another time he literally turned the show on its head when the director told him he had an extra two minutes to fill. "There was no recording, no film to fall back on, no autocue – there wasn't anything," he recalled. "I said straight to the camera: 'I am terribly sorry, I can't think of another thing to do and I've been told to go on for another two minutes. All I can do is stand on my head.

"So do you mind awfully if I stand on my head and say goodnight from *About Anglia* upside down? And I hope this doesn't happen again tomorrow night.'" With that he did a headstand. There were plenty of other well known – and some surprising – names associated with *About Anglia's* early days. **Bob Wellings** went on to national TV prominence as a reporter-presenter on the BBC's Nationwide programme.

Wellings had a flare for the quirky and offbeat story. In one about the psychology of men who grow moustaches, he modelled five false versions in styles ranging from toothbrush to handlebar.

Double act...

AMONG Anglia's reporters in the mid-1970s was a young Mancunian called **Judy Finnegan** who came to Anglia from her first job in TV news with Granada, and settled in Norwich.

She married a fellow Anglia reporter, **David Henshaw**, and in March, 1977, gave birth to twin sons, proudly showing off the babies on *About Anglia* the next day. The couple subsequently divorced and Judy's second marriage to **Richard Madeley** forged the best known husband-and-wife television partnership of the 1990s.

Alfred Hitchcock being interviewed for *About Anglia* **during the making of a feature film in Cambridge in the early 1960s.**

Judy Finnegan proudly showing off her twin sons on *About Anglia.*

Offbeat and quirky was also a fair description of a man who achieved something of a cult following on *About Anglia* for around ten years from 1964. **Kenneth Robinson** presented a satirical canter in words and music through the week's events in an insert called *Look At It This Way*. He also took a sideways look at British institutions, from seaside holidays to the *Ideal Home Exhibition*.

Two eminent TV men who gained their earliest experience on *About Anglia* were **David Dimbleby** and **David Frost**. Dimbleby joined the programme in 1960 during a summer vacation from Oxford University. Frost, whose father was a Methodist minister at Beccles, in Suffolk, was also employed as a reporter in 1960, after graduating from Cambridge University. His first recorded interview was with two Cambridge councillors about a plan to build shops in Lion Yard. But his contract was not renewed – executives felt he had no future in regional television...

Kenneth Robinson, looking at it his way.

Then, as now, *Anglia News* never let an opportunity slip for an interview with a major public figure visiting the region, whether from the world of politics or showbusiness. Among the early visitors to *About Anglia* was **Bruce Forsyth**, the energetic young compere of Val Parnell's *Sunday Night at the London Palladium*. And the first of many Prime Ministerial interviews took place in June, 1962, when **Harold Macmillan** faced the camera on a visit to Luton Hoo.

Prince Philip and **Prince Charles** are among members of the Royal Family who have been interviewed in the *About Anglia* studio, while **Bob Hope**, **James Stewart** and moon-walking astronaut **Neil Armstrong** were famous American visitors.

By the start of the 1970s, there was a new partnership in place to anchor the *About Anglia* programme in the form of **Graham Bell** and **Jane Probyn**. Bell remained as a senior presenter on the programme for the next 18 years, making him by far its longest-serving presenter.

Dame Edna – one of Graham Bell's many star interviewees.

He interviewed many celebrity guests such as **Stefanie Powers**, **Deborah Kerr**, **Dame Edna Everage**, **Cannon and Ball**, **Paul Daniels**, **Ralph McTell** and **Alan Price**. He and Probyn also took a weekly look at viewers' letters in *Midweek Mail*.

During his 31-year career at Anglia, until his untimely sudden death at 57, in 1997, Bell also presented the *Portrait of a Village* show, compered the *Miss Anglia* contest and introduced many religious and documentary programmes. In later years he switched to continuity announcing and was the voice behind the crime-fighting series *Crimestoppers*. He also became known to a new generation of viewers as the man who appeared with *Birthday Club* puppet **BC**, sending birthday greetings to children in the region.

Probyn spent nine years in Norwich and introduced some important new feature inserts into *About Anglia*, notably *Heirloom* which she presented with Hertfordshire antiques dealer **John Bly**, and a fashion feature called *Trend*. The latter reflected the growing importance of the British fashion scene, and for some time was the only regular weekly fashion spot on British TV. Probyn was associated with many other Anglia programmes, including *Where Are They Now?* – co-presented with **David Jacobs** - *Regional Flavour* and *About Women*.

Bruce Forsyth with Dick Joice in the *About Anglia* studio.

Christine Webber interviewing Prince Philip.

Christine Webber and Pam Rhodes – minstrels reunited.

In 1976 new presenter **Pam Rhodes** arrived and was joined three years later by **Christine Webber**. Coincidentally both were former *Black and White Minstrel* showgirls – Pam as a dancer and Christine as lead singer. Rhodes revealed: "We used to dance six miles a night – I measured it with a pedometer."

About Anglia was only her second presenting role, but she quickly became a firm favourite with viewers, despite having a testing introduction . . . her first interview was with arm-flailing science boffin **Dr Magnus Pyke**. "We started talking about nutrition and finished up discussing eyeballs," she recalled.

Rhodes was with the programme for seven years and later teamed up with erstwhile *About Anglia* colleague **Paul Barnes** to front the network leisure series *Anything Goes*. In the 1990s she achieved great popularity as presenter of the BBC's *Songs of Praise*.

Christine Webber came from Southern Television, where she had been an announcer, and stayed at Anglia for 11 years, during which she introduced several innovative features. Chief among them were the fortnightly social and medical inserts *Round Robin* and *On Call*. A key element of the former was *Round Robin Child*, an adoption and fostering appeal. **Brian**, a four-year-old autistic boy from Northamptonshire, was the first child featured, and over the years Webber was instrumental in placing almost 40 youngsters with families. *Round Robin* also gave advice on social problems affecting people of all ages – left-handedness, teenage gambling and bereavement among them.

On Call, launched in 1983, was co-presented with **Dr David Delvin**, medical editor of *General Practitioner* magazine, and covered a wide range of medical matters. After working together for five years, its two presenters cemented their personal as well as professional partnership with marriage at Thorpe Register Office in Norwich. They have continued to work together ever since in a number of media spheres.

Seasonal appeal...

IN the 1980s, *About Anglia* introduced a number of other feature strands, including a consumer affairs item *Checkout*, presented by **Tony Adams**, and *Get Up and Go*, a competition for young business entrepreneurs in the region. The first winner, who received a prize of £2,500, was **David Palmer**, a Norwich computer hardware designer, who had produced the smallest and cheapest voice synthesizer of its type in the world.

By this time, *Midweek Mail* had become *Write Now* with viewers' letters being reviewed by **Paul Barnes** and **Helen McDermott**, who had joined Anglia as a continuity announcer in 1979. She also became a newsreader on *About Anglia* and, in 1988, one of the regular presenters. She also formed a personal relationship with her *Write Now* partner Paul Barnes. And the effigy of **Kaiser Bill** — known as **'Spike'** — to which viewers' letters were ceremoniously consigned after their airing on *Write Now*, today adorns their Norwich home.

Newsroom journalist **Tim Child** launched a computer software review called *The Soft Spot* in 1985. Aimed primarily at young computer users, it gave him the idea for a new computer-based television game for youngsters. He set up his own company and, among other successful projects, worked with Anglia to develop the innovative *Knightmare* series that ran for many years on the ITV network.

Helen McDermott and sports presenter **Kevin Piper** teamed up for an additional magazine show, *About Anglia Xtra*, in February, 1989. The programme launched a

search for new faces to join the reporting team. Dress designer **Victoria Way**, 24, from Topcroft, in Norfolk, was the first one chosen from more than 2,500 hopefuls.

There was another search for would-be TV journalists in 1996 when secondary school students were invited to submit ideas for stories in their own localities for broadcast on *Anglia News*. The best were able to research and film the items for the programme. First on was 15-year-old **Sean Gilbert** who looked at what life was like for young people growing up on Peterborough's Welland Estate.

Helen McDermott and Caroline Oldrey launching the Christmas Gift Appeal.

Reporter Timothy Evans outside the Essex News Centre.

Community action...

THE *About Anglia* programme launched a new community service to help voluntary organisations in August, 1985, and it heralded the start of a major new development in the company's links with its region.

Eighteen months later an *Anglia Action* unit was set up at the Ipswich News Centre, in partnership with the national charity CSV Media, to provide information and back-up services on social action, community, health and welfare projects.

Anglia Action has continued to provide and expand its role in the 1990s, including roadshows in support of on-screen campaigns, such as fostering, carers, disability benefits and drugs and alcohol issues.

A community relations co-ordinator was appointed in Norwich in 1997 to oversee new projects. Among these has been a partnership scheme launched in 1998 to help and encourage community activities in the region. Anglia offers practical assistance, advice and the opportunity for on-screen back-up to organisations both large and small, including voluntary groups trying to get a community project off the ground.

A 'partnership programming' initiative has been added to the scheme, comprising a weekly five-minute programme and a monthly half-hour magazine, *Take It On*. These focus on problems, personalities, and achievements within the community, tapping into places, people and topics other programmes do not normally reach.

Graham Donaldson.   Fenella Hadingham.   John Francis.   Rebecca Jones.   Richard Swallow.   Jeremy Hands.

New faces for the nineties news...

NEW faces and voices ushered in the biggest changes to Anglia's news programmes in 1989/90.

As well as the departures from the programme of **Graham Bell** and **Christine Webber**, another senior anchorman, **Alastair Yates**, left in 1989 to join the fledgling *Sky News*. He was replaced by **Jeremy Hands**, a top reporter with ITN earlier in the decade, notably during the Falklands War and the Iranian Embassy siege.

When the dual news service began the next year, Hands became a programme editor and **John Francis**, who had been working for the BBC in the West Country, arrived back in Norwich, his home city, as a reporter-presenter on *Anglia News East*, along with newcomer **Fenella Hadingham**, later replaced by **Rebecca Jones**.

Caroline Oldrey, who originally came from Northamptonshire and had joined Anglia in 1985 as a continuity announcer and newsreader, became one of the west presenters along with newcomers **Stephen Chambers**, who had links with Peterborough, and **Richard Swallow**, who arrived from the BBC in the South-West.

In 1998 – the year which saw *Anglia News* take another giant stride forward with the move to a purpose-built unit at the Magdalen Street studio complex – sports editor **Kevin Piper** became one of the main programme presenters for the east service. He was renewing a partnership with **Helen McDermott** forged ten years earlier on *About Anglia Xtra*. The third member of the east squad was **Clare Weller** who arrived in 1997 from the south of England broadcaster Meridian as a replacement for **Rebecca Jones**. And in 1999 **Greg Milam** joined the regular team of presenters as Kevin Piper moved into other programming areas.

Helen McDermott, meanwhile, launched a new-style *About Anglia* in 1999 when the programme title – dropped in 1990 – was revived as a twice-weekly 5.30 pm regional magazine.

The west presentation team has enjoyed even greater continuity through the 1990s, with Caroline Oldrey and Stephen Chambers being joined by **Tim Curtis** as the third senior member.

In addition to the main news programme at 6 o'clock each weekday and bulletins throughout the day, *Anglia News* also produces news and sport bulletins at weekends, plus a half-hour *Sunday Supplement* in which **John Francis** and **Graham Donaldson** look at business and political stories affecting the region. There have also been many special programmes produced by the news team. Recent examples include an eye-opening report on drug abuse in the region, an award-winning follow-up to the disastrous Easter floods of 1998 and a profile of non-League soccer club **Stevenage Borough's** giant-killing FA Cup run.

And finally. . . one of the most enduring and endearing features of *Anglia News* and *About Anglia* for more than 30 years has been the annual Christmas Gift Appeal on behalf of needy children. Thousands of disadvantaged youngsters across the region benefit from the generosity of viewers in providing toys and other gifts as Christmas presents. Anglia works closely with social services and voluntary organisations to make sure the toys reach the youngsters in most genuine need. In some cases it may be the only present a child receives. All the presenters lend their support to the appeal, but its chief promoters in recent years have been Caroline Oldrey and Helen McDermott.

East is east and west is west...

DIVIDING the region into east and west in the summer of 1990 was probably the biggest change to Anglia's news service.

It meant splitting the region into two new areas and setting up separate news services to cover them, each with its own presenters, reporters, and production teams.

Viewers in Luton were no longer obliged to linger over events in Lowestoft, and citizens of Colchester were saved the confusion of catching up with affairs in Corby.

More importantly, the east-west split meant that news coverage within each patch was effectively doubled, providing a new and unrivalled local television news service to viewers living on both sides of the region.

Anglia's director of news at the time, **Jim Wilson**, said: "We asked viewers what they wanted from the regional service and almost without exception they said they wanted more local news about their towns and communities. We believe the dual service reflects the fact that East Anglia has a different culture, background and outlook from counties in the west of the region."

The name of the main flagship half-hour evening programme changed from *About Anglia* to become the new-look *Anglia News*, moving from 6pm to the later time of 6.25pm. It was presented by **Helen McDermott**, **John Francis** and **Fenella Hadingham** in the east and by **Caroline Oldrey**, **Stephen Chambers** and **Richard Swallow** in the west.

The hub of all this activity was based at Anglia's headquarters at Anglia House, in Norwich. A new purpose-built studio and new newsroom were part of the £6 million extension and improvements to the complex in the 1980s, but as Anglia's news operation continued to grow it became increasingly difficult to accommodate it all adequately.

In 1998, as part of a further £7.5 million investment, the company moved its Norwich news operation to its other studio base in Magdalen Street, where *Anglia News*, *Sport* and *Weather* now share new surroundings in one of the most advanced television newsrooms in Europe. The move was a huge undertaking, but careful planning over two years and a staged changeover, made sure the transition went smoothly. Not a bulletin was lost.

As well as the studios, control galleries, open-plan newsroom and news offices there are dressing rooms, edit suites, a graphics studio and news library. More than 100 staff made the move, including those members of technical staff who were to join the news team permanently instead of continuing as part of a central facilities pool.

In 1999 the ITV network ceased to screen *News at Ten*, moving the main evening ITN news bulletin to 6.30pm. As a result, *Anglia News* moved back to a 6pm time-slot.

Anglia News East – Helen McDermott, Greg Milam and Clare Weller.

Anglia News West – Caroline Oldrey, Stephen Chambers and Tim Curtis.

Anglia News gets a new home as part of a £7.5m refurbishment

Work on converting what had been a scenery workshop and storage area beneath Anglia's largest studio began in 1997. Builders had to sink the floor to create enough headroom for the two new studios where east and west would broadcast, separately but simultaneously. One major task was moving the heavy duty lift and lift shaft which had once carried scenery and props to the studio above – including the car viewers saw on *The Sale of the Century*.

Walking out in style...

ANGLIA expects much from its presenters, and looking back it mostly seems to have been the girls at the front of the action.

On one occasion – and for one night only – **Christine Webber** found herself taking to the flying trapeze at Yarmouth's Hippodrome Circus with a troupe called the Flying Cherokees from South Africa.

But her worst moment came when she agreed to interview a knife-thrower – while being a target for his act. "I was paralysed with fear," she confessed later.

Jane Probyn took up horse racing but parted company with her mount in the Newmarket Town Plate, at the time one of the few races open to women riders.

Probyn recalled: "Immediately before the race the owner/trainer and I were called before the stewards who doubted my competence to ride in the race. My heart stopped. *About Anglia* had a five-minute slot allocated for the event and I envisaged a blank screen if they forbade me to enter." The stewards reluctantly agreed to let her take part in the four-mile event but their misgivings were justified when she fell off from exhaustion after three miles – though fortunately it was only her pride that was hurt.

Fourteen years later another Anglia reporter took to the saddle in the same race, and also came to grief.

Rebecca Atherstone had already proved her pluck with a number of daring assignments, including being strapped to the top of a stunt plane to experience 'wing walking' with a flying circus. In 1985, she undertook a period of intensive training for her debut as a jockey. *About Anglia* charted her progress in reports dubbed 'Rebecca's Gamble', and at the time she admitted being more nervous about riding in the race than anything she had done in television before.

Unfortunately, her nerves proved justified. She was unseated, knocked out cold, and finished up in hospital nursing her injuries, after her horse, **Surprise Attack**, tried to jump a road.

Rebecca Atherstone eventually ended up owning the thoroughbred herself, after Newmarket trainer, former top jockey **Eric Eldin**, generously asked if she would like to have him.

Approaching 20 years of age now, **Polo**, as he became known, still lives in Suffolk with the family and is even trusted with their six-year-old daughter on his back. "He's the most wonderful horse and a great character," said Atherstone. "I only fell off him once, and that was in style. It was the only ungentlemanly slip he made."

In **Helen McDermott's** case it was more likely to be her colleagues who were in danger. Her sense of humour gained her a reputation as a practical joker, and she would often pull surprises that left her companions in the studio struggling for composure.

The set of false boobs she strapped on, while the camera was turned away from her, understandably reduced poor weatherman **David Brooks** to the giggles. And her fellow presenter **John Francis** was no doubt similarly nonplussed when she suddenly decided to attempt the splits as a follow-up to a news item about a dance school.

Her early ballet training may have stood her in good stead for doing the splits, but it wasn't until she was preparing to run in the London Marathon – a feat she completed in 1994, and again in 1995 – that it was revealed she had never mastered the art of riding a bike. "I was told that cycling would help in the training programme," she explained. "People don't believe me when I tell them I can't ride. Because I was a ballet dancer people think I have natural balance, but that's not the case as far as cycling is concerned!"

Talking of balance, it is only politically correct to point out that the boys have not been entirely absent from Anglia's annals of derring-do. **Tim Curtis** was 12,000 feet up at the controls of a stunt plane when he tried looping the loop. Unfortunately, he didn't get it quite right, and ended up slumping the slump over the joy stick instead. Luckily the pilot with him was able to take over and they both got down safely.

Rebecca Atherstone's wingwalk.

Christine 'flyer' Webber.

Rebecca Atherstone, Eric Eldin and Surprise Attack.

Jane Probyn – pride before the fall.

Christine Webber's night of the long knives.

That's the end of the news...now here's the weather...

ANGLIA became the first regional ITV company to set up its own weather department in September, 1961, when **Michael Hunt** was appointed station meteorologist.

"The new service will be based on information supplied by the Air Ministry Meteorological Office and will be locally interpreted in terms which will lay special emphasis on the needs of the holiday industry and the agricultural community," Anglia announced.

Michael Hunt was himself an *Air Ministry* meteorologist, and came to Anglia from RAF Dishforth, in Yorkshire, where he was a lecturer and examiner of senior aircrew in RAF Transport Command.

He headed the Anglia weather department for the next 23 years, developing it into a unique regional service by building up a network of almost 100 local weather correspondents who supplied information about local weather patterns, statistics and freak conditions.

Their reports helped Hunt became one of the first meteorologists to recognise that tornadoes were not as uncommon in Britain as people supposed. The "twisters" were only minor affairs compared with their American cousins, of course, and many of them passed unnoticed over uninhabited areas.

Hunt was able to recount one day that it had been raining not cats and dogs, but frogs. A mini tornado

passing over a fen area had sucked up the amphibians and deposited them on to nearby houses. On another occasion he revealed that a skein of wild geese found dead in a Norfolk field had been killed by a tornado. With his trademark handlebar moustache and clipped RAF tones, Hunt was one of Anglia's most instantly recognisable personalities for more than 20 years. He was also respected for his straightforward and honest approach to what he recognised was sometimes an inexact science. One day his opening remark to viewers was "Well, I'm afraid yesterday's forecast was a load of codswallop..."

"Well, I'm afraid yesterday's forecast was a load of codswallop..."

David Hughes and Karin Giannone.

Michael Hunt — tornado man.

Jim Bacon.

David Brooks and
Peter Walker.

Jim Bacon, who became head of Anglia's weather department in later years, told how, as a schoolboy in West Norfolk, he had been inspired to take up meteorology by watching Hunt's forecasts. "He had the knack of making it interesting, especially for us people in the Fens where there's more sky than ground and more weather than anything else," he said.

Michael Hunt retired in 1984 when most of the local weather correspondents – most of whom he had never actually met – attended a party and presentation at Anglia's studios. He continued as a relief forecaster until his sudden death the next year.

David Brooks, who had been Hunt's deputy for many years, headed the department for the next eight years followed by Bacon, who joined Anglia in 1986 after seven years as a weatherman and *Travel Show* presenter on national BBC television.

Brooks holds the dubious distinction of being probably the only TV weather forecaster struck by lightning – a case of the elements biting back, perhaps. It happened while he was playing golf but, luckily, although he felt a powerful shock go through his body, he was unhurt.

He was also involved in one of the most memorable *It'll Be Alright on the Night* clips involving a forecaster. Back in the 1970s, before the days of computerised charts, a member of the stage crew was stationed behind the set to slide the weather maps in and out of view on cue from the forecaster. One night, when the time came to show the chart summarising the Anglia weather for the next day, the requisite chart was missing, and all that appeared was a blank board.

Brooks was struck by a fit of giggles. He manfully tried to continue with the forecast, before eventually muttering, "It's good here, isn't it?" Recalling the incident Brooks says: "The whole studio collapsed in hysterics. The floor manager hid behind a camera and all I could see was his hand waving. **Pam Rhodes** was presenting *About Anglia* that night and she was still trying to compose herself as she introduced the next item, which was a very serious news story. As I left the studio I was told the programme controller, **Philip Garner**, wanted to see me – and it wasn't to offer me a pay rise!"

On a more serious note, Brooks and Bacon introduced big technological improvements to *Anglia Weather*, based on investment in the latest satellite and computer equipment that helped change the face of forecasting and give viewers a comprehensive, modern regional service.

One of the most significant was in 1986 when Anglia pioneered the introduction of computer graphic weather charts in the ITV regions. "It meant for the first

time we were able to draw charts electronically instead of by pen and ink," said Brooks.

Technology was also behind a big change in the Anglia weather at the start of 1999 when Anglia's contract with the Met Office for the supply of forecasting data ended. A new company, Weather Services International, was signed up to provide a package that included screen-ready forecast maps prepared by its own meteorologists.

It signalled the end of Anglia's long tradition of in-house meteorology and a sad farewell from the local TV screens for Jim Bacon and fellow meteorologists **Andy Cutcher** and **Clare Nasir**, whose scientific expertise was no longer required.

Two journalists from the *Anglia News* team were appointed as environment correspondents to present the forecasts and report for the news programme on weather-related stories. As the new dawn appeared on the horizon, **David Hughes** and **Karin Giannone** pledged to uphold the high standards associated with the company's weather service over the preceding 38 years.

These days there are as many, if not more, female weather presenters as male on our television screens, but it was not always so. Clare Nasir, from Northamptonshire, and Karin Giannone, a graduate of Cambridge University where she edited the student magazine, ended a long-standing male domination of Anglia's weather presentation.

A forecaster called **Jennifer Rouch** served briefly as assistant to Michael Hunt in the early 1960s, but from that time until Nasir made her debut in 1997, all Anglia's forecasters had been men, reflecting the fact that meteorology was for many years a male-dominated profession.

Claire Nasir.

In addition to those already mentioned, **Eric Dudley**, **Peter Walker** and **Colin Corkerton** are forecasters many viewers will recall.

The risque factor...

ONE day in 1997 two Aussies arrived, all jeans and jet-lag, at Anglia's Norwich studios. Few people had heard of them here, but back home their comedy chat shows were compulsive Saturday night viewing for much of Australia.

'Rampaging' Roy Slaven and HG Nelson (real names **John Doyle** and **Greig Pickhaver**) had been signed up for a three-programme pilot series.

In Australia, the dinner-jacketed duo's anarchic show was called *Club Buggery*. But in deference to translation difficulties, the UK version went out under the title *Roy and HG's Bughouse*. The format, however, was similar: 'Competitive interviewing', as one critic called it, of well-known people.

By the time the two returned in 1998 for an eight-week run, the Norwich connection had gained national and international recognition through the re-titling of their series as *Roy and HG's Planet Norwich*, the glitzy studio set masquerading as top night-spot, 'Star City'.

The show went out in the Anglia region on Thursday nights, Channel 5 on Fridays and ABC in Australia on Saturdays. Guests from the world of sport and entertainment, including England cricket captain **Alec Stewart**, former Wonderbra model **Caprice**, boxer **Chris Eubank**, and actors **Richard E. Grant** and **Stephen Fry**, were all subjected to the Roy and HG treatment – probing questions inducing non-malicious send-up. Some guests fared better than others.

In an interview with *The Independent*, HG said of their style: "We make mountains out of molehills and vice versa. We make the trivial serious and the serious trivial." And Roy added: "Language is really all we have. We use it as a sort of battering ram, brutal and blunt."

The men from Down Under... John Doyle and Greig Pickhaver otherwise Roy and HG.

Kathy Kirby in action in the Sixties.

Their brand of risque satire was a world apart from the light entertainment of Anglia's early days.

In the Sixties, the genre was dominated by music shows. Singers **Frank Ifield** and **Kathy Kirby** were among guests on shows that included *Come In, The Glen Mason Show, Rehearsal Room* and *The Sound of Summer.*

Johnny Dankworth and his orchestra appeared in a series called *Crescendo*, which also featured stars of the time such as **Ronnie Carroll, Bobby Rydell** and **Sheila Southern**. **Dankworth** and his singer wife, **Cleo Laine**, have enjoyed a long association with Anglia, from

entertainment shows to arts programmes and embracing music for *Survival* wildlife films along the way.

In 1961 singer **Sheila Buxton** presented *Showdate*, a series that featured pop stars like **John Leyton** and **Marty Wilde**, an amateur talent competition and a beauty contest with the title of 'Miss Anglia' up for grabs. The two top prizes of £100 were awarded at a final, broadcast from the Britannia Theatre, Great Yarmouth.

A year later the 'Miss Anglia' contest became an hour-long show in its own right.

The early Sixties also saw Anglia producing the first version of *New Faces* with **Kenneth Horne** compering a talent show for TV newcomers. The idea was later taken up by Midlands-based ATV and became a long-running network series.

There followed plenty of other opportunities for people from the East of England to take that first step on the ladder to showbusiness success with an appearance on Anglia.

Bobby Rydell... *Crescendo* **guest.**

Kent Walton spins a disc in *Top Twenty.*

Out and about... a *Disc Quiz* **outside broadcast.**

Introducing new faces...

City Sounds **presenter Steve Blacknell.**

Diane Solomon with Pete Sayers.

CITY SOUNDS was a 1980s music competition hosted first by **David Jensen** and then **Steve Blacknell**. It offered a half-hour TV special on Anglia for the best musical acts. Another series for regional talent was transmitted in 1995. Called *The Front Row*, it was hosted by stand-up comedian **Sean Meo**. The acts in the six shows ranged from Ipswich samba dancers to a Norfolk didgeridoo player. Poets, singers and comedians also featured.

In 1997 *Streetwise*, fronted by up-and-coming comedian **John Moloney**, introduced 30 street entertainers – from jugglers to harpists and can-can dancers to fire-eaters – and gave them the chance to perform to a wider audience.

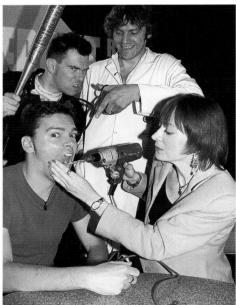

Open wide... regional comedy in *The Front Row*.

The popular following for folk and country music in the region has been recognised by numerous series, the longest-running being visits to the annual *Cambridge Folk Festival*.

Diane Solomon at the Maltings, in 1981, featured the American singer in a specially-recorded concert before a capacity audience at Snape in Suffolk. Her special guest was country singing compatriot **Glen**

Campbell and also featured were Newmarket's **Pete Sayers** and Solomon's backing group, **Paradox**.

Anglia has kept abreast of contemporary pop music, most recently with a series from the *V98* rock festival at Chelmsford. And in 1996 the Magdalen Street studio reverberated to *After Hours With Tom Robinson*, in which the Cambridge-born singer/songwriter was joined by rock stars such as **The Manfreds, Beth Orton** and **Alisha's Attic**.

Up The Junction, in 1992, was a live music and comedy extravaganza hosted by comedian **Rowland Rivron** at THE JUNCTION in Cambridge. Guests included **Beats International, The Levellers, Mark Lamarr, Jo Brand** and **John Hegley** and the **Popticians**.

Contemporary comedy has been well represented by Cockney **Lee Hurst**, who devised his own panel game show *Bring Me the Head of Light Entertainment*, which Anglia turned into a big success for Channel 5 in 1997. Hurst's early television appearances included stints on two Anglia shows called *Shark Tank* and *The Warehouse*.

Diane Youdale – alias 'Jet' from ITV's *Gladiators* **– swapped physical combat for verbal sparring in** *The Warehouse*.

Lee Hurst (centre) tries to muscle in on the act in *Shark Tank*.

Shark Tank was a part talk, part game show and *The Warehouse* a topical late-night mix of news, gossip, comedy and celebrity guests. In the first series of the latter, Hurst was the funnyman alongside co-presenters **Chris Donat** and **Diane Youdale**. Youdale was more accustomed to physical rather than verbal combat as **Jet** in ITV's *Gladiators* series. Subsequent series were fronted by comedian **Sean Meo** along with **Amanda Redington** and **Lowri Turner**.

Comedy of a different kind had featured eight years earlier in the capable hands of **Roy Hudd** and a show for Channel 4 called *Hudd's 'Alf 'Undred*, marking the comedian's 50th birthday. The one-off New Year's Eve special took a look back over half a century. It brought together actress **June Whitfield** and her daughter, **Suzy Aitchison**, for the first time on TV, and also featured Radio 2 *Huddlines* colleague **Chris Emmett**.

Singers Tom Robinson and Beth Orton.

Roy Hudd and June Whitfield go punk for *Hudd's 'Alf 'Undred*.

On cue... **Steve Davis with Kenny Lynch and Jimmy Greaves.**

Love Call **presenters David Jensen and Sam Norman with Tracey Thomas and Martin Moore who met through the programme and became engaged.**

Cue for a new role...

A FRAME WITH DAVIS, which started on Channel Four in 1983 and ran for three years, gave then World Snooker Champion **Steve Davis** his debut as a television presenter. In each of 20 programmes Davis chatted and joked with two celebrities, acting as referee and coach for a light-hearted game of snooker between his guests.

First to take up their cues were soccer pundit **Jimmy Greaves** and singer-comedian **Kenny Lynch**, with **Bernie Winters**, **Frankie Vaughan**, **Jeffrey Archer**, **Rodney Bewes**, **Willie Carson**, **Dennis Waterman**, **Richard O'Sullivan**, **Tim Brooke-Taylor**, **Mike Reid** and **Duggie Brown** following them up to the table.

It was a maximum break of comedy in the second series with **Lennie Bennett**, **Bernard Manning**, **Barry Cryer**, **John Junkin**, **Michael Barrymore**, **Don Maclean**, **Alfred Marks**, **Stan Boardman**, **Ted Rogers**, **Willie Rushton**, **Jim Bowen**, **Dave Wolfe**, **Norman Wisdom** and **Max Boyce**.

Welshman Boyce was back to lead off the third series with soccer star **Emlyn Hughes** and the remaining frames were potted out by **Bernie Clifton**, **Bobby Davro**, **Lennie Bennett**, **Derek Jameson**, **Duggie Brown**, **Bill Tidy**, **Leslie Thomas**, **Bernard Bresslaw**, **Chris Serle**, **Bernie Winters** and **Kenny Lynch** – plus the only female in the series, **Suzanne Danielle**.

Chatty entertainment had really got under way at Anglia in 1981 when Anglia industrial journalist **John Swinfield**, who was more used to grilling heavyweights of the business world such as **Lord King** and **Robert Maxwell**, hosted a light-hearted talk show called *Side By Side By Swinfield*. Guests were from many walks of life, among them **Suzi Quatro**, **Brian Rix**, **Douglas Bader**, **Mary Whitehouse**, **Gary Glitter** and *Spitting Image* creators **Fluck and Law**.

And they called it puppy love...

ANGLIA broke new ground with *Relationships*, launched in January, 1991, and billed as Britain's first serious television dating show.

From March, 1993, until May, 1995, an extended and updated version went out under the name of *Love Call*. The programme, transmitted live but part-recorded, featured people from the Anglia region looking for their perfect partners.

At first, written responses were passed on to the people featured but later the 'lonelyhearts' appearing on the show were able to take phone calls direct from viewers. The programme was originally hosted by **Mariella Frostrup** and **Paul Thompson**, then by Frostrup and **David Jensen**. Jensen was then partnered by **Jayne Irving**, followed by **Sam Norman** and finally by former *Dr Who* assistant, **Sophie Aldred**.

Four marriages resulted from early series and later there were several proposals of marriage and acceptances live on air. One of the most strikingly successful pieces of match-making, however, came after a Norfolk woman wrote asking the team to find a mate for her dog – boxer bitch Gucci. The problem was that the woman was against tail-docking and many breeders would allow their dogs to mate only on condition that the pups were subjected to this practice.

Eventually, after pointing out the problem on air, *Love Call* turned up two potential suitors and, after they had been 'vetted', one helped Gucci produce several fully-tailed pups.

Beauty and the best...

BOXING DAY 1987 marked Anglia's most ambitious and costly arts and entertainment production – an hour-long version of **Tchaikovsky's** classic ballet, *Sleeping Beauty*, on ice.

It cost £1 million to make and starred two of the world's finest skaters – Britain's Olympic gold medalist **Robin Cousins** and **Rosalynn Sumners**, a silver medal winner for America – along with a 50-strong cast.

Huge sets created by top film designer **Michael Seymour** – the man behind the look of *Alien* – were transported in a convoy of 40 lorries from London to a war-time aircraft hangar at Snetterton in Norfolk where the spectacular show was recorded.

By that time 300 tons of concrete had been used to level the floor and 10 miles of plastic freezer pipes laid and sprayed with thousands of gallons of water until the ice built up to a thickness of four inches. Lighting the production and running the ice-freezing plant was one of the biggest operations ever mounted in British television. It required more than one million watts of electricity – enough to power 10,000 ordinary light bulbs. In addition to the mains supply, the bulk of the power was provided by five generators, including the biggest mobile unit in Britain, consuming 400 gallons of diesel a day.

Sleeping Beauty won awards – for the best achievement with an entertainment special and best lighting – in the 1988 International Monitor Awards at Los Angeles. It also sold to 45 countries, including the United States and China, making it one of British television's biggest export successes.

How Anglia got to the bottom of a mysterious tragedy...

The Gaul.

THE sensational discovery of the sunken wreck of the missing Hull trawler the Gaul in 1997 was a crowning moment in Anglia's distinguished record of factual programming.

Only a year earlier the Ministry of Defence said it would be too difficult and too costly to undertake a successful search, but an Anglia team found the fishing vessel, which had vanished without trace 23 years earlier in the Barents Sea, between Norway and Russia.

Ever since the trawler's disappearance, there had been intense speculation about her fate. One persistent theory was that the Gaul had been involved in espionage and her 36-strong crew were casualties of the Cold War.

The Anglia crew which made the documentary, *Secrets of The Gaul*, for Channel 4's *Dispatches* programme included cameraman **Paul Bennett** and sound recordist **Richard Laughton**, working with producer **Norman Fenton** and reporter **Callum Macrae**.

Following an earlier link-up for another programme about the Gaul, independent producer Fenton and Anglia set out to make a second film with the intention of finally answering questions the trawlermen's families had been asking since the night the vessel disappeared.

"The Anglia team achieved what the Ministry of Defence only a year earlier had said was impossible," said executive producer **Bob Ledwidge**. "We located

the wreck of the Gaul and filmed it using a remotely-operated vehicle nearly 1,000 feet down on the bed of the Barents Sea."

Painstaking research work by Anglia's team – including studies of the last reported sightings of the Gaul by Norwegian trawlermen – pinpointed the likely area. After three days at sea, and a six-hour sonar search, the wreck was discovered.

Describing the moment when they saw the first shadowy pictures of the lost trawler, Paul Bennett said: "The camera drifted along the side of the wreck and we saw the number which confirmed it was the Gaul. It was a strange mixture of emotions. Any elation we felt was strongly tempered by the human tragedy it represented, and bewilderment that there had been no survivors as the vessel appeared quite intact."

The evidence from the seabed ended speculation that the Gaul had been arrested by the Soviet navy and her crew held captive. But the programme also built up a dramatic dossier on how civilian trawlers were used extensively to spy on the Soviet navy off the coast of Norway – revelations that caused intense embarrassment in Whitehall where successive Labour and Conservative governments had always denied that fishing boats were used for spying.

Secrets of The Gaul was voted the year's best current affairs programme in the Royal Television Society's journalism awards.

The early days...

THIRTY-SIX years earlier, Anglia's first networked current affairs programme was also concerned with a former enemy power. *Germany, Friend or Foe?*, shown on ITV in September, 1961, looked at the British public's attitudes towards Germany in the post-war era of new-found allegiance.

Among those taking part were the historian **A J P Taylor** and **Sir Richard Gale**, deputy commander-in-chief of Nato forces in Europe. Filming took place in East Anglia, Wales and the blitz areas of London, and among the questions raised was how people reacted when they saw German naval vessels anchored at Great Yarmouth and a Panzer unit stationed in Pembrokeshire.

Factual programmes have come a long way since that documentary, which some critics complained was inconclusive and ineffectual.

Martin Brundle.

A new factual dimension...

IN THE 1990s, the factual genre has taken on new dimensions, as demonstrated by *Great Escapes*, which Anglia introduced to the ITV network in 1998. Presented by former Formula One racing driver **Martin Brundle**, the programmes featured news footage and amateur video, capturing dramatic incidents from around the world in which death and disaster were averted by courage, skill, quick-thinking or sheer good fortune.

They included a boy resuscitated after being submerged in a frozen lake for 45 minutes – he survived because his body went into suspended animation in the icy

water – an 18-month-old toddler brought out alive after 58 hours trapped 20 feet below ground in a vertical shaft just nine inches wide, and a 70-year-old woman saved by firefighters after spending 15 minutes balanced on a narrow window ledge outside her burning flat on the 25th floor of an apartment block.

As a man for whom danger has been a frequent companion, Brundle readily identified with them all. "The programme celebrates survival," he said. "It's very positive. It gives you hope to know that individuals are prepared to risk their lives to save somebody else."

A key influence...

A KEY influence in the development of Anglia's factual output was **Brian Connell**, who was appointed programme adviser in 1963. He had been a respected foreign correspondent on Fleet Street newspapers, a presenter of ITV's *This Week*, and later ITN's special events commentator, in which role he commentated on the funeral of **Sir Winston Churchill**.

Over the next 20 years, Connell presented many regional and network Anglia documentaries, but the two series for which he is best remembered are *Arena* and *The Brian Connell Interviews*.

Arena was a long-running political series which had started in 1960 as an academic discussion programme. At that time it was staged in Cambridge but then moved into the Norwich studio and turned its attention to world events. Each week Connell introduced two guests, usually MPs, but occasionally peers and political journalists, to debate issues on the national and international agenda.

In 1970 came *The Brian Connell Interviews*, a chat show tailored to the style of its presenter which, Connell pointed out, was quite different from some other exponents of the genre. "I feel sure there must be a place in television for intelligent conversation with people of accomplishment," he said. His policy, he added, was to seek guests who were "at the top of their particular trees, people from business, arts and sciences, experts who for one reason or another do not normally appear on television."

Among the dozens of top people who obliged him over the next ten years were **Dame Rebecca West**, **Cardinal Basil Hume**, **Sir Frederick Ashton**, **Alan Ayckbourn**, **Sir Geraint Evans**, **Helen Mirren**, **Penelope Keith**, **Joyce Grenfell**, **The Duke of Wellington**, **Reginald Maudling** and **Bernard Levin**.

Leaders from the business world were profiled by **John Swinfield** in his series *Enterprise*, launched in 1977. **Sir Adrian Cadbury**, of the chocolate company, **Sir Alex Alexander**, of Lyons, **Peter Wilson**, of Sotheby's, **Sir Charles Forte**, **Clive Sinclair** and American banker **David Rockefeller** were among his subjects.

Swinfield was named industrial radio and TV journalist of the year in 1983 for the *Enterprise* series and, also in that year, *Enterprise* was screened on Channel 4 for the first time, with subjects including Virgin boss **Richard Branson**, Royal wedding dress designers **David and Elizabeth Emmanuel** and Habitat chief **Sir Terence Conran**.

The next year Swinfield produced *Enterprise Specials* with **Lord Weinstock**, of GEC, and **Robert Maxwell**. The latter was filmed extensively at home and at work, and was also accompanied by the cameras on a visit to Israel.

Maxwell, the millionaire publisher and newspaper proprietor whose death eight years later exposed the wayward financial dealings that left hundreds of his employees with depleted pensions, insisted in the programme that he was a man of the people. "I don't care about wealth or things. I care more about people, providing jobs for people and encouraging their initiative," he said.

In *King's Flight*, a 1986 documentary networked on ITV, Swinfield spotlighted **Lord King**, the British Airways chairman who was embroiled in a long-running battle to privatise Britain's state-owned airline. It was a fight he was always going to win, and the tough-talker demonstrated why in a candid discussion of his methods.

More leading figures from a number of different walks of life were featured in a 1990 series titled simply *Leaders*. It set out to discover the qualities possessed by people with that special ability to make things happen. Among those taking part were mountaineer **Chris Bonnington**, industrialist **Sir John Harvey-Jones**, cricketers **Alan Border** and **Clive Lloyd**, former England rugby skipper **Bill Beaumont** and soccer manager **Graham Taylor**.

Anglia had established a reputation for networked ITV documentaries in the 1970s with programmes such as *The Voices of Apollo*, in which **Brian Connell** introduced spectacular sequences shot by American astronauts from space and on the surface of the moon, along with programmes produced by the *Farming Diary* team on national and international issues and others made in the region for series such as *About Britain*.

> "I don't care about wealth or things. I care more about people, providing jobs for people and encouraging their initiative".
>
> **Robert Maxwell**

Brian Connell and
Joyce Grenfell.

In Troubled Waters...**Malcolm Allsop investigates.**

The following decade, however, saw a significant increase in documentary production for national viewing. *In Troubled Waters*, screened in 1980, took **Malcolm Allsop** to ports and sea lanes of the North Sea to investigate the threat of a major disaster after the worst year on record for oil tanker accidents.

The Medicine Men, a 1981 eight-part series written and produced by **John Lloyd Fraser**, examined the growing interest in alternative medicine and therapies such as herbalism, homeopathy, hypnosis and acupuncture. It showed sportsmen, including athlete **Seb Coe**, receiving treatment from an osteopath. It also filmed a woman giving birth under self-induced hypnosis.

The same year saw a timely feature on the uncertainties facing one of the last outposts of the British empire, the Falkland Islands. *More British Than The British* examined islanders' fears that the British government might be ready to do a deal with Argentina which was again pressing its claims to sovereignty over the islands. Five months later their concerns were resolved when Britain's Task Force was dispatched to deal with Argentina's attempt to take over the islands.

The vintage period for Anglia documentaries continued with *The Haunt of Man*, a one-hour programme shown in 1982. Two years in the making, it gave a grim warning about the plundering of the earth's dwindling natural resources. It was also one of the first television programmes to examine the new theories on global warming and the implications for future generations.

Two years later, Anglia travelled to another British outpost in the South Atlantic, the island of St Helena, whose inhabitants were also feeling fearful about their future under British rule. *St Helena – Island in Exile* looked at the economic and social problems faced by the islanders, and their anger at being deprived of full British citizenship, preventing them from settling in the UK. Producer **Graham Creelman** described St Helena as 'an island on the dole'.

He said: "Britain pays out £7 million a year – the cost of two miles of motorway – to keep the population from starvation. Total British support for the Falkland Islanders is now running at £750 million a year."

In *Animal Passions*, **Joanna Lumley was among those arguing against experiments in the beauty industry, with a practical demonstration of cosmetics developed without animal testing.**

Below: A young baboon having its blood pressure taken at an animal reseach lab.

Animal passions...

ANIMAL PASSIONS, another 1982 programme for ITV, tackled the emotive and controversial subject of experiments on live animals. It included the first film from an institute in Cambridgeshire which had once been described as 'Frankenstein's Farm'.

The programme, narrated by **Nigel Havers**, was allowed into Babraham Hall to film 'Babycham', the first successful crossing of a goat and sheep. But the Anglia team was not allowed to film a goat which had a mammary gland successfully transplanted onto its neck. The institute's director, **Dr Barry Cross**, did, however, agree to talk about the operation, carried out to study milk production. The programme also filmed at other laboratories and showed experiments on baboons, beagles, rabbits and rats.

Protests, opinions and debates...

Cover Story: **protesting against animal exports.**

Roberta Kray, campaigning for her husband's release.

CHANNEL 4 took a major three-part documentary from Anglia in 1983 called *Prison* which producer **Geoffrey Weaver** promised would be "full of opinions, historical information and comment" about the crisis facing Britain's jails at that time. It was certainly hard-hitting, with the first programme putting blame for the crisis on both the judiciary and government reluctance to take on the judges and make changes to the penal system.

Although networked programmes inevitably achieve the highest profile, there have been hundreds of other equally noteworthy Anglia documentaries made for regional screening. Some were made into series and others stood alone as single documentaries. . . some of general regional interest, and others covering more specialised or localised subjects.

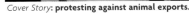

Dr Mary Archer introducing *Frontiers* **from Duxford.**

Current affairs have been at the core of much of this programming. In 1981, Anglia started a regular strand of regional documentaries under the title *Anglia Reports*, and it has run every year since. Later, it became known as *Anglia Tonight*, and the current version is *Cover Story*. Subjects in the 1999 series included the increasing threat from coastal erosion, the smuggling of tobacco and alcohol through east coast ports, and speculation about the future of one of Britain's most notorious prisoners, **Reggie Kray**.

In the past 15 years, the rapid economic growth of the East of England has prompted a diversity of regional factual programmes on themes such as industry and employment, politics, relations with Europe, social, consumer and environmental issues.

Just the Job, fronted by **Su Ingle** in 1990, explored employment and business issues such as skill shortages, self-employment, welfare at work and the wider role of women in the workplace. It also featured a special link-up between Anglia and the Open College, with a travelling roadshow visiting 11 towns in the region to provide a shop window on training opportunities.

In the same year, *Anything to Declare* was a six-week series offering viewers a window on Europe, with reports from Holland, France, Belgium and Germany on subjects ranging from street cleaning to conscription.

Livewire, a series presented by **Malcolm Allsop**, sought out clever inventions and bright business ideas in the East of England. The series signed off with awards for the best projects. And, in 1997, the KPMG Anglia Enterprise Awards rewarded companies from the region for their success in areas of manufacturing, leadership, innovation, motivation and customer dedication.

Science had first featured in the 1960s when *Survey* looked at projects going on in Cambridge University, and again in 1979 when six programmes were made on the work of Cambridge scientists under the title *Frontiers of Discovery*. In 1987, **Dr Mary Archer**, a fellow of

Newnham College, and one of the region's foremost scientists, made her debut as a TV presenter, introducing a series called *Frontiers* which looked at the latest scientific and technological research being carried out regionally in medicine, food, transport, communications and the environment.

The past 20 years have also seen an increase in studio-based factual discussion programmes with strong audience participation. Anglia has been at the forefront with daytime talk shows like *The Time...The Place* and *Trisha*, but has successfully used similar formats at the opposite end of the day's programmes.

Frontline, presented by **Malcolm Allsop**, involved the audience in debates on such topical issues as euthanasia, tabloid newspapers, nuclear power and embryo research.

In 1998, Anglia introduced a new series called *Heroes and Villains*, exploring news stories to pinpoint the nation's goodies and baddies of the week. Presented by **Paul Ross**, it mixes serious issues with the not-so-serious, each programme putting people making the news into the hot seat. A trio of guest panellists — among them **Germaine Greer** and Agony Aunt **Anne Atkins** — help frame the arguments which are put to a studio audience to decide if the person in the hot seat deserves hero or villain status.

Air crew enjoying their *Big Day* **at Luton.**

Reporter Bob Ledwidge (right) on a Suffolk safari in *Livewire*.

Sarah Willcoxson (left) and Sharon Freakley find construction work *Just the Job*.

Deckchair Bob and Mandy relaxing in *Trippers*.

Fly-on-the-wall documentaries and docu-soaps, those TV phenomena of the 90s, have had a part to play, too. A series called *The Big Day* in 1993 went behind the scenes with staff at Luton airport on a busy summer Saturday and joined the unsung holiday heroes who keep the trippers happy on Yarmouth seafront. The next year cameras met the winners and losers on a race day at Newmarket, told the inside story of production at one of the region's leading newspapers, the *Cambridge Evening News*, and joined adoring **Elvis** fans paying homage to 'The King' at their annual convention.

In 1999, *Trippers* turned the spotlight on the people who make life sunny for visitors to Southend – from **Bob**, king of the deckchairs, to **Mandy**, flamboyant mother of two, who is a waitress in the VIP bar of one of the town's smartest nightspots.

The cameras also took a close-up look at women police officers working in Essex in a six-part 1996 series, *Fair Cops*, produced for Anglia by independent company Media Futures.

Anglia gained special access to one of the region's top hospitals for *Nurses*, a six-part 1997 series focusing on seven nurses and their everyday dramas on the wards of the Norfolk and Norwich Hospital. The nurses, six women and one male, talked candidly on camera about the joys and heartaches, satisfactions and frustrations of their jobs.

Probing questions...

CONSUMER issues regularly feature in *Cover Story*, *About Anglia* and the regional news programmes, but at times have also occupied series in their own right. One was *Help*, launched in 1991, with presenters **Graham Donaldson** and **Jayne Irving**. It demonstrated that actions can speak as loud as words through television. It featured people who had rolled up their sleeves to get a job done in their local communities, and it offered practical help with problems like overcoming phobias, reforming ill-behaved pets, and dealing with the law.

Politics have appeared in many guises, from comprehensive coverage of every General Election since 1963 to profiles of leading politicians in the region. One was a 1989 portrait of the new Chancellor of the Exchequer, **John Major**, who welcomed **Malcolm Allsop** and the *Anglia Reports* cameras to his home near Huntingdon where, among other duties of state, he was filmed doing the washing up with his wife, **Norma**.

Politicians really began answering to their electorate on Anglia in 1968 with the launch of *Probe*, chaired by **Richard Clarke**. The main element was a confrontation between a politically-mixed audience and one of their MPs. Later, under **Bill Norris**, a phone-in was used. Anglia's switchboard opened for calls two hours before the programme and, on an average evening, there were 80 questions from which about a dozen were selected.

When **Geoff Druett** took over as presenter, the phone-in was replaced by film reports and a studio interview and *7 Days*, which first appeared in 1980 with Malcolm Allsop as editor and presenter, followed a similar format.

Allsop also introduced *Cross Question*, which started life as a political debate conducted in front of a jury. In one 1980 programme, **Jack Straw MP**, who became Home Secretary 17 years later, tried to convince the jury that the community should have more say in the running of police forces, while Police Federation chairman **John Jardine** argued against him.

Later *Cross Question* became a regular forum for a studio audience to quiz three or four leading people of different political persuasions about issues of the day. As well as regional MPs and peers, the programme attracted visiting heavyweights from Westminster, union leaders and employer representatives.

In 1989, *Cross Question* went on the road for the first time, being produced as an outside broadcast from towns and cities all over the Anglia region. Said Allsop: "People have travelled from all over the region to be members of the studio audience, and we felt it was time to take the show out to them."

Cross Question featured election and party conference specials, plus programmes from Brussels. An annual feature, which continued even after the series proper ended, was the *Cross Question Christmas Quiz* in which politicians let their hair down in a light-hearted contest between the Government and Opposition benches.

John and Norma Major tackle the dishes.

Malcolm Allsop chairing *Cross Question*. Panellists include the late Labour leader John Smith (left) seated next to Charles Kennedy, later to be the leader of the Liberal Democrats, and Conservative Minister Douglas Hurd (right).

Crimestoppers

Reconstructing a knife incident for *Crimestoppers*.

IN JULY, 1988, Anglia started screening a new initiative in the fight against crime. Called *Crimestoppers*, it pioneered in the ITV regions the use of short, sharp, filmed reconstructions of crimes to encourage viewers to come forward with information. Each item occupied only about 30 seconds, but was screened around ten times in a week during programme breaks. *Crimestoppers* proved hugely successful, leading to scores of arrests and convictions and the recovery of thousands of pounds worth of property. Later, the technique of reconstructing serious crime for the camera was also employed for a series of 15-minute programmes called *Crime Night*, presented by **Clare Weller** and **Tim Curtis**.

The bare essentials of humanity...

FULL FRONTAL IN FLIP FLOPS, screened on ITV in January, 1999, was another documentary first for Anglia – the first time it had devoted a programme to naturists (as opposed to naturalists) and certainly the first time that members of a programme-making team had removed all their clothes in the course of their duties.

One of them, director **Don Boyd**, wrote of his undressing experience in the *Daily Telegraph*: "My own great moment of truth occurred at a naturist wedding... I stripped off in front of my crew in a caravan owned by the bride and groom. My first feeling was pure exhilaration – and no one was unkind enough to laugh. By the end of the filming most of the rest of my team had stripped at various stages. Only the sound recordist refused, arguing that he would have nowhere to put his equipment."

Such escapades would have been unthinkable 40 years earlier. Nudity had no place in documentary or any other programming in Anglia's formative years. It was not until arts and drama programming achieved liberation in the 1980s that Anglia first depicted the bare essentials of humanity.

A rear view of the action.

And the bride wore. . .

And one-off success stories...

THE full range of Anglia's regional factual programming is demonstrated throughout this book. But it is the single, one-off documentary – revealing, entertaining, startling or quirky – that has been a particular feature of Anglia's output. They are too numerous to mention in their entirety, but here are some examples from the past 30 years:

King's Thousand (1970), a celebration of 1,000 years of the King's School, Ely.

John Constable (1970), a chronicle of his life, with **Roy Dotrice** as the painter.

Portrait of a Villain (1971), the story of **Victor Carasov**, who had spent more than 50 years in prison.

A Beautiful Way to Live (1971), with members of hippy communes explaining their choice of lifestyle.

Royal Day in Essex (1971), The Queen opening a £9 million scheme to pump water from Norfolk to Essex.

Test Case for Paradise (1972), the problems caused by holidaymakers descending on the Norfolk and Suffolk Broads.

Muddle and Go Nowhere Railway (1972), an affectionate look at the Middle and Great Northern Joint Railway, part of the East Anglian scene for 80 years.

Piers of the Realm (1973), **Roy Hudd** treading the boards of our seaside piers.

Come to the Fair (1973), a look at some of the travelling fairs of the East of England.

The Making of a City (1975), examining the state of Milton Keynes with a live debate between the planners and their critics.

The Day the Taxis Went to the Seaside (1976), **Mike Reid** (later Frank Butcher in *EastEnders*) describing an annual event when London cabbies treat East End children to a day-out at Southend.

The Royal Tour of East Anglia (1977), highlights of the Royal Silver Jubilee tour through the region.

Last Chance (1981), the inside story from the alcoholics' unit at Severalls Hospital, Colchester.

De Havilland 100 (1982), highlights from Hatfield of the de Havilland aircraft company's centenary.

Promised Land (1985), a graphic picture of the problems affecting the West Indian community of Luton.

Land for the Living (1989), a revealing insight into the business of cremation.

In Search of Space (1989), the Royal Greenwich Observatory's move to Cambridge.

East Coast Arcadia (1989), the story of one of England's strangest villages, Jaywick Sands, Essex.

Fruit and Nuts (1989), what was on the menu at the Tyringham naturopathic clinic, near Newport Pagnell.

Once Upon a Time (1990), spotlight on Britain's biggest amateur panto, with the Ipswich Co-op Juniors.

No Turning Back (1992), a tribute to Caister lifeboat coxwain **Benny Read**.

An Indian Summer (1992), the life and work of **Leonard Cheshire**, including his final pilgrimage to India.

Moving Targets (1995), Norfolk surgeon **Robin Coupland's** campaign on behalf of the innocent victims of modern weapons of war.

The Club (1996), behind the scenes with staff and customers at Dukes nightclub, Chelmsford.

Norwich Cathedral – History in the Making (1996), Nigel Havers narrating a celebration of 900 years of one of the region's finest buildings.

Brawn Beautiful (1998), the extraordinary life of **Gayle Moher**, top body builder with a tragic past.

Ray Davies – Visions of England (1998), the world premiere of the singer and composer's first major work for orchestra and chorus.

Spitfire (1998), the 60th anniversary of the RAF fighter plane with exclusive film from the Spitfire airshow at Duxford.

The Big One (1999), behind the scenes with supporters, police, stewards and officials at a local derby between Norwich City and Ipswich Town.

A sense of history...

WHEN, in 1997, **Prince Edward** wrote and presented a six-part series about links between the East of England and his royal ancestors through the ages, he was following a long tradition of historical documentaries on Anglia Television.

The series, *Crown and Country*, made for Anglia by the Prince's production company, Ardent, visited historically important towns, castles, houses and antiquities, and featured interviews with local experts, re-enactments of significant events and investigation of some of the most fascinating stories from the region's past.

During the making of the series, Edward revealed that the ancestor he would most like to have met is **Henry VIII**. He acknowledged that Henry was "a man who revolts so many because he was a tyrant who killed two of his wives". "Yet", said Edward, "he was also a remarkable sportsman, had a creative flair and was, by many accounts, extremely able.

"He intrigues me because of all the contradictions and I would love to know what sort of man he really was. I regard kings and queens as mere mortals who, by fortune or misfortune, depending on which way you look at it, are thrown into an extraordinary position.

"Some excel, some fail and others just survive. That perspective makes me want to know the personalities more, thus making them three-dimensional rather than the one-dimensional characters of so many text books."

The series began at Britain's oldest royal burial site, Sutton Hoo in Suffolk, one of the archaeological discoveries of the century.

Archaeology has been an important component of Anglia's delves into the past, especially in its early years when Cambridge archaeology professor, **Glyn Daniel**, was both a director of the company and an

Prince Edward takes part in an historical re-enactment for *Crown and Country.*

experienced programme-maker, having been voted Television Personality of the Year in 1955 when he was a regular team member on the BBC programme *Animal, Vegetable or Mineral.*

His first Anglia programme was *Town and Gown*, a series about life in Cambridge. In 1962, he presented *Once a Kingdom* which was television's first in-depth look at the history of the East of England. It led Anglia on to more ambitious ventures.

Who Were the British?, supervised by Daniel and narrated by another Cambridge lecturer, **Dr Brian Hope-Taylor**, in 1966, was Anglia's costliest documentary series up to that time. The six, half-hour documentaries about life in the Stone, Bronze and Iron Ages, and during the Roman occupation, took more than a year to make.

Film crews travelled widely in Britain and Europe and the first major location was the Colosseum in Rome. One unit, using a six-seater aircraft, lunched in the Orkneys, had supper the same day in Norway and breakfasted next morning in Denmark.

A sequel, *The Lost Centuries*, spanned the Dark Ages between the fall of Rome and the beginning of the Renaissance. It was even more costly and took four years to make, camera teams going to Israel and Jordan as well as many parts of Europe.

In a desert near Amman, in 1968, the team was caught up in the Arab-Israeli conflict when the Israelis crossed the Jordan river. The crew headed towards the fighting and shot news film of it. They were then hijacked by Palestinian guerrillas who thrust a grenade under the nose of the cameraman and demanded to be driven to Amman. The unit complied.

Digging for Yesterday, presented by **Dick Joice** in 1977, focused on industrial archaeologists involved in saving national treasures. It included a visit to County Durham, birthplace of Britain's railways, and Anglia helped finance the building of a replica of George Stephenson's pioneering steam engine, Locomotion.

Prince Edward demonstrates an historical leaning as photographed by Cati Majtenyi during the filming of *Crown and Country.*

A 1980 series was digging into the past much closer to Anglia's home. *The Dig on Our Doorstep*, directed by archaeologist **Paul Jordan**, a new addition to Anglia's programme-making team, detailed the excavations carried out before new offices were built at the back of Anglia's Norwich studios.

Anglia donated £21,000 towards the cost of the dig, undertaken by the Norfolk Archaeological Unit. It revealed a Saxon church which had graves, some with well-preserved skeletons, many of children.

The resulting programme, narrated by **Rene Cutforth**, also looked at some of the medieval discoveries on the site including personal items like a bowl, a comb and a pair of tweezers.

Excavations unearth a Saxon graveyard behind Anglia House.

Glyn Daniel introducing *North Sea Saga.*

Paul Jordan and the cameras were back for a much bigger archaelogical operation on an adjacent site during construction of Norwich's Castle Mall Shopping Centre. *Digging Deep*, screened in 1993, revealed the host of fascinating finds made during the four years of painstaking study. Three years earlier, *Lost and Found in Fenland* had revealed the story behind the discovery of the 3,000-year-old Bronze Age settlement at Flag Fen, near Peterborough.

North Sea Saga was a 1982 four-part archaeological series – with an introduction by **Glyn Daniel** – looking at the links between East Anglia and north-west Europe. It traced evidence dating back more than 8,000 years to a time when there was a land bridge across the North Sea which meant our ancestors could have walked to the continent.

Eastern Approaches, presented by archaeologist **Tony Gregory**, in 1986, highlighted the vulnerability of East Anglia's coastline to foreign invasion through the ages. Gregory was also the first presenter of *Look What We've Found*, a 1983 series about the latest finds made by archaeologists in the East of England. A second series was screened in 1985 and introduced by *Mastermind's* **Magnus Magnusson**, himself a keen archaeologist.

Glyn Daniel returned to the screen in 1985 to present *Myth America*, a documentary for Channel 4, in which he traced the facts and fantasies surrounding the true origins of the American nation.

War and peace...

Juliet Stevenson with *Anglia at Peace* producers Carolyn Schagen and Nigel Flynn.

WARTIME recollection has figured highly in Anglia's output, largely because the region was so closely affected by both world wars. Award-winning series *Anglia at War*, first shown in May, 1992, recalled, in vivid detail, sights and sounds of the second world war in the East of England.

Narrated by **Sir Ian McKellen**, *Anglia at War* was a four-year project commissioned by Anglia from Norwich-based independent producer Fourth Estate. It made extensive use of archive footage, photographs and first-hand accounts of people who lived through the period.

It was followed, in 1996, by a series from the same producers called *Anglia at Peace*, this time narrated by actress **Juliet Stevenson**, in which she recounted the story of how the region emerged from the dark days of war into a new era of hope, change and expectation. The next year found **Timothy West** providing the commentary for another retrospective series *Life and Times*, which reflected on the amazing changes that took place in the East of England in the first 70 years of the century.

Among other wartime stories covered by Anglia was *Woodbine Willie – His Life and Times*, networked on ITV on Remembrance Sunday, 1983. It traced the moving story of First World War chaplain, the **Rev. Geoffrey Studdart Kennedy**, who became a national hero in the first world war for his ministry to British troops on the bloody battlefields of France.

In *The First Casualty*, a 1989 production, film historian **John Huntley** looked at the battle for the hearts and minds of the British public waged on cinema screens up and down the country during the 1914-18 war. It was the first time the screen had been used as a mass propaganda weapon.

And *Woburn at War*, screened in 1987, featured actor **Marius Goring** recalling his real-life role as one of the staff operating a "black propaganda" radio station broadcasting into the heart of Nazi Germany from Woburn, in Bedfordshire.

A 1994 programme, *Flight from Colditz*, recalled the famous wartime escape attempts, including the first British TV reconstructions of events in the notorious Nazi fortress. Five former PoWs took part in the programme, reliving their experiences on an emotional return to Colditz Castle.

War in the air was recalled in *The Men Who Flew the Liberators*, a 1972 film looking at the impact the United States 8th Army Air Force made on local communities when they arrived in the East of England during World War II. And in a 1985 programme, *Bomber*, veterans of the RAF's 7 Squadron made a nostalgic return to their old base at Oakington, near Cambridge, from where they flew Lancasters on raids over Germany. *The Forgotten Bomber*, in 1989, focused on the Bristol Blenheim, and attempts to get the last surviving operational plane flying again after it crashed two years earlier.

A flyer of a different era was featured in *A Magnificent Man in His Flying Machine*, a much-acclaimed profile of pioneer 19th century aircraft designer **Sir George Cayley**. Anglia had a wooden glider built to Cayley's specifications, using the same materials which had been available to him in 1852. And cameras recorded an historic moment when the 39ft-long aircraft, with a 30ft wingspan, flew at Brompton Dale, in Yorkshire, where Cayley had carried out his experiments 120 years earlier.

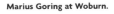

Wartime Norwich recalled in *Anglia at War*.

Former PoWs returing to Colditz.

Marius Goring at Woburn.

The replica Cayley glider in flight.

Actor **Robert Hardy** lent his history expertise to a 1982 Anglia programme called *Treasures of the Tower*. Hardy, an authority on the English longbow, gave viewers a guided tour of an exhibition of armoury from the Tower of London – on display at the Sainsbury Centre at the University of East Anglia.

There was a very different feel to Anglia's most recent retrospective series. *The Sixties*, screened in 1998, looked back at the decade that marked huge changes in the nation's way of life – its social attitudes, environment, technology and culture – and recalled some of the landmark issues and events of the era in the eastern counties.

The programmes, narrated by local broadcaster, **Ian Masters**, used film from the Anglia archives – most of it not seen since it was first broadcast more than 30 years ago – with then and now interviews to show what the decade meant to ordinary people in the towns and villages of the region.

Magnus Magnusson presenting *Look What We've Found.*

Robert Hardy filming *Treasures of the Tower.*

Summer of discontent down on the farm

FARMERS were up in arms in the summer of 1991 when Anglia announced it was axing a programme that had been an agricultural institution in the East of England for 32 years.

For many, *Farming Diary* had become as much part of a traditional Sunday down on the farm as roast beef and Yorkshire pudding. It was Anglia's longest-running series, having started within days of the station's 1959 opening, and the agricultural community had come to regard it as their own.

The decision to end it was described as 'incredible' by Norfolk National Farmers' Union chairman, **William Brigham**. More than 300 farmers and growers in the county signed a protest petition, and the *Eastern Daily Press* published an editorial questioning the wisdom of the decision.

But there were sound broadcasting reasons for the move. Anglia pointed out that far fewer people were employed in agriculture than in earlier times, and *Farming Diary* – as a show for, by and about farmers – was too narrow in its perspective for the 1990s.

Heralding a new programme devoted to rural issues, **Bill Smith**, who had produced *Farming Diary* since 1977, told the *EDP* that Anglia would continue to cover major farming stories. "There is tremendous general interest and concern about what happens in the countryside. We expect to make the news as well as report it," he said.

And so *Farming Diary* was gone, replaced by *Countrywide* and its successor, *A Place in the Country*, both of which successfully achieved Anglia's aim of appealing to a wider audience by covering a greater diversity of countryside stories.

Farming Diary occupies a special place in Anglia's history. At the height of its powers it achieved international eminence, reporting widely from abroad – particularly the United States and Europe – and its programme-making team produced a number of award-winning documentaries for regional and network transmission.

In 1959, Anglia's directors, led by their farmer-chairman, **Lord Townshend**, regarded a farming programme as essential. Agriculture was still by far the main occupation in the region, and they had the ideal man to present the new programme – a personable young West Norfolk farmer called **Dick Joice**.

Farming Diary had the same signature tune throughout its 32 years – *Folk Songs from Somerset* – and its regular Sunday lunchtime programme was followed

Peter Longstaff at work on his farm.

particularly keenly by farmers and growers for news of the latest machinery and cultivation techniques.

Over the years, programme topics ranged from the spread of Dutch elm disease to the problems of workers in tied cottages; from the effects of import levies to the technicalities of a blackcurrant harvester.

Once Britain took the Common Market plunge in 1973, reports from and about Brussels became a regular feature. And the EC (or EEC as it was known in earlier times) gave rise to many special programmes.

They included *Too Much of a Good Thing* that looked at the reasons for food surpluses in Europe, and *The Place That God Forgot*, showing how Euro funding was helping a backward area in southern Italy. Another special, *Once Bitten*, highlighted the threat of rabies entering Britain from the continent, while *Going Dutch* examined the trend towards farmers from the continent – and particularly Holland – buying up prime agricultural land in Britain.

The intriguingly titled *Switch on the Chickens, Put the Cows on the Roundabout*, featured in the Top Ten programme ratings when shown on the ITV network. It showed the latest food-producing units in use on the continent. The switched-on chickens

were in an automated hen house in Germany, where 120,000 were tended by just one man, while the revolving cows were in Venice where a thousand were carried to the milking parlour on a turntable.

In 1975, the *Great Grain Drain* investigated the rise in world food prices after Russia bought up American grain.

On the home front, *Farming Diary* reported on some all-too-familiar problems facing the British pig and dairy industries in 1979, the implications for farmers of the 1981 Wildlife and Countryside Act, and, in 1985, how agriculture was – or rather was not – responding to the latest medical advice on the advantages of low-fat diets and healthy eating.

A remarkable farmer featured in one special documentary. **Peter Longstaff**, of Plumstead Green, near Norwich, was a victim of the drug thalidomide which led to 450 deformed babies being born in Britain in the early Sixties.

Green Farm told how, despite having no arms, he ran his own successful pig farm and used his feet to tackle every activity, from driving a tractor to shaving and even throwing darts in his local pub. "If you have a positive attitude you will get on. That's how you have to look at it," he said.

Oliver Walston taking grain to Eritrea.

Oliver Walston, always colourful and never afraid to challenge established thinking, made some memorable contributions to Anglia's documentary output. The most vivid was in 1984 when he organised a famine relief appeal among Britain's farmers for the starving people of Eritrea, the war-torn rebel territory of Ethiopia.

A special 1983 programme, 'The Last Straw', dealt with the heated debate over straw burning. Cambridgeshire farmer, writer and broadcaster Oliver Walston, who had joined the *Farming Diary* presentation team, investigated other possible uses for the millions of tons of straw produced in Britain each year – including animal feed, fuel and fibre-boarding.

Udder to butter – the *Farming Diary* team record the action.

He travelled to Eritrea with an Anglia crew to report on the first shiploads of wheat from the *Send a Tonne to Africa* appeal arriving in Port Sudan. They brought back moving footage of the grain reaching desperate refugees in camps controlled by the Eritrean People's Liberation Front.

The *Farming Diary* team was one of the first western TV crews to enter the war zone, and they had to travel by night along hazardous mountain roads to avoid the fighting.

On a lighter note, in 1986, Walston's farm was the scene of an off-beat achievement by *Farming Diary* in setting up a new bread-and-butter-making record. Part of a wheat field was harvested and **John Stubbing**, of Norwich millers Read, Woodrow and Sons, sliced 11 minutes off the world bread-making record by producing two loaves of bread from the grain in a field-to-loaf time of 29 minutes and 37.94 seconds.

And Cambridgeshire dairyman **Stan Gillett** and Norfolk farmer's wife, **Mrs Greta Allen**, set the first udder-to-butter record at 17 minutes and 23.5 seconds for milking a cow and producing butter in the field. The attempts were overseen by the High Sheriff of Cambridgeshire,

Dr Irwin Peck, and the claims submitted to the *Guinness Book of Records*.

But there was a hiccup a couple of days later when the previous bread-making champion, Cambridgeshire baker **Owen North**, claimed his record stood because the *Farming Diary* team should have baked 13 loaves – a baker's dozen – and not just the two loaves produced by John Stubbing.

However, producer **Bill Smith** said the *Farming Diary* claim would be for the fastest bread-and-butter-making record, which had never been set before.

Back on the serious side, a 1988 one-hour special, *Living Off the Land*, looked at the crisis looming over land surpluses and over-production. One expert predicted that 20 million acres – an area the size of England's 25 largest counties – could be out of production by 2015. The programme examined how farmers were diversifying into butterfly and llama farming – and some taking alternative employment altogether.

With agricultural issues becoming increasingly international in the 1980s, Anglia's farming team was more occupied than ever by what was happening beyond the field boundaries of the East of England.

A 1987 documentary featured one of the biggest – and most controversial – farmers in America. **John J. Greytak** was a 'sodbuster' – a man who bought up and ploughed vast tracts of prairie (or sod), using his huge 525 horsepower tractors and 70ft-wide cultivators. The programme cited growing fears that such practices caused considerable damage, such as soil erosion, to the environment.

An earlier trip to the great grain belt of the American mid-West had yielded material for another ITV network documentary, *The Food War*, which examined the potential for a trade war between the United States and the European Community. The kind of tensions examined in the programme have resurfaced a number of times since, and 15 years after the programme was made a 'food war' is still regarded as likely between the two agricultural superpowers.

A crew spent two weeks in the Soviet Union in 1988 as the first western TV programme allowed full, unfettered access to Communist farms. They went to Latvia, Lithuania and Ukraine to report on the effects of **Mikhail Gorbachov's** restructuring programme on Soviet agriculture – and the implications for EC farmers. Four years earlier the programme had gained permission to go into East Germany to film on a state farm and at a nearby co-operative venture.

Dr. Irwin Peck samples the finished products of the bread-and-butter making record.

When *Farming Diary* celebrated its 30th birthday, in 1989, the occasion was marked by the first interview with the new Agriculture Minister, **John Gummer**, who was asked about the changed emphasis of his department to a ministry of food rather than food production. And **Dick Joice** returned to chat to **David Richardson** about the early days of *Farming Diary*.

Richardson was one of the presenters most associated with the programme. A farmer from Wymondham, Norfolk, he was a much-respected figure in agricultural broadcasting, and was named Communicator of the Year by the Guild of Agricultural Journalists in 1989. He had started his broadcasting career with Anglia in 1960, left for the BBC three years later, but returned to *Farming Diary* in 1979, at which time his co-presenter was Cambridgeshire farmer **John Jenkins**. Richardson also presented many of Anglia's countryside programmes for the ITV network series *About Britain*.

In addition to Richardson and **Oliver Walston**, the regular presentation and reporting team in the final ten years of *Farming Diary* and the associated special documentaries, included Cambridgeshire journalist **Barry Wilson** and associate producers **Richard Foxton** and **Kim Whittaker**.

Another part of *Farming Diary's* output for many years was a quiz and public speaking contest for young farmers called 'Face the Camera'. The winner received a trophy and cheque, and in most years, a kiss from the reigning 'Miss Anglia' who made the presentations. Contestants had to answer questions on farming, and then give a one-minute talk on their chosen agricultural topic.

Dick Joice and David Richardson.

Animal crackers...

ANIMAL programmes – whether about wild creatures or pets – attract a wide audience and Anglia was one of the first ITV companies to tune in to this appeal.

Several of the early series were presented by Norfolk naturalist **Philip Wayre**, known chiefly in recent years for his efforts to re-establish the otter in the wild in Britain.

In December, 1963, he launched one of the earliest programmes of its kind, *Pets' Club*, with East Anglian children bringing their charges to the studio and discussing their care and welfare with him. Three years later Wayre hosted *Nature Trail*, in which teams of boys and girls from secondary schools in the region showed off their powers of observation.

Then, in 1968, he introduced *The Survival Game*, a network round-Britain quiz about the world's wildlife. The top prize for the first series winners – a team of girls from Stoke on Trent – was a ten-day safari to East Africa. Cameras followed the winners on their trip for *Schoolgirl Safari*, which was shown the following year and a second series of the quiz followed soon after.

Naturalist Philip Wayre hosting one of the early animal programmes.

With one of Europe's largest open zoos – Whipsnade – being in the Anglia region it was not surprising that a series of programmes looking at its animals and aims was launched in 1973. Twenty five years later cameras returned to the 600 acres of rolling countryside just outside Dunstable, in Bedfordshire, for a 13-part visit with *EastEnders* star **Pam St Clement**.

For six months the cameras captured the behind-the-scenes activity. Joining the routine, and not-so-routine, work brought presenter Pam into close contact with some of her favourite animals, including elephants, giraffes, hippos, zebras, rhinos and cheetahs.

"These days zoos like Whipsnade are the key to protecting our wildlife for the future," she said. "They work hard at breeding endangered species and are actively involved in releasing animals back into the wild so they can roam free and, hopefully, carry on breeding."

Presenting her first television wildlife series was a project close to the heart of the keen conservationist and animal lover.

"Animals have always been a passion with me," she admitted. "I was brought up on a farm and it taught me the beginnings of the relationship between people and animals.

Pam St Clement makes friends with one of Whipsnade Zoo's residents.

"I wanted to be a vet when I was a youngster. My pride and joy was a copy of *Black's Veterinary Dictionary* which was given to me on my sixteenth birthday and was carried around constantly."

During the series viewers were introduced to several of the keepers, vets and the animals they cared for, including Marcus the baby giraffe, Anna the elephant with a bad toe, Bert the hand-reared vulture who thought he was human and Sydney, the macaw who couldn't fly.

Fly-on-the-wall...

Desmond Morris with a basketful of Somali cats.

THE VET, shown in both the Anglia and Meridian regions, was a six-part fly-on-the-wall series which focused on the Essex practice of **Andrew Scott**, an experienced veterinary surgeon with a practice at Purleigh, near Maldon. One of the first cases to be introduced by Mr Scott, a leading figure in the Animal Welfare Foundation and British Veterinary Association, was bad, ugly and certainly made a big impact. The 'patient' was a Vietnamese pot-bellied pig which needed worming.

An innovative aspect of the series at the time was following cases home from the surgery so people could see the animals in their normal environment: "It really helps to show what they mean to their owners," said Mr Scott.

One of the longest-running series of the genre in recent years on Anglia has been *Animal Country*, introduced by **Desmond Morris** and **Sarah Kennedy** for the first time in 1991 and for the last in 1996.

Said Morris, whose interest in zoology was first sparked by the discovery of his great grandfather's old microscope, slides and a natural history book in a trunk in the family attic: "This sort of programme has been missing from British television and we thought it was time to bring it back."

The man who started his animal TV career in 1956 with Granada's long-running *Zoo Time* added: "There is a huge interest in companion animals – with over seven million dogs and a similar number of cats in this country – and it is important that people are kept in touch with them."

The very first programme visited the Otter Trust at Earsham, near Bungay, in Suffolk, and called in on a Norfolk woman who had spent more than 20 years looking after everything from dogs and donkeys to gulls, hawks, owls and pigeons on their five acres of land.

"I joined the RSPCA as a little girl before the war – and they got me for life," **Brenda Shaw** explained.

Celebrities who featured with their animals included **Alexandra Bastedo**, from the Sixties action series *The Champions*; best-selling novelist **Jilly Cooper**; broadcaster, organic farmer and Council for the Protection of Rural England president **Jonathan Dimbleby**; explorer **Ranulph Fiennes**; actress **Susan George**;

broadcasters **Paul Heiney** and **Libby Purves**; TV presenter **Matthew Kelly**; *Born Free* actress **Virginia McKenna**; comedy writer **Carla Lane** and biologist and naturalist **Roger Tabor**. **David Attenborough** appeared in one programme and naturalists **Gerald** and **Lee Durrell** (**David Bellamy** took over after Gerald's death in 1995) were regulars in the end-of-series judging programmes. The real point of the series, however, was the ordinary unsung heroes to be found working away from the spotlight to improve the lot of animals. Each series featured one person judged to have done most for animals. They received a £5,000 prize to be ploughed into their chosen animal project.

An amusing incident during the last but one series came when **Desmond Morris** went to point out an innocent-looking, orange-coloured fish in a lily pond during filming at some tropical gardens. As he spoke to camera the fish leapt from the pool and attached itself firmly to his finger with its teeth. Fortunately, it soon released its grip and no great damage was done, despite a fair amount of blood. Eventually the shocked and bemused presenter discovered that the fish in question was often fed on bananas and had simply mistaken the Morris finger for one of its favourite snacks.

"I was attacked by a number of creatures during *Zoo Time*, and once had an uncomfortably close scrape with a shark. But it's the first time I've ever been bitten by a fish," laughed Morris.

Helping hand... Carla Lane tends to a baby squirrel.

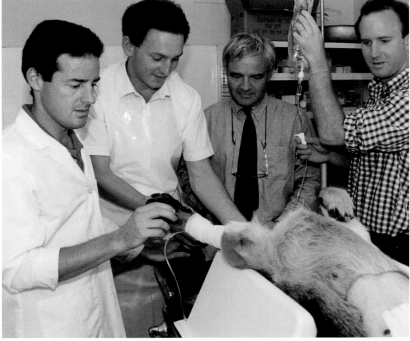

Essex vet Andrew Scott (second right) with colleagues in the operating theatre.

A kiss for Sarah Kennedy from an angora kid in *Animal Country*.

All in the line of duty... a cameraman gets more than his feet wet.

Paul Heiney and his Suffolk Punches in *Animal Count...*

Ironically, he was doing some fish behaviour studies at the time, in preparation for a book: "This might make a useful contribution to the project," he added.

Wildlife Rescue joined Anglia's menagerie in 1997, with vet **Mark Evans** taking a look at everyday problems faced by the wildlife on our doorstep – and again at the role played by humans who set out to save them. Evans became a TV presenter only by accident, after seeing a TV-am item about its search for the fattest cat in the country.

As one of the first vets in the country to run weight clinics for dogs and cats, he didn't see the funny side of the piece and, although he had never before contacted a newspaper or radio or TV station, was so furious that he called TV-am.

"Amazingly, I got straight through to the researcher and gave her a mouthful about irresponsible programme-making," he recalled.

"About ten weeks later they rang and said they'd found one of the fattest cats in the country and wanted me to talk with the owner."

The fact that he got very angry in the studio obviously went down well and he received several invitations back before working on other

Michaela Strachan with Britain's rarest amphibian, the Natterjack toad.

Vet Mark Evans examines an injured badger in *Wildlife Rescue*.

programmes such as *Wild Bunch*, *Good Morning with Anne and Nick*, *Playdays* and *The Holiday Programme*.

For the second series, in 1998, Evans was joined by *The Really Wild Show's* **Michaela Strachan**, whose role as a wildlife presenter grew out of programmes like *The Wide Awake Club* and *Owl TV*. Despite travelling the world to be filmed with all kinds of exotic animals, she was glad to be banging the drum for Britain's wildlife.

"I think it is important to make people realise what's around them, particularly when it is endangered. You can't really go round telling other people to save their wildlife until you start saving creatures on your own doorstep."

Vet Evans also featured as host of *The Wildlife Quiz*, produced by Anglia for Channel 5's *Wild on Five* evening in December, 1997. In it, two teams of animal show celebrities found a new habitat for their talents and tested their knowledge during rounds involving 'true or false' statements, mystery animal sounds and objects, identification of young animals, endangered species and 'video nasties'.

Taking part were **Terry Nutkins** (*Pets Win Prizes*), **Jamie Crittall** (TV vet), **Shauna Lowry** (*Animal Hospital*), **Nick Baker** (*Really Wild Show*), **Wendy Turner** (*Pet Rescue/Absolutely Animals*) and **Simon Tonge** (London Zoo curator).

Thanks for the memory...

David Dimbleby
Broadcaster who worked for Anglia during his summer vacation when he was at Oxford

"A glorious summer at the end of the 50s. Huge East Anglian skies. Strange stories to cover. And *About Anglia* trouncing the BBC's *Tonight* from the start. BLISS."

Derek Jacobi
Actor

"One of the first television plays I ever did was from Anglia, called *The Photographer* – since then I returned for several *Tales of the Unexpected* and voiced *Survival* episodes. I loved working in Norwich – the combination of that beautiful city and those warmly welcoming studios was knockout. Good restaurants, too."

Edward Woodward
Actor who appeared in some of Anglia's early dramas and lent his distinctive voice to several Survival *narratives*

"Anglia was one of the companies all actors desperately wanted to work for – its standing far outweighed its size. Anglia always had the best dramas and the best directors and everyone wanted to work with them."

Anthony Valentine
Actor

"Working for Anglia has very strong associations for me. Perhaps foremost in my mind is *Survival*... 38 years of the most incredible wildlife programmes, and I've been lucky enough to be involved with quite a few of them. I never cease to be amazed at the talent and dedication of the people at the sharp end who often spend years in a difficult, sometimes hostile, situation to bring back for us a world we would otherwise never see.

"Being an actor I should perhaps have put drama first. Again working for Anglia has always been a very happy experience. Anglia has always loved drama. It's never been just another part of its output, it's been special. Perhaps the strongest feeling I have about Anglia is a feeling of family. Whatever you're doing everyone is involved and everyone seems to care.

"If I had to find three words that mean Anglia to me they would be quality, creativity and care. Oh and let me throw in a fourth, enjoyment. I've always enjoyed working for Anglia."

Malcolm Bradbury
Writer and academic who lives in Norwich

"Besides the wonderful regional and countryside programmes, and the splendid history of *Survival*, I most fondly remember the great Anglia drama department of Sir John Woolf and John Rosenberg. The amazing output of *Tales of the Unexpected*, the fine record of PD James, even a series of my own (*Anything More Would Be Greedy*). Anglia then had its distinct TV theatre, which nourished both TV and the region. I hope it comes back."

John Bly
Antiques dealer who presented Heirloom

"Working with Anglia Television for the duration of the *Heirloom* programme was a great privilege and huge fun. From the short inserts for *About Anglia* with Jane Probyn, to the live appearances at the County Shows, and the networked half-hour series, I learnt all the broadcasting skills I have in the hands of the best ever people in the business. Thank you Anglia."

Sir Clement Freud
Politician and broadcaster

"I always thought my 1963 appointment as football correspondent to Anglia TV – with the provision of a bicycle to get me from Carrow Road to the studio – would be the beginning of a famous career. Alas."

Bobby Robson
Football manager who expressed his "appreciation of the coverage Anglia has given to sport in general, and football in particular – especially the coverage of Ipswich Town – at home and abroad."

"One particular incident I recall was after a match at Portman Road at the end of December, when I was being interviewed by Gerry Harrison. Gerry asked me what I would like to see in the New Year. I replied 'brighter soccer' – just as the floodlights were turned off and left us in the dark! There must be footage of this in your archives."

Martin Brundle
Racing driver turned TV presenter

"As a Norfolk boy, Anglia has played a big role in my life, getting all the news and sport as a youngster. Many a time a camera crew has been round my house for interviews about the latest trials and tribulations of Grand Prix racing. Indeed, it was through Kevin Piper (Anglia's Head of Sport) that I was introduced to the idea of being involved with the new Formula One production – that was as a consultant and I ended up working on the programme. Another pleasant surprise was that last year Malcolm Allsop (Anglia's Director of Programmes) asked me to present a couple of pilots of *Great Escapes*. You will, therefore, not be surprised to find that I am rather fond of Anglia Television, even if they are reminding me of my own imminent 40th anniversary."

Gerald Sinstadt
Sports commentator

"Anglia will always have a place in my affections. It was at Anglia that my career as a television commentator began, under the most genial and inspirational of directors, Bob Gardam. From Colchester, Lincoln and Northampton to the World Cup Finals may seem like a giant leap but it wouldn't have happened without those first small steps."

Christine Webber
Writer, broadcaster, agony aunt, psychotherapist and former About Anglia *presenter*

"When I presented *About Anglia*, I really thought that I had the best job in the entire world. One day I interviewed Prince Philip about the Duke of Edinburgh Award Scheme and the next I was at the circus in Great Yarmouth learning how to be a trapeze artist. It was never dull.

"I was also given responsibility for all social action and medical content in *About Anglia*, which helped pave the way for my present career. We ran all sorts of campaigns – like buying a guide dog – and ended up buying 14. We helped to raise money for the first full body scanner at Addenbrooke's Hospital in Cambridge as well as the new lifeboat for Aldeburgh.

"We also worked with various adoption agencies to bring 'difficult to place' kids to the public's attention. It was a huge success, not just in terms of the children who appeared on the programme, but also for many other youngsters languishing in care throughout the region who were adopted as a result of our viewers' new awareness.

"My time at Anglia also provided me with some wonderful mates, including my closest friend, Helen McDermott, and an extra special one in Dr David Delvin, who used to present the medical slot with me. Our liaison was such a happy one that we made it legal – and have been married for 11 years."

Jane Probyn (now Jane Bishop)
Presented About Anglia *in the 1970s, and started* Heirloom *with John Bly*

"I first heard of Anglia Television when my agent called and said they were looking for a reporter for the six o'clock magazine programme. 'Where are they based?' I asked. 'Norwich,' came the reply. 'Where's that?' (O-level geography was not on my CV). 'Well, dear,' she said in her soft Irish brogue, 'you get on a train at Liverpool Street and when it stops, you get off.' I did – and stayed for nine years.

"I have some great memories of my time at Anglia – and some amusing ones, too. Christmas at Woburn is one in particular. *About Anglia* invited viewers to Woburn Abbey to find out what Christmas with the Duke and Duchess of Bedford would be like. After a tour of the house and interviews with their graces and staff, the grand finale was Christmas Eve dinner in the Canaletto Room.

"My part was to ask the Duke about the wonderful paintings while helping myself to the fish course from a large salver held by the butler. As the cameras rolled, however, I had extreme difficulty in getting to grips with the elaborate piece of haute cuisine. It was only when the butler helpfully whispered, 'The fish madam, the FISH', I realised I had been struggling to serve myself the inedible decorative centrepiece."

Potato unearths a future in the past...

IT was one of those moments that happens to all presenters of live TV shows sometime. Back in the Sixties, **Dick Joice** was introducing an edition of *About Anglia* when suddenly there was a major technical hitch and he found himself facing the camera with no idea what was happening next.

As every broadcasting professional knows, the important thing in such circumstances is not to 'corpse'. Joice, a collector of curios all his life, happened to have a potato shaped like a duck in the drawer of the studio desk – no one knows quite why to this day – so he fished it out and filled in the crucial time by talking about odd-shaped vegetables.

It was a moment of destiny for Joice and for Anglia. The humble potato gave rise to *Bygones*, a programme that ran

for 20 years and remains one of the best-remembered and most popular Anglia ever produced.

Joice explained later: "It made me realise I always needed to have something to hand to talk about – just in case. So I started taking funny little domestic things, like old apple peelers and lamp-glass cleaners, into the studio and putting them up as puzzle items. They did so well and we had so much correspondence that we realised we had something for a slot here, and gave it 15 minutes."

In 1967, the slot became half an hour, and spun off from *About Anglia* as a programme in its own right, with Joice as presenter. "It was my wife Jean who thought of calling the programme *Bygones*," said Joice. "It was not a word that was used a lot in general terms in those days, even by museums."

The programmes continued to include weekly 'mystery objects', some from Joice's own assortment of agricultural and domestic gadgets he had started collecting as a boy, others supplied by museums or sent in by viewers.

So popular did *Bygones* become, it gave rise to a series of books and even its own museum. And, nine years after Anglia had apparently consigned the programme to television history, it was reincarnated as *Bygone Days*, now presented by **Helen McDermott**, but still with its original *'Wheels'* signature tune evoking images of a Victorian fairground or street-corner barrel organ.

Bygones featured a weekly 'mystery object', which often came from Joice's own collection of old gadgets.

Gamekeeper Basil Goffin with Eddie Anderson.

Seventeen *Bygones* books, published over five years from 1976 by the Boydell Press, gave detailed accounts of many of the crafts and customs of the past featured in the TV series. And the introduction printed inside the front cover summed up perfectly what *Bygones* was all about: "A series of programmes that looks at life as it used to be yesterday . . . about people, their work, their memories, their everyday life."

The museum is the *Bygones Collection* housed at Holkham Hall, in North Norfolk, seat of the Earl of Leicester, who provided a permanent home for many of the artefacts collected by **Dick Joice** and others over the years. The exhibits, from traction engines to corkscrews, number several thousand items.

Bygones was both entertaining and educational. It gave viewers glimpses of crafts and skills fast disappearing from the towns and villages of the East of England as technology and cheap, disposable goods rendered them obsolete.

The series threw up some wonderful country characters. Early on there was peg-legged **John Bone**, a North Norfolk smallholder and 'dicky dealer' who toured the villages around Cley-next-the-Sea with a donkey-driven cart that looked like a chicken house on wheels. He had a dog called **Toby** and as they passed the village shop,

Bone would give the dog a penny which it would carry in its mouth into the shop, place on the counter and wait to be given a bar of chocolate. Then Toby would chase after his master who would divide the chocolate between the dog, the donkey and himself.

Some unlikely philosophers were discovered, too, among the craftspeople and agricultural workers of the region. Gamekeepers like **Basil Goffin** and **Jack Rumsey** were never short of an opinion on any subject, particularly poaching, and Fenland railwayman and molecatcher **Arthur Randell** had a wealth of knowledge of country ways.

In the city, **Jack Amis** and his partner **Dolly** made a meagre living grinding knives on the streets of Norwich. But Amis loved the independence the way of life gave him. "I am a spring-born bird. I want to be free. I don't want to bow down to anybody and I enjoy every minute," he said.

Veteran Suffolk cider worker **Harry Sparrow** gave a moving account for the camera of war, comradeship and humour during the dark days of 1914-18. An equally evocative testimony was by former Royal Flying Corps pilot **Tim Harvey** who described what it was like to see action in the air, where life expectancy could be counted in days, if not hours.

Humour was an essential feature of *Bygones*. Eccentricity often went hand in hand with individuality in the days when tradespeople were not required to conform to the kind of rules and regulations that exist today. Health and safety officers, for instance, would probably take Suffolk chimney sweep **Doddy Diggens** to the cleaners nowadays if they found him firing a 12-bore shotgun up the chimney to loosen the soot, as he demonstrated for a 1971 *Bygones*.

There was usually something to smile about as well in the musical item that signed off most of the programmes – like **Jolly Jack Andrews** singing to his pigs, **Bill Taylor**, a spoons-playing butler, or those makeshift musicians who got tunes (of sorts) out of a handsaw, a broom or a row of bottles.

Even an undertaker got in on the comedy act. **Hubert Aldridge**, of Walpole, with jokes like: "What's the difference between a laundryman and an undertaker? A laundryman stiffens collars and an undertaker collars stiff 'uns!"

Jolly Jack Andrews singing to his pigs.

George Lamb, gipsy pegmaker, in 1975.

Worldwide appeal...

The Rev W Awdry, creator of *Thomas the Tank Engine*.

Billy Connolly with Eddie Anderson.

Naughty girl... Helen Mc Dermott gets a taste of Victorian school discipline at Stomarket's Museum of East Anglian Life.

COLLECTIONS featured on *Bygones* knew no bounds. In the 1984 series, for instance, ornamental bath feet, milk bottles, tractor seats and garden syringes were among those to rank alongside the comparatively common-place such as musical instruments, teddy bears and woodworking tools.

Bygones tackled many weightier matters, too, and often devoted a whole programme to a single topic. There were tears of the clown, for example, in a 1978 report about circus closures. The story of Chelmsford wireless pioneer Marconi was told in 1988 on the occasion his widow and daughter performed the official opening of an Essex local radio station, and the farming revolution in the eastern counties over the previous 40 years was reviewed in a special programme called *Acres of Change* in 1984.

The programme frequently travelled beyond the Anglia region for a good story. It met *Thomas the Tank Engine* creator, the **Rev. W. Awdry**, on the Talyllyn narrow gauge railway in North Wales. During the filming he marvelled at the number of 'takes' it took to satisfy a TV director's quest for perfection, and is reputed to have mused: "I never realised spontaneity took so much planning."

Cameras went to Perthshire to seek out one of the last commercial makers of paperweights, charted the restoration of a unique Victorian theatre in Newcastle, visited the world's largest water wheel on the Isle of

Man and featured one of the country's oldest working steam mill engines at a museum in Wigan.

There were even occasional sorties overseas, including a report about fishermen on horseback netting shrimps on the beaches of Flanders, a nostalgic visit to Bavaria by a group of East of England rail enthusiasts for a steam weekend marking the 150th anniversary of German railways, and two trips to America to cover stories with links back home to the East of England. Anglia's resident cook **Patrick Anthony** joined the team for a taste of the wine-making tradition on the island of Madeira.

There was good commercial reason for *Bygones* spreading its wings. The programme was not merely for Anglia consumption, but was taken by a number of other ITV companies and sold abroad. It was screened by *Discovery* in the United States and even travelled as far as Australia. In its regular seven o' clock Tuesday slot on Anglia, it often achieved an excellent 40 per

cent share of the audience. For some reason it was even more popular in Ulster, where a whopping 65 per cent share was not uncommon. Not unnaturally, *Bygones* made three visits to Ireland to cement this loyal following.

The series also had a number of famous guests over the years. **Billy Connolly** took part in a 1985 programme talking about his affection for the People's Palace museum in Glasgow. **Roy Hudd** told the stories of music hall star **George Robey** – known as The Prime Minister of Mirth in a near 60-year career. And writers **J B Priestley** and **John Osborne** were among those taking part, along with Hudd, in a programme about 'Cheeky Chappie' comedian **Max Miller**.

Wisbech and Upwell Tramway Centenary in 1983.

Hinge and Bracket make a guest appearance.

Former postal workers' union leader Tom Jackson.

Dick Joice demonstrates a portable shower.

J.B. Priestley who spoke about Max Miller.

Les Dawson and **Lord Delfont** were contributors to a programme in 1987 about Blackpool Tower. And in 1989 former postal workers' union leader **Tom Jackson** joined **Dick Joice** to talk about his passion for collecting old cookery books.

Although **Dick Joice** was undoubtedly 'Mr Bygones', others to have especially close associations with the programme were **Eddie Anderson**, who wrote and introduced many of the location reports, **John Huntley**, a regular contributor of items about transport and early film and cinema, and **David Kenten** who, as producer and director, developed and shaped the series from the late 1970s onward. But *Bygones* was one of the programmes almost everyone wanted to work on, and many others made sterling contributions to its success.

The programme's audience had a big influence on the content as well, as David Kenten acknowledged in 1986. "The fund of subjects seems to keep on growing, thanks largely to the number of viewers who write in with information and ideas."

It came as a surprise to many, therefore, when Anglia decided to take *Bygones* off the air two years later. It was felt the series had come to the end of its useful life and it was time to make way for new programme ideas – not a view shared by those most closely associated with the show, especially its presenter.

No one was happier than Joice, however, when the films he had introduced over the years were taken off the shelf and dusted down for screening again in two series of *Bygone Days* in 1997 and 1998. "I'm absolutely delighted it's coming back," he said. "I think interest is increasing in things of the past, particularly among young people." *Bygone Days* was presented from a different location each week by **Helen McDermott**, who provided updated information on many of the original items and sometimes interviewed those who

had taken part in earlier programmes. A new element was introduced in the form of material, previously unseen on television, from the files of the East Anglian Film Archive where, incidentally, the original *Bygones* programmes are now lodged for posterity. Among the clips introduced by curator **David Cleveland** was an early home movie shot in Southend by professional cameraman **George Woods-Taylor** between 1919 and 1924, featuring his toddler son 'Bobbie'. Eighty years later, Bobbie was still living in Southend and was interviewed about his memories of early stardom.

There was an especially happy link between past and present when **Dick Joice** made several contributions to *Bygone Days*, talking to McDermott at his home in West Norfolk and at the *Bygones Collection* he founded at Holkham Hall.

**Past and present...
Helen McDermott
and Dick Joice in**
Bygone Days.

Images of old Framlingham in Suffolk... old films and stills were a regular feature of *Bygones*.

Filming steam threshing at Aslacton, Norfolk.

Football crazy...

Anglia's first soccer commentators John Camkin (left) and Gerald Sinstadt.

This sporting life...

FROM basketball at Hemel Hempstead to pro-am golf at Sheringham, Anglia has covered a huge variety of sporting events across its region, either as part of the daily sports service in the regional news, or as programmes in their own right.

Leading the way, of course, has been football, with all the triumphs and disappointments of the region's League clubs chronicled on screen. In the early days, Anglia cameras were there when Norwich City beat Southend to win promotion to the Second Division in April, 1960, and when Ipswich Town were elevated to the old First Division a year later.

They were there, too, when Town, under **Alf Ramsey**, achieved the remarkable feat of becoming League Champions in their first year in the top flight – clinching the title by beating *Aston Villa* in April, 1962.

Alf Ramsey.

As England's World Cup-winning goalkeeper **Gordon Banks** said: "Alf took them from the lower levels of the league and made them the very best. Absolutely incredible – it had never been done before and I'm not sure it will ever be done again".

The 1961/62 season was important in terms of Anglia's growing commitment to football, because Norwich also brought their campaign to a successful conclusion, beating Rochdale 1-0 at Carrow Road to win the League Cup by a four-goal aggregate.

Mindful of these successes and the high profile football was enjoying in the region, Anglia made television history the next season by reaching a special agreement with the Football League to start its *Match of the Week* programme, becoming the first TV station in Britain to broadcast regular weekly coverage of League football.

TV soccer came a lot cheaper then than in today's era of multi-million pound wheeler-dealing for screening rights. Anglia paid the League just £1,000 for the exclusive rights to recorded highlights of 30 games that season involving four East Anglian clubs – Ipswich, Norwich, Peterborough and Colchester. The first match screened was between Ipswich and Wolves, but Ramsey's team were unable to rise to the occasion, losing 3-2. **Len Caynes**, who went on to become a *Match of the Week* director and then Anglia's head of sport, was a cameraman at that match along with **Stuart McConahie**, later editor of ITV's *World of Sport*.

Eighteen years later, the cost of screening *Match of the Week* had risen a few thousand per cent, but still not to the astronomical heights paid for Premiership coverage these days. By November, 1980, each programme was reckoned to cost Anglia about £7,000,

of which the Football League's fee was £1,500. And the League paid each of its 92 clubs £25,000 a season out of the revenue it received from ITV.

Match Of The Week's regular commentator in the early years was pipe-smoking **John Camkin**, a former newspaper sports writer who had also covered soccer for the BBC. A director of Coventry City, he was a much-respected figure in the game and his commentaries helped win many admirers for the fledgling Anglia service. He was followed by another top commentator whose voice is still familiar to millions of football followers – **Gerald Sinstadt**, now with the BBC's *Match of the Day*.

In the 1970s, former Army second lieutenant and *Daily Express* war correspondent, **Gerry Harrison**, became Anglia's voice of football, a role he performed for more than 20 years, including six times with ITV's World Cup commentary team.

Working with Harrison on the Anglia sports team for five years, from 1979 – 84, was a young reporter/presenter called **Steve Rider**, now one of the linchpins of the BBC's sports coverage as presenter of *Grandstand* and the big golf tournaments. Despite being only 27 when he took his first television job with Anglia, he was already the author of two books, one on football and the other on boxing, collaborating with **Henry Cooper** on the latter. No one would think it now of one of the coolest presenters on television, but Rider, who came to Anglia from local radio, admitted having an attack of nerves when he first stepped in front of the camera.

Another sports-mad presenter who has gone on to achieve national TV fame was briefly part of the Anglia team in the late 1960s – chat show host supreme and Barnsley devotee **Michael Parkinson**.

Gerry Harrison reporting on a Norwich City Match.

Michael Parkinson... part of the sports team in the late '60s.

Gerry Harrison outstayed them all and became the station's head of sport. So it came as a shock to colleagues and viewers when he left Anglia in 1993 to take a job producing worldwide football coverage for an American-owned TV company. Harrison cited ITV's losing out to Sky and the BBC in the soccer rights war as the main reason for his move.

But though Anglia lost out in the Premiership battle, the station has continued to take every opportunity to bring top soccer to the screen. A regular Sunday afternoon soccer programme returned in 1996 with *KICK-OFF!*, which showed either live games or an hour of highlights. And midweek *KICK-OFF!* programmes have continued to cover action from games involving local clubs as well as other top matches from outside the region. Anglia's day-by-day sports coverage has also included comprehensive highlights of goals and key incidents at weekend and midweek fixtures, plus follow-up stories and behind-the-scenes features.

Tony Jones is Anglia's main commentator today, with **Kevin Piper** or **Richard Futter** presenting in the studio, usually accompanied by former Ipswich striker **Alan Brazil** as the expert summariser. Other top names from football to give Anglia viewers the benefit of their knowledge over the years have included **Bobby Robson**, **Geoff Hurst**, **Martin Peters**, **Mike Walker**, **Bryan Gunn** and **Barry Fry**.

Fry is known today as the flamboyant boss of Peterborough United whose giant-killing exploits of the past have been responsible for some of Anglia's most exciting soccer coverage. It started in 1963 when the 'Posh' scored a 2-1 home victory over the mighty Arsenal in the FA Cup 4th round on their way to the quarter-finals in which they lost to Chelsea. Peterborough were back on the giant-killing trail in the 1991/92 season, producing a remarkable Rumbelows Cup run that swept aside Wimbledon, Newcastle and Liverpool on the way to eventual defeat by Middlesbrough in a quarter-final replay.

Heads you win... former Ipswich and Scotland striker Alan Brazil teams up as a pundit with *KICK-OFF!* **presenter Kevin Piper.**

World Cup hero, Geoff Hurst, shares his knowledge.

Giant killers and cup winners...

Golden Canaries **of '59.**

Norwich City's Mick Channon shows off the Milk Cup in 1985.

ANOTHER giant-killing act, which took place just before Anglia went on air, was celebrated on screen in 1963. Third Division Norwich had reached the semi-finals of the FA Cup in 1959 with a remarkable run that included victory over Manchester United. They eventually succumbed to Luton, in a replay. But their achievement in getting to within kicking distance of Wembley was celebrated in an Anglia programme *Golden Canaries '59*, for which the entire cup-run side – with the exception of winger **Errol Crossan**, who was in Canada – were gathered together in the studio.

The 1959 team, this time including Crossan, but sadly minus central defender **Barry Butler**, who was killed in a car accident, got together again in front of the Anglia cameras in 1999 for a 40th anniversary celebration of that Cup run.

Colchester United. were the giant slayers in the 1970/71 season when Anglia cameras were at Layer Road to record the famous 3-2 victory over Leeds that earned the 'U's' a cup draw with Everton. The same season saw more celebrations in Norwich when the Canaries won the Second Division championship to enter football's top flight for the first time.

Ipswich achieved another of their finest hours in 1978 when they lifted the FA Cup by beating Arsenal at Wembley. Anglia devoted a special programme to the celebrations when the team rode in an open-top bus through ecstatic crowds to a civic reception . There was even better to come for Ipswich and manager **Bobby Robson** in the 1980/81 season when they beat Dutch club AZ 67 Alkmaar 5-4 on aggregate to win the UEFA Cup.

In 1985 it was Luton's turn to dominate Anglia's FA Cup coverage when they earned a semi-final place against Everton. Meanwhile, the Milk Cup glory was Norwich's as they beat Sunderland in the final, and Anglia recorded another open-top bus journey through wild celebrations.

Ipswich's signing in 1989 of **Sergei Baltacha**, the first Soviet footballer to play in the English league, was marked by an Anglia sports documentary *Sergei – Home And Away* looking at his new life in England and the one he left behind in Russia.

UEFA Cup winner... Bobby Robson, former Ipswich and England boss.

There was more football from foreign fields in May, 1991, when Anglia screened *Bobby Robson PSV*, an account of the former Ipswich and England boss's first year as coach of Dutch club PSV Eindhoven. And Norwich fans were treated to coverage of their team's first European campaign in the 1993/94 season, which included a 2-1 victory over Bayern Munich in Germany followed by a 1-1 draw in the second leg at Carrow Road.

The away leg gave Anglia's **Tony Jones** the chance to stage a remarkable display of initiative. When colleague **Richard Henwood** had to return unexpectedly on match day Jones was left to get into the Olympic Stadium without accreditation. Having gained admission to the Press box he bluffed his way into the dressing room area with cameraman **Chris Warner**. He then sneaked on to the pitch, despite not having the requisite red bib. A camera borrowed from Norwich freelance photographer **Roger Harris** made Jones look the part and helped him stay in place until the final whistle, allowing him to get immediate reaction from manager

Heroes' welcome...
Ipswich Town team with the
FA Cup after beating Arsenal
at Wembley in 1978.

There's Only One Barry Fry... the
Peterborough manager was the subject
of an hour-long documentary.

Mike Walker and second goalscorer Jeremy Goss. Not only that, but Jones the cameraman captured the shot used in the Canaries' club programme of Mark Bowen's headed first goal.

Norwich's next opponents were just as awesome – Inter Milan. A goal from Dennis Bergkamp gave the Italian side a single goal advantage from the first leg at Carrow Road. And the Canaries – urged on by 2,000 of their own supporters – achieved a creditable draw in the San Siro stadium. Sadly it was not enough to see them through.

The controversial sale soon after of Norwich striker Chris Sutton to Blackburn for a record £5 million was chronicled in a special Anglia programme, *Going? Going? Gone!,* which included contributions from Sutton's new manager, Kenny Dalglish, and his old one – Mike Walker, by then manager at Everton – who scoffed at the price put on the player's head.

Earlier Anglia had featured the move of Canaries' goalkeeper Chris Woods to Glasgow Rangers with a programme that linked up with former Ipswich captain Terry Butcher, who had also made the journey from East Anglia to Ibrox Park.

Away from the higher echelons of regional football, Anglia has also celebrated notable achievements on the non-League scene, with the FA Vase producing particular highlights. Stamford were winners of the competition in 1980 and runners-up four years later. Sudbury were beaten finalists in 1989 and Norfolk team Diss – managed by former Canary Bill Punton – lifted the trophy in 1993, their achievement being celebrated in an *Anglia Sport Special.* The next year it was the turn of Arlesey Town to taste success.

There have also been soccer specials like the *Anglia Television Five-a-Side Football Championship* – two programmes which brought together the winners of county FA finals held in the region during the 1996/97 season.

Back at Peterborough, the ebullient Barry Fry, fresh from a series of successes and disappointments in other high-profile football jobs, took the reins and found himself the club's owner for a time as well. Anglia cameras accompanied him for every traumatic twist and turn in the club's fortunes in the 1996/7 season for an hour-long network documentary *There's Only One Barry Fry.* The number of expletives, as Fry gave vent to his feelings on

the touchline and in the dressing room, led to comparisons with a controversial documentary on former England coach Graham Taylor a few years earlier. But the amiable former Barnet, Southend and Birmingham manager came out of it much better – thanks to his larger-than-life personality and sense of humour.

Fry discovered the club's debts were worse then he thought and, with a £210,000 loan secured on his home, he faced the prospect of financial ruin. "Looking at the worst scenario, the club could go bust," he told the Anglia cameras. "My wife always said she'd live in a tent with me – she may well have the opportunity!" Eventually, however, tax and legal problems intervened to prevent him from continuing with the double burden and a new owner was found. He likened the relief to having a Boeing 707 fly off his shoulders.

Fry's troubles in the 1996/97 weren't entirely over, with hopes of promotion becoming fears of relegation, but 'Bazza' still managed to laugh. "When I came to Peterborough United, I promised entertainment and plenty of goals – what I didn't promise was which end the goals would be scored," he quipped.

Straight bat... Graham Gooch with Gerry Harrison.

International rugby sevens at Cambridge University's Grange Road ground.

The region's cricket pitches, both major and minor, have been well-trodden by Anglia cameramen over the years. **Colin Milburn**, the big-hitting Northants opening batsman, who lost an eye in an accident that effectively ended his career and who then died tragically young, was one of the batsmen often in the frame – not least when he was picked for England in June, 1966.

The region's other senior county cricket team, Essex, have also figured regularly in Anglia's coverage, particularly when providing England captains like **Keith Fletcher**, **Graham Gooch** and **Nasser Hussein**. Cameras were at Chelmsford, too, when Gooch played his last game for the county against Worcestershire in 1997.

A particularly good season for the two county sides came in 1992 when Anglia followed Northamptonshire's victorious campaign in the Nat West Trophy and Essex's success in the County Championship. The achievements of the Chelmsford-based players were also in sharp focus in 1998, when they took their place in the history books by beating Leicestershire at Lords to become permanent holders of the last B & H Cup.

On the rugby scene, Anglia has profiled many of the top players and clubs in the region. Bedford schoolteacher **Neil Bennett** was in the spotlight in 1974 when he was picked for England. Varsity matches have always figured prominently in Anglia's rugby coverage and **Alastair Hignall**, captain of both the rugby and cricket teams at Cambridge University, was the subject of a special profile.

In 1986, Anglia celebrated a prestigious international rugby occasion in a 45-minute programme presented by **Stuart Jarrold** from the Greene King International Invitation Sevens, played at the University's Grange Road ground. "It's the first time we've had the opportunity to cover international class rugby on our own doorstep and we're delighted," said Jarrold.

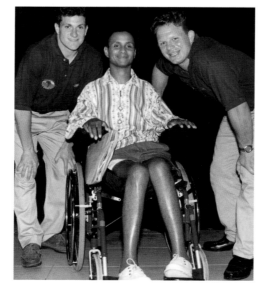

Into Africa, a special August, 1996, documentary, recorded an altogether different and quite unique rugby event. For a start, some of England's leading players, including **Dean Richards, Kieran Bracken, Damian Hopley, Martin Johnson** and Northampton internationals **Tim Rodber, Matt Dawson** and **Paul Grayson** were taking the game into Ghana for the first time. They were there to raise money for former Ivory Coast international **Max Brito**, who broke his back in the previous world cup and was confined to a wheelchair, receiving only £250 a month disability pension to support himself, his wife and two young sons. But the tour was also historic as one of the last reasonably light-hearted excursions before rugby union entered its new age of professionalism.

The presence of horse racing's headquarters at Newmarket in the heart of the region has made the 'Sport of Kings' high on the list for regular Anglia coverage. Fixtures on the Flat at Newmarket and Yarmouth, and over jumps at Huntingdon, Towcester and Fakenham, have been an important aspect of the Anglia regional sport service. And for many years, the company provided outside broadcast facilities and personnel for networked coverage of the bigger meetings from Newmarket and other courses for ITV and Channel 4.

Some of racing's most important developments have been chronicled on Anglia screens, such as those at Newmarket in 1966 and 1967 – first the pioneering introduction of closed-circuit TV and video tape equipment to record the last three furlongs (now a routine feature on all British racecourses) and then the introduction of starting stalls. The work of equine scientists in the town has also been featured, covering issues like the war against doping and advances in the treatment of sick and injured racehorses.

Anglia looked at the workings of the Jockey Club in a 1971 programme and later in the same year investigated the ruling body's decision to license women riders for the first time.

Newmarket legends like **Lester Piggott** have regularly featured on Anglia screens – in more ways than one in the case of the century's most celebrated and controversial jockey who, towards the end of his career, served a spell in local prisons for tax offences. In 1996 Anglia produced a special report on the remarkable feat of Newmarket-based **Frankie Dettori** who rode all seven winners on the Saturday card at Ascot's Festival meeting.

Rugby stars Paul Grayson (left) and Harvey Thorneycroft with former Ivory Coast player Max Brito in *Into Africa*.

An unusual racing link occurred in 1983 when international footballer **Mick Channon**, then a Norwich City player, indulged his passion for the Turf by giving viewers of *About Anglia* Friday evening tips for the weekend. Channon, who owned a horse called Jamesmead in training with **Alan Bailey** at Newmarket, knew his stuff and sometimes his 'Friday Flutter' had the bookies running for cover. It was no surprise when, after his retirement from football, he set up as a horse trainer. Now he is one of the most successful in the country. Others to try their hand at the 'Friday Flutter', with varying degrees of success, included comedian **Tom O'Connor**.

Norwich City's Mick Channon
with his horse Jamesmead.

Sport for all...

ATHLETICS coverage has included many highlights – from **Bob Thirtle's** 1965 world championship marathon victory through to and beyond **Paul Evans's** 1996 Chicago win over the same distance. **Paula Radcliffe**, of Bedford, was in focus for her 1992 world junior cross-country championship victory in America along with her 1997 and 1998 achievements in breaking two records at a Brussels meeting and winning the European cross-country championships in Italy.

Anglia cameras were also at **Thurrock**, in Essex, in 1993 for a meeting with a star-studded list of British athletes, including **Colin Jackson, Sally Gunnell** and **Tony Jarrett**. Tony Jones interviewed the President of Thurrock Harriers, newly-retired javelin thrower **Fatima Whitbread**.

In *The Running Programme*, a six-part series screened from August, 1987, international stars revealed the secrets of their training programmes. Presenter **Cliff Temple**, athletics correspondent of *The Sunday Times* and a qualified coach, said it was the first programme made specifically for runners. "It's all about how to enjoy and improve your running – and what to do if things go wrong," he said.

Plenty of other sports have had a regular look-in on Anglia, particularly in the past two decades with an increasingly wide range of top events being staged in the East of England. Among them badminton, snooker, billiards, bowls, cycling, darts, golf, squash, show-jumping, tennis and even minority pastimes such as archery.

Snooker made its mark in a big way in the 1980s when Anglia mounted one of its largest outside broadcast operations for a sports event. Nearly 70 technicians were needed to produce 26 hours of live and recorded action for ITV and Channel 4 from the Hofmeister World Doubles held at the Derngate Centre, Northampton. Five cameras were trained on the table and there were another two in an adjacent studio where **Dickie Davies** did the introductions and interviews. For many of the crew it was a concentrated 12-hour shift each day. "The only breaks we see are on the table," said producer Len Caynes.

The Tolly Cobbold Classic in Ipswich was another regular snooker tournament covered by Anglia, and in 1983 **Fred Davis** and **Rex Williams** competed in the final of the World Professional Billiards Championship televised from Peterborough.

Top players from the world of darts have appeared regularly on Anglia over the past 15 years, coinciding with the emergence of the game as a TV attraction. The Seashore Holiday Village, at Yarmouth, was one of the regular venues in the 1980s for a *Festival Of Darts* featuring competition for the British Matchplay title. And more recently the Lada UK Masters has been fought out in front of the Anglia cameras.

Norfolk's Wymondham Dell bowls club has been the location for one of several top bowls tournaments televised by Anglia. *The CIS Insurance International Pairs* attracted most of the game's top players, and was a sell-out among local bowls fans who packed the audience.

Golf coverage has included the *Bernard Matthews Pro-Am* tournament at Sheringham in 1980 when American star **Lee Trevino** was among the players. Twelve years earlier, **Gary Player** had been the main draw when the cameras covered an exhibition match at Ramsey, near Huntingdon. And **Nick Faldo**, who lived in Hertfordshire, has regularly featured on Anglia through his years of success, including a special profile presented by **Gerry Harrison** in 1984.

Anglia pioneered coverage of *City Centre Cycling* in towns across the region, and was the first ITV company to show *Roller Hockey* with the final of the Dex-O-Tex Senior Challenge Cup held in Cambridge in 1983.

Fatima Whitbread being interviewed by Tony Jones.

On target for the Lada UK Masters.

What a Player!... Gary at Ramsey, near Huntingdon, in '68.

Nick Faldo in a special profile with by Gerry Harrison.

Lee Trevino at Sheringham in 1980.

International bowls at Norfolk's Wymondham Dell Club.

On cue... top players line up for the **Tolly Cobbold Classic in Ipswich** – from left to right: John Virgo, Dennis Taylor, Terry Griffith and Alex Higgins.

Cycle racing on the streets of Southend.

Squash was always considered difficult to televise because of the problems of getting suitable camera positions in the enclosed court and following the small ball at high speed. But Anglia helped pioneer innovative coverage.

First, in 1976, came an instructional series called *Play Squash Jonah's Way*, introduced by the sport's most famous exponent, **Jonah Barrington**, from a court specially designed to give cameras an unobstructed view. Next, in 1981, was the *Dunlop International Supasquash Championship*, held at Welwyn Garden City. It involved an exciting new version of the game, devised for television, and the brainchild of Hatfield businessman **Mike Palmer**.

Three years later, an all-glass portable court was used at the Marina Centre, Yarmouth, for televising the *Pro-Kennex Classic* which featured a clash between British champion **Gawain Briers**, who lived in Norfolk, and Australian number one **Dean Williams**. "It will revolutionise squash from a spectator's point of view," predicted Anglia's **Len Caynes**.

In a region bordered on one side by the sea, and streaked with rivers and lakes, it is hardly surprising that watersports have figured large in Anglia programmes. Sailing activities covered have included the national Seafly class championship success of Blakeney's **Maurice Arthur**, in 1971, the World Speed Sailing record by **Timothy Colman**, of Norwich, at Weymouth, in 1972, and the Felixstowe welcome for Hong Kong 505 champions **Peter White** and **John Davies**, in 1973.

Cameras were also at Wyboston Lakes, Bedfordshire, to cover **Mike Hazelwood's** British Waterski championship win in 1974 and the arrival at Lowestoft the same year of **Claire Francis's** all-girl crew in the round-Britain yacht race. Suffolk sailboarder **Gary Aldous's** North Sea crossing was celebrated in 1982 and the next year British windsurfing champion **Nick Tillett** was given a send-off as he left to compete in America.

On the swimming scene, **Jackie Willmott's** return home to Southend with a world championship silver medal caught the attention of the cameras along with clubmate **Sarah Hardcastle's** achievement in gaining a third place British ranking.

Darren Hall at the English National badminton championships at Norwich Sport Village.

Chris Serle took over the helm of *Sailaway* in 1994.

Hooked on success... John Wilson presenter of 13 *Go Fishing* series.

In earlier Anglia days there was a 1961 demonstration by Olympic diver **Brian Phelps** when he helped open a new pool in Norwich.

More recently, the spotlight shone on **Karen Pickering**, of Ipswich, as she became Britain's first woman swimmer to become World Champion in 200-metre freestyle in 1993, then took the 100 metres freestyle gold in the 1994 Commonwealth Games and, along with Haverhill's **Jessica Craig**, was part of the British team which broke the national 4 x 200 metres freestyle relay record at the Perth World Championships in 1998.

Undoubtedly one of Anglia's greatest and longest-running successes has been *Go Fishing* which hooked Anglia viewers for the first time in 1987. Since then, presenter **John Wilson** has notched up 13 series, some featuring celebrity fishing enthusiasts such as **Bob Carolgees** and **Roger Daltrey**. And the programme, which went nationwide on Channel 4 for a time, has helped make Wilson Britain's best-known angling broadcaster.

Another on-screen regular for several years was *Sailaway*, Anglia's series on watersports in the East of England, which was launched in March, 1989. ITN weather girl **Trish Williamson** charted a new course in her wide-ranging TV career when she introduced the first run of programmes. Later presenters included tennis star **Annabel Croft**, who met her yachtsman husband **Mel Coleman** while learning to sail for a TV programme.

Former *That's Life* co-presenter **Chris Serle** took over the helm in 1994, renewing his

romance with the East Coast which he had already explored in a converted lifeboat for *Secret Coastline*, another Anglia series two years earlier. He got hooked on sailing after taking a coastal skipper's certificate and tackled the Fastnet Race for his *In at the Deep End* series on BBC.

"Until then I rather turned up my nose at the 'Snotty Yachty' brigade," he admitted. "I thought they were all a bit peculiar in their funny-coloured plimsoles and their strange shell suits."

In June, 1997, a new six-part series *Waterlines* hit the screen with *Sunday Times* yachting correspondent **Keith Wheatley** and top marine photographer **Kos Evans** presenting. As well as featuring stories about local sailors and people making their living from boats and the sea, the programmes explored a wide spectrum of topics from ocean racing to the little-known boating interests of celebrities, including **Lorraine Chase, Gary Glitter, Sir Freddie Laker, Warren Mitchell** and **Peter Stringfellow**.

Airline tycoon Sir Freddie revealed why he was inclined to kiss his motor yacht but kick the tyres of his aeroplanes, while nightclub entrepreneur Stringfellow – filmed in Majorca with his Sunseeker powerboat and leggy lovelies – admitted he was a "fair-weather, posey boater."

The long and the shorts...

THE long and shorts of being an Anglia sports presenter... (left) **Steve Rider** looking vertically challenged beside one of the basketball players at a Cambridge event, and (right) **Stuart Jarrold's** cover is blown as (almost) all is revealed behind his desk. News presenter **Helen McDermott** recalls trying to expose the legs of the sports presenters: "In the summer people like **Gerry Harrison** and Stuart Jarrold sometimes wore shorts in the studio, but as their legs were under the desk, the viewers saw their shirts and ties and had no idea they were wearing shorts. So I was always trying to get them to stand up or walk away from the desk while they were still on camera."

Ringside with Anglia

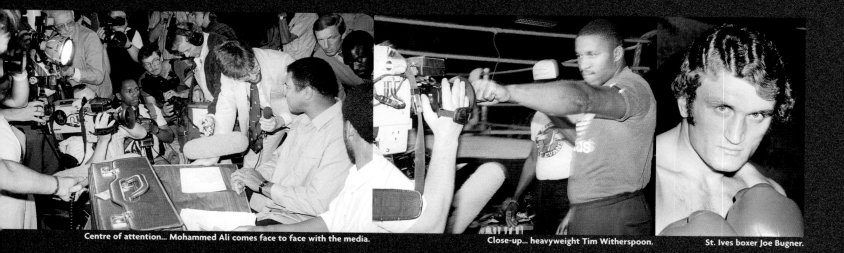

Centre of attention... Mohammed Ali comes face to face with the media.

Close-up... heavyweight Tim Witherspoon.

St. Ives boxer Joe Bugner.

BOXING fans have been well catered for, too. There was even coverage, back in the early Sixties, of **Randolph Turpin**'s return to the ring at Wisbech, where he stopped American **Eddie Marcano** in the sixth round.

And in 1967 the legendary **Tommy Farr** introduced *Knock-Out*, a 26-part series highlighting some of boxing's greatest moments.

Since then, however, the big names to crop up on camera most regularly have been **Joe Bugner**, originally from St Ives, **Dave 'Boy' Green**, from Chatteris, and Norwich's **Herbie Hide**.

In the Eighties, fans of the noble art were treated to regular doses of their favourite sport in *Seconds Out*, a series co-produced by fellow ITV broadcasters Thames and HTV. Norwich Lads' Club was a regular venue for the fights, which were introduced by **Tony Francis** with commentary by former world champion **Barry McGuigan**. One of the boxers beginning to make a name for himself in the programmes with some stunning knock-out performances was a young **Nigel Benn**.

Anglia cameras and reporter **Gerry Harrison** were part of the Press scrum when American heavyweight **Tim Witherspoon**, accompanied by 'The Greatest' himself, **Mohammed Ali**, arrived at his UK training camp to prepare for a title defence against **Frank Bruno** in 1986.

Dave 'Boy' Green in action.

Anglia's Piper calls the tune...

Martin Brundle talks to Kevin Piper, *A Race Against Time.*

Winning driver Jan Brise receives the Anglia TV Trophy from 'Miss Anglia', Heidi Lohschelder, at Snetterton.

ANGLIA emerged on the world stage of motor sport in 1996 as part of the consortium that won the new ITV contract to cover Formula One racing.

MACH 1 – a combination of Anglia, its sister company Meridian and independent specialist Chrysalis Sport – beat off stiff competition from several rivals with a proposal which included a number of technical innovations. Anglia's head of sport, **Kevin Piper**, played a key role in the successful pitch, which also outlined the consortium's aims to make Grand Prix coverage more personal and accessible.

Piper started to put together a plan for Anglia to provide the service as soon as ITV won the F1 rights and his proposals, in a paper compiled after research with the likes of **Martin Brundle**, **Ron Dennis**, **Eddie Jordan** and **Murray Walker**, formed the backbone of MACH 1's tender document.

A key change was for each Grand Prix to be presented from its location, allowing the production team to capture the atmosphere and excitement and involve the audience. Informative features were introduced, giving viewers the chance to become more familiar with the personalities, the teams and the circuits.

Martin Brundle, who had demonstrated a talent for laconic delivery during Anglia's regular coverage of his own racing career – including a 1995 documentary *A Race Against Time* – was one of the first names in the frame to pair up with veteran commentator **Murray Walker**.

Brundle, whose amazing escape from a spectacular crash in the 1996 Australian Grand Prix remains a vivid memory for many viewers, was always keen on the idea but delayed taking up the job offer until he was convinced his own Formula One racing career had reached the end of the road.

Happily for MACH 1 and ITV the two things came together at the start of the 1997 season and the former world sports car champion and Le Mans winner has established himself as an accomplished and popular broadcaster since he took up the mike at the Australian Grand Prix in March of that year.

Overall coverage has also been acclaimed and the broadcast from the 1997 British Grand Prix won the Royal Television Society's award for Best Live Sports Outside Broadcast. MACH 1's contract with ITV was extended during 1998 to the end of the 2001 season.

It is not surprising that Anglia has paid attention to motor sport over its 40-year history. The region has major racing circuits Silverstone and Snetterton along with several leading manufacturers, as well as the country's premier drag racing strip and other smaller venues.

Pole position among the manufacturers must go to Lotus, whose fluctuating fortunes have been followed closely over the years. Anglia has been a regular visitor to the car manufacturer's Hethel headquarters, near Norwich, ever since the legendary innovator **Colin Chapman**, who had moved his business from Cheshunt, in Hertforshire, laid the foundation stone in July, 1966.

Among those watching that ceremony was top driver **Jim Clark**, whose name was synonymous with Lotus for many years, but with its Hethel base for only a tragically short time. It was long enough for him to win the 20th British Grand Prix at Silverstone, the former wartime bomber base which had become one of the world's leading motor racing circuits.

Within two years, however, the cheers had turned to tears as, in April, 1968, Anglia covered the return to Hethel of Clark's wrecked Lotus Cosworth – its driver having been killed while racing in Germany. It was not the only Lotus tragedy to have been covered by Anglia. Another black day came with the death of **Ronnie Peterson** after he was badly burned in a crash in the 1978 Italian Grand Prix.

But there were many triumphs, too, for Lotus and drivers who included such names as **Fittipaldi**, **Herbert**, **Piquet**, **Rindt** and **Senna**. Anglia's *The Fittipaldi File*, screened in September, 1972, focused on the star Brazilian, his mentor Chapman, and their rivals.

Most notable among Lotus's successes, perhaps, was the 1978 world championship win of **Mario Andretti** in the John Player Special, which he drove through the streets of Norwich when the company was honoured for its achievements by Norfolk County Council. The victory was celebrated in an Anglia documentary *Three Days at Monza*.

Andretti, along with **Stirling Moss** and **John Watson**, was among those who took part in *Golden Lotus*, a 1998 Anglia celebration of the company's 50 years. The programme, presented by **Kevin Piper**, paid tribute to the innovations of founder Chapman and traced the compelling story of the company which rose from humble workshops in a converted stable block to become a world-beater.

Chapman's widow and son took part in the programme along with some of his original engineers and Formula One team manager **Peter Warr**. Andretti remembered the Lotus supremo as "an innovator and a maverick". To Watson he was simply inspirational: "People would have worked 25 hours a day for him!"

Sadly, of course, Lotus no longer runs a Grand Prix team, although it has announced plans for an F1 return – and even the cherished collection of rare models, which had stood for years in the company's own museum, went under the hammer in 1998.

A champion of speed in an earlier era was recalled by Anglia in *Full Throttle*, screened in June, 1983. It told the remarkable tale of motor racing hero **Sir Henry ('Tim') Birkin**, who crammed his brilliant career into six short years in the late Twenties and early Thirties.

He was only 36 when he died from septicaemia, as a result of burns from a hot exhaust pipe. But, by then, he was the undisputed leader of 'The Bentley Boys', a dashing band of drivers whose thundering green, supercharged machines thrilled racing enthusiasts around the world.

His daring determination brought him wins at Le Mans in 1929 and 1931 and made him a favourite with crowds at home and abroad.

Birkin had two homes in Norfolk. He had a particular affection for Blakeney, where he honeymooned, delighted in speedboating and shooting and where he is buried. In 1983, on the 50th anniversary of his death, Anglia covered a cavalcade of Bentleys and other cars he drove when they took part in a Birkin Memorial Rally.

Sir Henry ('Tim') Birkin, undisputed leader of 'The Bentley Boys' recalled in *Full Throttle*.

The *Lombank Trophy* **event at Snetterton in 1961.**

The region is still represented at the pinnacle of motor sport by the Silverstone-based team of **Eddie Jordan** who were the subject of a 1999 documentary profile for the ITV Network, *Driving Ambition – A Season with Eddie Jordan* – and comparative newcomers Stewart Racing, based at Milton Keynes, whose cars are powered by Northampton-based Ford Cosworth engines.

Anglia's focus on the Jordan Grand Prix operation was timely. Set up in 1991, Jordan was still waiting for its first Grand Prix win which came with a vengeance in 1998 at the Spa circuit in Belgium – former world champion **Damon Hill** taking the chequered flag first, followed by team-mate **Ralf Schumacher** for an amazing 1-2.

But Lotus and Jordan are not the only manufacturers in the region who have had outstanding success in motor racing reported on Anglia. Huntingdon-based Lola won a world championship title in America's Indycar series. A much earlier success story was chronicled in April, 1962, when cameras focused on the development and manufacture of the famous BRM racing car at Bourne and Folkingham, in Lincolnshire, then part of Anglia's transmission area.

The BRM Story covered the full period of the company's history, from its inception before the Second World War to the completion and testing of the new.1½-litre model in readiness for its 1962 racing debut. Producer of the programme was **Maxwell Boyd**, motoring correspondent of *The Sunday Times*.

The next year Anglia was back at Bourne to cover a civic reception for BRM's world champion **Graham Hill** and members of his team. Hill figured in the news again the following year when he crashed at 90 mph while testing his F1 BRM at Snetterton. Fortunately he was not seriously hurt.

In 1974, *Lord off the Wheels* shone the spotlight on the third **Baron Hesketh of Hesketh**, who was backing Britain to win on the international Grand Prix circuits with the help of driver **James Hunt**. A later documentary, for the *Anglia Reports* series, chronicled Hesketh's similarly high-powered bid for success on the motorcycling scene.

Another leading name in motor racing, albeit in Formula Three, is **Van Diemen** – based near the Snetterton circuit in Norfolk, where it wheeled out what was Britain's newest racing car for trials in 1973. Snetterton is home, too, to **Martin Donnelly** racing – the team set up by young Irishman Donnelly after his own career was ended by an horrific 160 m.p.h. crash in practice for the 1990 Spanish Grand Prix.

Snetterton may be a poor relation to the glamorous Silverstone, but it has had many successful associations with Anglia over the years, including an annual Formula Ford race for the *Anglia TV Trophy*. In the 1970s, there was an added incentive for the winning driver – he received a congratulatory kiss, along with the handsome cup, from 'Miss Anglia'.

The Norfolk circuit, which is just eight years older than Anglia itself, has also had many of the great names of motor racing burn up its surface – and Anglia cameras have been there to capture the occasions. Among them were **Stirling Moss**, **Jim Clark** and **Graham Hill**, who won the Archie Scott Brown Memorial Trophy there in July, 1962, at an average speed of 97.24 m.p.h. One of local television's earliest associations with motor racing was in March, 1961, when there was a special programme on *The Lombank Trophy* race at Snetterton, featuring **Jack Brabham**, **Roy Salvadori**, **John Surtees** and **Innes Ireland**.

Stirling Moss made a nostalgic return to the circuit in 1982 for *The Willhire Historic Race Meeting*, which Anglia televised. He was at the wheel of a Chevron B19, and told presenter **Steve Rider**: "These cars are beautiful to drive, and also they have a lot of character."

Other Snetterton competitors have included **Ayrton Senna** – racing then under the name of **Ayrton da Silva** – and Norfolk's **Martin Brundle**, who clashed in 1983 Formula Three events before graduating to the Grand Prix grid.

Colin Chapman checks out the Lotus.

Fittipaldi and companion *The Fittipaldi File.*

Mario Andretti with Colin Chapman *Three Days at Monza.*

Stirling Moss and Steve Rider at Snetterton in 1982.

Colin Chapman's son Clive and former Formula One driver John Miles *Golden Lotus.*

Eddie Jordan filmed at the
British Grand Prix in 1998
for *Driving Ambition*.

Dicing with death...

TWO-WHEELED track stars, including **Giacomo Agostini**, **Mike Hailwood**, **Ron Haslam** and **Barry Sheene**, were also regulars at Snetterton. Sheene, who broke a large percentage of the bones in his body during his career, was the subject of a special documentary, *Life and Fast Times*, shown on Anglia in March, 1977. A less frequent visitor was stunt star **Eddie Kidd**, who was interviewed at Snetterton in July, 1982, as he prepared for a world-record leap over 34 cars at Silverstone. .

One of Anglia's most unusual motor sport reports came from Silverstone when **Roberta Cowell**, a sex-change racing driver, began her track career as a woman at the age of 54.

Drag racing has also featured regularly on Anglia screens. Presenters, including **Gerald Sinstadt**, **Guy Michelmore**, **Steve Rider** and, more recently, **Kevin Piper**, **Richard Henwood** and **Stuart Jarrold**, have risked their eardrums to help those unfamiliar with the sport understand its nerve-jangling action and trans-atlantic jargon.

Such a high-speed sport has had its share of disasters. Some have unfolded on camera, with several deaths,

including that of **Alan Herridge** in what was to have been his last competitive race in 1983. There have also been amazing escapes over the years. Two of the most spectacular were those of **Darrell Gwynn**, who somehow avoided serious injury in 1990 when his car hit a barrier and erupted into a ball of flames, and **Rico Anthes**, who overturned at 260 mph during the 1993 world finals.

Other motor sport regularly covered by Anglia, often in its long-running *Wheels* series, includes speedway and hot rod racing from Ipswich, King's Lynn and Peterborough as well as moto-cross from Elsworth, in Cambridgeshire, and Wakes Colne, in Essex.

In 1965, Anglia's camera teams were in Monte Carlo following the gruelling course of that year's rally and taking a look at karting with **Chris Kelly** in a new series called *GO*. Another series, introduced by **David Jensen** in 1996, featured aspiring young Grand Prix cars. *Champions of the Future* brought together 80 of Britain's best young kart racers, aged between eight and 16. Coverage of the racing came from three major British karting venues including, in the Anglia region, Kimbolton, in Cambridgeshire.

Karting at Kimbolton.

Drag racing at Santa Pod.

Moto-cross at Elsworth.

Speedway at Peterborough.

The Anglia Years...

1959

Anglia goes on air at 4.15 pm on October 27, broadcasting from the Mendlesham transmitter in Suffolk. **Susan Hampshire** is one of the first on-screen celebrities as a singer in *The Midday Show*.

Special police security arrangements are laid on between Norwich railway station and Anglia House in November for the transfer of £25,000 worth of jewellery being displayed on *The Midday Show*.

Hughie Green interviews celebrated one-legged fighter pilot **Colin Hodgkinson** in *Battle Formation* from RAF Coltishall in December.

1960

Anglia's first major outside broadcast takes place in January as five cameras cover the enthronement of new bishop, **Dr Launcelot Fleming**, at Norwich Cathedral which has to be specially lit for the occasion.

About Anglia begins in May as a twice-weekly programme. In September, it is extended to four nights a week.

David Dimbleby gets first broadcasting job in May as an interviewer on *About Anglia* during his summer vacation from Oxford University.

Peter Scott and **Julian Huxley** are first guests on *Countryman*, a nature series introduced by **Aubrey Buxton** in June. It is the forerunner of the *Survival* series.

Anglia selects first female announcer in July – 20-year-old **Valerie Oldfield**, who had joined the company in January as a shorthand typist.

Politician **Tony Benn** gets early television experience in December as chairman of religious discussion programme *Food For Thought*.

1961

First *Survival* programme screened on ITV in February. Introduced by **Aubrey Buxton**, it features the wildlife of London.

The programme title *New Faces* is first used by Anglia for a talent show introduced by **Kenneth Horne** in April. (Idea later taken on by ATV in Birmingham).

Anglia is one of first ITV companies to screen a chart show, *Top Twenties*, introduced by **Kent Walton** in September.

Germany – Friend or Foe? is Anglia's first networked documentary in September. It discusses British attitudes to the Germans 16 years after the end of the war.

In October, Anglia becomes first regional TV company to transmit a late-night news headline feature.

Anglia becomes first ITV company to set up its own weather forecasting department with appointment of former RAF meteorologist **Michael Hunt**.

Programmes severely disrupted by strike involving actors' union Equity.

1962

Top of the Class, a general knowledge schools quiz, is launched in March under the chairmanship of **Peggy Wright**, a teacher and local councillor from Dereham, Norfolk.

Anglia's first interview with a Prime Minister takes place with **Harold MacMillan** at Luton Hoo in June.

First *Cambridge Footlights* show is screened as a highlights programme in August. Covered from Edinburgh Festival Fringe as outside broadcast.

Anne Gregg takes up her first job with mainland TV, arriving from Northern Ireland in September.

Anglia pioneers screening of regular weekly League football in September after paying £1,000 for the exclusive rights to 30 games during the season.

What? Where? When? panel game in which experts, under **Dr Glyn Daniel**, try to identify unusual objects is launched.

First Anglia programme especially for women, *Monday Date*, begins in October, introduced by **Shaw Taylor**.

1963

Police Call, one of the first programmes to provide "a new avenue of communication between the police and the public", launched in January.

Muriel Young launches *Music Match* quiz.

Chris Kelly joins Anglia as an announcer/news reader in April.

Anglia pioneers experimental early morning educational programming on British TV with *Dawn University*.

Brian Connell, former ITN foreign correspondent and *This Week* presenter, joins as programme adviser for special projects and current affairs in December.

Pets' Club, one of British television's first programmes on pets, starts in December.

1964

Satirist **Kenneth Robinson** makes his Anglia debut in April with *Look At It This Way*, a sideways glance at life.

Romper Room, with **Miss Rosalyn**, launched in June.

Portrait of a Village first appears in December.

1965

New transmitter at **Sandy Heath**, in Bedfordshire, serving the west of the region, is opened in July.

Special programme devoted to **Allan Smethurst**, the 'Singing Postman', broadcast in September.

1966

New late-night news bulletin begins in January, with up-to-the-minute coverage of Anglia's extended area, now stretching from Hull in north to Luton in south and from Northampton in west to Great Yarmouth in east.

Anglia's only networked 'soap' *Weavers Green*, is launched twice-weekly in April.

Cameras go to Italy, Denmark, the Orkneys and locations all over Britain for documentary series *Who Were The British?*, screened in July.

Rene Cutforth introduces *Home Sweet Home*, a series depicting life in urban communities in East of England in August. In September, **Cutforth** and **Bob Wellings** front *Mild and Bitter*, a pub chat show filmed in East of England 'locals'.

Under the Clock, with **Michael Partington** looking at the week's events in Parliament with East of England MPs, begins.

1967

Boxing legend **Tommy Farr** introduces *Knock Out*, a 26-part series looking at some of the sports greatest moments.

1968

Radio DJ **'Diddy' David Hamilton** begins East of England tour in January with *Try for Ten* quiz game.

Michael Parkinson and **Gerald Sinstadt** present new regular regional sports programme with the launch of *Eastern Sport* in April.

Transmissions switch from 405 to 625 lines in readiness for colour transmission.

1969

Bygones, introduced by **Dick Joice**, is screened for the first time in April.

In August, *The President Meets The Premier at Mildenhall*, an *About Anglia Special*, features **President Richard Nixon's** visit to the US air base at Mildenhall, Suffolk, where he held talks with **Prime Minister Harold Wilson**.

Mr and Mrs, a new 26-part matrimonial quiz game hosted by **Norman Vaughan**, is launched in October.

1970

Actor **Roy Dotrice** portrays **John Constable** in a documentary about the life and work of the Suffolk artist in April.

Disc jockey **Pete Murray** takes over as compere of the *Music Match* quiz in May.

Anglia programmes transmitted in colour for the first time in October.

1971

In July, **Brian Hope-Taylor** introduces *The Lost Centuries*, an eight-part historical series examining the enemies who brought down the Roman Empire.

Sale of the Century quiz show begins in October.

1972

Anglia marks the 50th anniversary of the BBC in November with **Brian Connell** talking to director general **Sir Hugh Carleton Greene**, and **Professor Asa Briggs**.

Sequences shot by American astronauts in space are shown in *The Voices of Apollo*, a documentary introduced by **Brian Connell** on the ITV network in December.

1973

Roy Hudd takes an affectionate look at the region's seaside piers in *Piers of the Realm* in June.

The Big Question, a late-night discussion between churchmen **Alan Webster, Eric Doyle** and **Edmund Banyard**, is networked on ITV for the first time in November.

Survival's film *The Incredible Flight of the Snow Geese* wins two Emmy awards.

1974

Movie giant **Orson Welles** makes his international TV debut, presenting a 26-part drama series *Orson Welles' Great Mysteries* in April.

Survival wins a Queen's Award for exceptional overseas sales.

1975

Card game quiz *Gambit* starts in July with Fred Dinenage as compere.

Anglia marks the start of East Anglia's first – and Britain's smallest – commercial radio station in November with *Switched On In Ipswich*.

1976

The **Syd Lawrence Orchestra** features in *Salute to Glenn Miller*, a programme recorded in September at an open day at the US air base at Mildenhall.

September also sees the start of *David Niven's World*, a networked series of adventure stories introduced by the actor and featuring mountaineers, racing drivers and explorers.

1977

Anglia's first situation comedy series, *Backs to the Land*, is launched in April. Based on wartime's Land Army girls it is dubbed 'Mum's Army' by the Press.

Chris Kelly introduces *Chatterbox*, a schools speaking competition series, in April.

Alternative 3, a spoof science fiction drama presented in the guise of a documentary, causes a sensation when screened on the ITV network in June. Many viewers take it seriously and TV switchboards all over Britain are jammed.

Station announcer **Patrick Anthony** demonstrates how to make Irish coffee on *About Anglia* in December and the 'Patrick's Pantry' cookery slot is born.

1978

An edition of *Sale of the Century* registers the highest audience recorded for a game show on British TV – 21.15 million viewers.

Anglia sponsors a yacht called *Anglia Pipedream* in the round-Britain yacht race. *About Anglia* follows its progress.

Anglia expands Norwich base with new premises in a former bowling alley in Magdalen Street. Included is the company's largest studio.

Mario Andretti's world motor racing championship win in the John Player Special Lotus is celebrated in a documentary *Three Days at Monza* transmitted in December.

1979

Tales of the Unexpected is launched on ITV in March with the first series of **Roald Dahl's** twist-in-the-tail short stories.

About Anglia is named Britain's best daily news programme by the Royal Television Society.

Two *Survival* programmes are sold to Communist China – the first by a British television company.

Survival marks the International Year of the Child in October with a special one-hour programme, *The Seas Must Live*, highlighting the need for conservation of marine environments. Broadcast simultaneously in the 31 member countries of the European Broadcasting Union in October.

Anglia programmes blacked out during three-month ITV pay dispute.

1980

In January, *The Dig On Our Doorstep*, featuring archeological discoveries made before work started on the extension to Anglia's headquarters, is screened. The finds include a previously unknown Saxon church which had burned down 1,000 years earlier.

The works of poet laureate **Sir John Betjeman** are dramatised on television for the first time in *Betjeman's Britain*, screened in August. Seven poems read by Sir John are enacted by stars including **Peter Cook**, **Eric Morecambe** and **Susannah York**.

Folio, a new regional arts series presented by **Chris Kelly**, begins in September. Suffolk author Hammond Innes takes part in the first programme.

1981

Heirloom, **John Bly's** antiques insert into the *About Anglia* programme, becomes a series in its own right in February.

More British Than The British, a documentary looking at growing tension between Britain and Argentina over sovereignty of the Falkland Islands, is screened in most ITV regions in October. (Six months later, the Argentine invasion of South Georgia sparks the Falklands War).

1982

Survival film-makers **Cindy Buxton** and **Annie Price** are stranded on South Georgia for a month in March after the Argentine invasion. They are rescued unharmed by the Royal Marines.

Filming starts in May for a seven-part drama serial based on a novel by crime writer **P.D. James**. **Roy Marsden** is cast as detective hero Adam Dalgliesh in *Death of an Expert Witness*, set in the East Anglian Fens.

Sandy Newman-Sanders, Anglia's first newsreader, retires in December. He had been the company's education officer for the past 16 years, providing back-up information and adult education programming to more than 4,000 educational establishments in the region.

1983

Sale of the Century reaches the end of the road in March after 13 series. More than 500 contestants appeared on the programme since 1971.

Sir Alec Guinness is cast in his first Anglia drama in April – as a crusty retired high court judge in **John Mortimer's** *Edwin*.

Shaw Taylor hosts new eight-part series, *Join Us for Bridge*, on the ITV network in October.

1984

Film producer **David Puttnam** becomes a director of Anglia TV in January.

Prince Michael of Kent makes hour-long tour of Anglia studios in October and sees new electronic news-gathering operation.

1985

Anglia becomes first major ITV company to go ahead with computerisation of its newsroom in January.

Michael Hunt, who pioneered ITV regional weather forecasts with Anglia in 1961, dies suddenly in October. He had continued as a relief forecaster after retiring as head of the weather department a year earlier.

Miss Anglia, the beauty competition that had run for 24 years, is held for the last time in July.

1986

Anglia pioneers computer graphic weather forecasts in ITV regions in April. Innovations include new symbols and mapping for any region of the world.

News stringers (freelance cameramen) are equipped with lightweight electronic cameras with ambient sound – another first for *Anglia News* in May. It follows a productivity agreement abolishing traditional demarcation lines and allowing the use of single electronic camera units (SCUs) on all programme production.

The **Marquess Townshend** of Raynham, chairman of Anglia since it was formed and longest-serving chairman in ITV, retires. He is succeeded in April by **Lord Buxton**.

1987

Go Fishing begins in May with **John Wilson** as presenter.

Survival becomes the first British programme to be screened simultaneously across the whole continent of North America in June. The one-hour film *Killer Whale* is shown by the CBS network in the United States and the Canadian Broadcasting Corporation in the same Friday evening slot.

Anglia launches all-night service in August with 37-year-old Bristol-born **Paul Lavers** (dubbed 'Mister Midnight') guiding viewers through to breakfast programmes from Monday to Thursday each week.

Anglia Action, a free service offering support and initiatives on community matters, is launched in September with a base at Anglia's Suffolk news centre in Ipswich which opened five months earlier.

1988

Anglia introduces a new corporate image in 1988, bidding goodbye to the silver knight which had been its emblem for almost 20 years.

Anglia chairman **Lord Buxton** warns in the company's annual report that Government plans to auction ITV franchises to the highest bidders could lead to despair and ruin for large numbers of employees in independent television.

Peter Gibbings, former chairman of *The Guardian*, takes over as chairman of Anglia in April on the retirement of **Lord Buxton**, last of the founder directors to leave the board.

Long-serving *About Anglia* presenter **Graham Bell** switches roles to become senior station announcer in March. **Helen McDermott** joins the *About Anglia* team full time, sharing presentation duties with **Christine Webber** and **Alastair Yates**.

A new initiative in the fight against crime starts with short film reconstructions in *Crimestoppers*.

1989

Plans are announced in November for separate regional news bulletins for the east and west of the region. Chief executive **David McCall** describes it as a major commitment to meet the broadcasting challenges of the 1990s.

Anglia buys £2.4 million stake in the Australian film and television production company Village Roadshow in May, gaining access to the increasingly important Australian market.

1990

Anglia's Education Department unveils 'Key Plus', a data package for use with school computers, in January. Anglia is a pioneer in the provision of computer-based learning systems for schools, and the business continues to grow as a major multi-media provider.

About Anglia presenter **Christine Webber** announces in January that she is leaving after 11 years to explore new ventures in television and journalism. **John Francis** joins the programme team in May from the BBC regional newsroom in Plymouth.

About Anglia is renamed *Anglia News* in July, coinciding with the introduction of a dual news service for the east and west of the region.

Unmanned, remote-control cameras are introduced to the news studios for the first time.

Sub-titling for deaf viewers is introduced on local news programmes for the first time.

1991

Food Guide, a new regional food and drink series, is launched in January with presenters **Patrick Anthony**, **Kay Avila** and **Denis Curtis**.

John Bacon, 56, Anglia's longest-serving newsreader, retires in June after 16,250 bulletins and 5,500 hours of broadcasting.

The curtain comes down on *Farming Diary* in September. It was Anglia's longest running programme – almost 32 years on screen.

Anglia wins ITV franchise for the East of England in October in the first auction of licences. It is top in a four-way bid with an offer of £17.8 million annually. A consortium headed by **Richard Branson** is among the under-bidders.

1992

Anglia takes over the running of ITV's popular morning talk show *The Time.... The Place...* in September

A pioneering addition to Anglia's arts output starts with the award-winning *First Take* series. Launched in association with Eastern Arts, it gives novice film-makers the opportunity to develop and demonstrate their skills.

1993

Dieter Plage, 57, a leading *Survival* film-maker for 25 years, dies in March after falling from an airship while filming above the forest canopy in Sumatra, Indonesia.

Anglia joins with Home Box Office, the American programme division of Time Warner Entertainment, in three partnerships in the United States and Europe for production and distribution.

Survival goes behind the scenes at the **Prince of Wales's** private estate in Gloucestershire on ITV in August for television's first in-depth look at the gardens, countryside and wildlife of Highgrove.

Anglia and independent producer Broadsword launch a new company, Televirtual, in October. It's the first in Britain to market a revolutionary new computer system, VActor, enabling animated characters to speak and move in real time, offering the prospect of cheaper animation production.

1994

Anglia Television is acquired in March for £292 million by the financial services and media company MAI plc which already controls south coast ITV licensee Meridian Broadcasting. Plans announced for a rationalisation programme resulting in 33 per cent job cuts at Anglia.

David McCall, who joined Anglia in 1968 as company secretary and became chief executive in 1986, succeeds **Sir Peter Gibbings** as Anglia chairman in April with **Malcolm Wall**, formerly deputy chief executive of Meridian Broadcasting, as managing director.

Vanessa Feltz launches new brand of daytime chat show on ITV in May.

Samantha Norman – daughter of film critic Barry – joins Anglia to co-present two series. She teams up with **David 'Kid' Jensen** on dating show *Love Call*, in January, and with *Breakfast TV's* **Michael Wilson** in March to launch *Weekend*, a leisure, arts and entertainment guide.

Futuristic children's series *Virtually Impossible* – made for Anglia by independent company Broadsword – becomes the first TV programme to be presented by a 'fish'. The host is a computer-animated character called **Codsby**.

1995

A consortium, including Anglia's parent company MAI, wins the licence for the new Channel 5 in January, opening up new production opportunities for Anglia.

Actor **Tony Robinson** looks at the wildlife, countryside and coastline of his native county in *Wild About Essex*, a six-part series made with the *Survival* team, starting in May.

Stephen Fry celebrates 100 years of the National Trust in the East of England by visiting many of properties in the Trust's care in *Mr Fry's Very Grand Tour* in June.

1996

Anglia's parent company, MAI, merges with United Newspapers, publishers of the *Daily Express*, to form United News and Media, one of the top 20 media companies in the world.

Anglia announces a major £7.5 million development programme for its Norwich studios in April – the most significant investment in site and technical facilities in the company's history. Plans for the Magdalen Street studios include a fully-integrated news facility geared to digital technology.

Survival film-makers are honoured with a special BAFTA award in April. The Special Award for Craft marks the outstanding quality of the camera teams' work for more than 35 years **Alan Root**, responsible for some of *Survival's* most memorable films in a 33-year association with the programme, receives the award on behalf of his colleagues.

Graham Creelman, director of programmes for two years, is appointed managing director of Anglia following Malcolm Wall's appointment as deputy director of the broadcasting and entertainment division of United News and Media.

A consortium comprising Anglia, Meridian and Chrysalis Sport wins the ITV contract for coverage of Formula One Grand Prix motor racing in September. **Murray Walker** confirmed as commentator, with former driver **Martin Brundle** giving expert opinion.

A new helping of TV cookery with a liberal sprinkling of Yorkshire relish is offered up when chef **Brian Turner** begins a new regional food series in November.

1997

Norfolk-based actress **Liza Goddard** takes on a new role with *Liza's Country* in January, travelling the region to seek out interesting people, places and events.

A six-part series written and presented by **Prince Edward** explores links between the East of England and his royal ancestors through the ages. *Crown and Country*, produced by the Prince's company Ardent Productions and screened in October, visits some of the region's most historically important towns, castles, houses and antiquities.

Bring Me the Head of Light Entertainment, Anglia's anarchic new comedy panel game devised by **Lee Hurst** and chaired by **Graham Norton**, establishes itself as Channel 5's most successful light entertainment programme when the new station goes on air in March.

Graham Bell, Anglia's longest-serving presenter, dies suddenly aged 57 in September.

Around 70 Muppet characters from **Jim Henson's** famous New York company arrive to work at Anglia's refurbished studio complex in November. They are taking part in *Jim Henson's Animal Show*, a series for pre-school children interlinking puppet characters and *Survival* wildlife footage.

1998

Vanessa Feltz, dubbed 'Anglia's Queen of Chat', is dethroned in a wrangle over money in August. She is replaced by Australian presenter **Trisha Goddard**. (Feltz subsequently joins the BBC).

Anglia wins a contract in August to produce *Guilty*, a series of 60 one-hour daytime talk shows for the satellite channel Sky One.

Changes in the weather are announced in October with the appointment of two new environment correspondents, **David Hughes** and **Karin Giannone**, to present weather bulletins and report on environmental and weather-related stories for *Anglia News*. Contractual changes in the supply of weather data results in the closure of the in-house meteorology department set up in 1961.

1999

EastEnders star **Pam St Clement** introduces the residents of Whipsnade Wild Animal Park in January for a 13-part series. *Whipsnade* captures the drama, excitement and occasional heartache in the lives of the animals and the staff who look after them.

The programme title *About Anglia*, abandoned nine years earlier, returns in January as a twice-weekly magazine show presented by **Helen McDermott**. *Anglia News* reverts to a 6 pm slot in March as part of changes brought about by the re-scheduling of *News At Ten*.

Oscar-winning film and TV producer **Sir John Woolf**, a founder director of Anglia and the man chiefly responsible for building the company's worldwide reputation for quality drama, dies in June, aged 86, and in August the death is announced of former presenter and programme adviser **Brian Connell**, 83.

Anglia marks its 40th anniversary in October with a series showing highlights from the extensive programme archives.

October also saw the death at 78 of **Dick Joice**, one of Anglia's most popular presenters. Joice was founder of the *Bygones* series which ran for over 20 years. He also presented *Farming Diary* and *About Anglia* before becoming a director of the company and its programme controller.

Index